KNOWLEDGE ELICITATION:
Principles, Techniques and Applications

ELLIS HORWOOD BOOKS IN INFORMATION TECHNOLOGY

General Editor: Dr JOHN M. M. PINKERTON, Principal, J. & H. Pinkerton Associates, Surrey (Consultants in Information Technology), and formerly Manager of Strategic Requirements, ICL

EXPERT SYSTEMS IN BUSINESS: A Practical Approach
M. BARRETT, Expertech Limited, Slough, and A. C. BEEREL, Lysia Limited, London
ELECTRONIC DATA PROCESSING IN PRACTICE, Vols. 1 and 2
M. BECKER, R. HABERFELLNER and G. LIEBETRAU, Zurich, Switzerland
EXPERT SYSTEMS: Strategic Implications and Applications
A. C. BEEREL, Lysia Limited, London
APPLICATIONS OF OPTICAL STORAGE*
A. BRADLEY, Congleton, Cheshire
SOFTWARE ENGINEERING ENVIRONMENTS
P. BRERETON, Department of Computer Science, University of Keele
SMART CARDS: Principles, Practice and Applications
R. BRIGHT, Information Technology Strategies International Limited, Orpington, Kent
PRACTICAL MACHINE TRANSLATION*
D. CLARKE and U. MAGNUSSON-MURRAY, Department of Applied Computing and Mathematics, Cranfield Institute of Technology, Bedford
ENCYCLOPAEDIA OF IT*
V. CLAUS and A. SCHWILL, FRG
KNOWLEDGE-BASED SYSTEMS: Implications for Human–Computer Interfaces
D. CLEAL, PA Computers and Telecommunications, London, and N. HEATON, Central Computer and Telecommunications Agency, London
THE CASSANDRA ARCHITECTURE: Distributed Control in a Blackboard System
I. CRAIG, Dept. of Computer Science, University of Warwick, Coventry
KNOWLEDGE ELICITATION: Principles, Techniques and Applications
D. DIAPER, Section of Psychology, Liverpool Polytechnic
KNOWLEDGE-BASED MANAGEMENT SUPPORT SYSTEMS
G. I. DOUKIDIS, F. LAND and G. MILLER, Department of Information Management, London Business School, London
KNOWLEDGE-BASED SYSTEMS: Applications in Administrative Government
P. DUFFIN, CCTA, Riverwalk, London
MULTI-LINGUAL SPEECH ASSESSMENT*
A. FOURCIN, Dept. of Phonetics and Linguistics, University College London
KNOWLEDGE ENGINEERING FOR EXPERT SYSTEMS
M. GREENWELL, Expert Systems International, Oxford
EXPERT SYSTEMS: Safety and Risks*
E. HOLLNAGEL, Computer Resources International, Denmark
KNOWLEDGE-BASED EXPERT SYSTEMS IN INDUSTRY
J. KRIZ, Head of AI Group, Brown Boveri Research Systems, Switzerland
ARTIFICIAL INTELLIGENCE: Current Applications*
A. MATTHEWS and J. RODDY, Aregon International Ltd, London
INFORMATION TECHNOLOGY: An Overview*
J. M. M. PINKERTON, J & H Pinkerton Associates, Esher, Surrey
PRACTICAL TOOLS IN HUMAN–COMPUTER INTERFACES*
S. RAVDEN and G. JOHNSON, MRC/ESRC Social and Applied Psychology Unit, University of Sheffield
EXPERT SYSTEMS IN THE ORGANIZATION: An Introduction for Decision-makers
S. SAVORY, Nixdorf Computer AG, FRG
ARTIFICAL INTELLIGENCE AND EXPERT SYSTEMS
S. SAVORY, Nixdorf Computer AG, FRG
BUILDING EXPERT SYSTEMS: Cognitive Emulation
P. E. SLATTER, Telecomputing plc, Oxford
SOFTWARE ENGINEERING MANAGEMENT
H. M. SNEED, FRG
SPEECH AND LANGUAGE-BASED COMMUNICATION WITH MACHINES: Towards the Conversational Computer
J. A. WATERWORTH and M. TALBOT, Human Factors Division, British Telecom Research Laboratories, Ipswich
THE IMPLEMENTATION OF COMPUTER SYSTEMS
R. J. WHIDDETT, Dept. of Computing, University of Lancaster

* In preparation

KNOWLEDGE ELICITATION:

Principles, Techniques and Applications

Editor:

DAN DIAPER, Ph.D.
Section of Psychology
School of Humanities and Social Science
Liverpool Polytechnic

ELLIS HORWOOD LIMITED
Publishers · Chichester

Halsted Press: a division of
JOHN WILEY & SONS
New York · Chichester · Brisbane · Toronto

First published in 1989 by
ELLIS HORWOOD LIMITED
Market Cross House, Cooper Street,
Chichester, West Sussex, PO19 1EB, England
The publisher's colophon is reproduced from James Gillison's drawing of the ancient Market Cross, Chichester.

Distributors:

Australia and New Zealand:
JACARANDA WILEY LIMITED
GPO Box 859, Brisbane, Queensland 4001, Australia

Canada:
JOHN WILEY & SONS CANADA LIMITED
22 Worcester Road, Rexdale, Ontario, Canada

Europe and Africa:
JOHN WILEY & SONS LIMITED
Baffins Lane, Chichester, West Sussex, England

North and South America and the rest of the world:
Halsted Press: a division of
JOHN WILEY & SONS
605 Third Avenue, New York, NY 10158, USA

South-East Asia
JOHN WILEY & SONS (SEA) PTE LIMITED
37 Jalan Pemimpin # 05–04
Block B, Union Industrial Building, Singapore 2057

Indian Subcontinent
WILEY EASTERN LIMITED
4835/24 Ansari Road
Daryaganj, New Delhi 110002, India

© **1989 D. Diaper/Ellis Horwood Limited**

British Library Cataloguing in Publication Data
Knowledge elicitation principles, techniques and applications. —
(Ellis Horwood books in information technology).
1. Expert systems. Design
I. Diaper, D. (Dan)
006.3'3

Library of Congress Card No. 88–34703

ISBN 0–7458–0451–9 (Ellis Horwood Limited)
ISBN 0–470–21410–4 (Halsted Press)

Typeset in Times by Ellis Horwood Limited
Printed in Great Britain by Unwin Bros., Woking

Table of contents

Preface

Expert systems and Knowledge-Based Systems (KBS) now form a market worth annually billions of dollars, yen and ECUs (European Currency Units). The technology associated with expert systems and KBS has progressed exponentially in the 1980s, both in terms of the systems themselves and with the specialist tools designed to support the building of these systems. However, at the core of the development of these systems remains the fundamental problem of being able to extract and represent the knowledge on the human domain experts on which the contents of expert systems and KBS must be based. The term 'knowledge elicitation' is used throughout this book to mean this process and is deliberately distinguished from the issue of encoding knowledge in machine form. Hayes-Roth *et al.* (1983) described knowledge elicitation as the bottle-neck in expert system development and at the end of the 1980s this remains the case. The principal problems of knowledge elicitation are physchological ones because they involve human experts, and also many other people, and as such are of a different type, and very much more complicated, than those associated with the software engineering problems of building systems and tools. Perhaps because of the very difficulty of knowledge elicitation, less effort, money and far fewer publications have seriously addressed the issue. This book sets out to partly redress this imbalance by being exclusively devoted to knowledge elicitation.

The seven chapters in this book arose from a one day meeting organised by the British Computer Society's Human–Computer Interaction Specialist Group held in February 1988. The aim of this meeting, which was attended by nearly 100 people, and also of this book, was to provide a coherent set of perspectives on knowledge elicitation. This book is not, however, merely a mini-conference proceedings but a fully edited book in which the chapters cross-reference each other. The organising principle behind the original selection and the order of the chapters is captured in the book's subtitle: Principles, Techniques and Applications. Thus one approach the reader may adopt is to work through the chapters in the order that they are offered and thus progress from the general, and at time quite complicated, theoretical background (Chapters 1 and 2), through a review of techniques for eliciting domain experts' knowledge (Chapter 3) and representing it (Chapters 4 and 5), to the application of knowledge elicitation to real world problems (Chapters 6 and 7). Such structuring is, of course, a nightmare for an editor and none of the chapters quite fit the above structural model and all stray further than would the chapters of a well written, single author tome. However, a considerable amount of editorial effort has gone into making the content of each chapter consistent with that of the others and agreements, and sometimes disagreements, between the authors are marked within every chapter. For readers, who for whatever reason, do not wish to tackle the chapters in the provided order there are many alternatives. For example, Chpater 6 provides a considerable amount of cross-referencing to the other chapters and this might be followed by Chapter 2 and then Chapter 7, which illustrate the points about organisational and human issues associated with expert system/KBS development. Then perhaps the reader might try the more theoretical approach of Chapter 1 before moving to Chapters 3, 4 and 5 on the techniques and knowledge representations associated with knowledge elicitation. Alternatively the reader may begin with Chapters 3, 4 and 5 before putting their content into the wider applications, organisational and psychological contexts provided by the other chapters.

If knowledge elicitation is indeed the bottle-neck preventing the more rapid development of expert systems then, even if I were not the editor, I might suggest that this book should be read by everyone involved in the development or application of expert systems or KBS. The book was developed because there was perceived to be a glaring hole in the published literature. The original intention was that the audience for the book would include not only those who are currently, or about to be, actually involved in knowledge elicitation but also to provide a single reference for those involved in other aspects of the development of expert systems so that they could appreciate the complexity of the whole issue and the limitations on what they could expect. However, the book is not a primer suitable for first year undergraduates, but it was intended that an able, modestly well read advanced undergraduate or postgraduate student would find this book an understandable and reasonably comprehensive volume from which to develop an understanding of the whole area of knowledge elicitation. The background of the intended readership is not meant to be restricted to those either in industry or academia, but to encompass both. Similarly, the book is crucial to those with a computer science background who are generally not well equipped to deal with psychological issues and for those who lack a sound background in computing this book is intended to show where the desperately needed contributions of the psychologists, sociologists, linguists, etc., are most needed. The contributions of the latter specialists will, however, depend on them possessing the technical computer knowledge necessary for working in the domain. This knowledge is not in this book but is widely available, and sometimes accessible, once one has a feel for what needs to be known.

Given the human nature of the problem of knowledge elicitation it is perhaps not surprising that virtually none of the experts who have contributed to the seven chapters have a principally computer science background, though all of us have worked on, or with, expert systems and KBS for many years. The authors present a balance between those with an academic background and those who are firstly involved with industrial and commercial ventures in the expert system/KBS domain, though happily, from the chapters it is not always clear which side of this traditional divide the authors come from.

Jill Bell is an independent consultant specialising in human skills training and with Bob Hardiman, who has been in the computer industry for 20 years, the last 14 with IBM, has developed their course 'The Human Side of Knowledge Engineering' for IBM. The course has been offered numerous times in the UK, the USA and also in the Far East. Betsy Cordingley has a social sciences background which she has deployed in both industrial settings and at the University of Surrey where, apart from her work on expert systems she teaches specialised, intensive courses about research design and computer-aided analysis. Nancy Johnson is a lecturer at Brunel University and has a background in mathematics and linguistics and is currently engaged in research in the areas of VLSI design and oncology. Michael Wilson has a research background first involving the mental representations that develop to support computer use and he is now a Senior Research Associate at the Science and Engineering Research Council's Rutherford Appleton Laboratory where he investigates techniques and representations to improve knowledge acquisition during expert system development. Geoffrey Trimble worked, prior to 1967 with civil engineering contractors, civil and structural design consultants and management consultants and was, until his appointment as Professor of Construction at Loughborough University of Technology, Deputy Chief Executive of the UK's National Building Agency. Since 1983 Professor Trimble has devoted his efforts to work on expert systems in construction and has concentrated particularly on the problems of knowledge acquisition. Jeremy Clare is a consultant in artificial intelligence (AI) and Human Factors with Cambridge Consultants Ltd and has been devoted for many years to understanding how people use and understand complex systems. He has worked on naval command systems, visual performance with optical and electro-optical aids and is currently involved with the transfer to Europe, from the USA, of experience with AI financial industry applications. Finally, I am a senior lecturer in applied psychology at Liverpool Polytechnic and have for most of the 1980s been involved with what has become known in the UK as cognitive ergonomics or cognitive engineering. Initially with training applications in information technology and, since 1983, I have been interested in the methodology of design of expert systems so that they support the needs of both their operators and the client organisations who purchase them. My research on intelligent interfaces and natural language has provided a rich test bed for my general interest in the area of expert systems and KBS technology.

Liverpool Polytechnic
September 1988

Dan Diaper

Introduction to:
Designing expert systems: from Dan to Beersheba

While divided into three sections, this first chapter aims to serve as an introduction to a book on knowledge elicitation by covering two major issues. First, a discussion of the psychology of people, and particularly those who are domain experts, is intended to acquaint those readers who lack a psychological background to the stupendous complexity of real people and the richness of all psychological issues. Secondly, the chapter tries to introduce to those new to expert systems and KBS development projects the way such systems are built.

The first section attempts to define expert systems and to place them in context with respect to other computer systems. The section deals with the application and functionality of expert systems, and generally leaves out any discussion of the nature of their architecture because this is not centrally relevant to either knowledge elicitation or their definition as intelligent systems.

The second section is divided into two parts. First, the current use of rapid prototyping as a development method is described and the disadvantages and limitations of this approach are characterised. Second, a more planned, general methodology for expert system design is presented and is used to place the knowledge acquisition stages in the overall design process.

The third section returns and extends some of the issues raised in the first section concerning the psychology of people. It characterises what little is known about human knowledge representation and attempts to explain why there are good reasons for expecting a mismatch between what people know and how they express this verbally. The section concludes with the claim that the central problems associated with knowledge elicitation are the same as those that have been tackled by the applied psychologists who have developed cognitively orientated methods of task analysis.

1

Designing expert systems: from Dan to Beersheba[†]

Dan Diaper
Section of Psychology, School of Humanities and Social
Science, Liverpool Polytechnic

1. DATA PROCESSING, ARTIFICIAL INTELLIGENCE AND EXPERT SYSTEMS

Just as Locke in his 'Essay Concerning Human Understanding' believed that 'It is ambition enough to be employed as an under-labourer in clearing the ground a little, and removing some of the rubbish which lies in the way to knowledge' (O'Connor, 1964) so it is appropriate at the start of a book devoted to knowledge elicitation for expert systems and Knowledge-Based Systems (KBS) to first describe and define these devices and to thus prepare the soil for the following chapters devoted specifically to the topic of knowledge elicitation: its principles, its techniques and their applications.

Expert systems were the first, commercially available computers that exhibit a modest degree of intelligence. Traditional computers, now referred to as the first to fourth generation of computers, are literal computational devices that exactly follow the instructions of their users. In the standard Data Processing (DP) environment a user is provided with a data base that contains a large number of records, usually held on backing store in files. Each record consists of a number of fields that contain numeric or string data and, admitting a considerable simplification and ignoring the actual input or use of the data, the user searches for records by inputting field descriptors in combination with some logical operators. This description provides us with a model of a data base that is virtually structured by the way which it is accessed and searched by the user. This is in contrast to the data base designers' actual structuring of the data base which has attempted to anticipate users' search requirements. The computer part of such a system exhibits no intelligence, which is provided entirely by the user. Such DP systems work perfectly satisfactorily when the relevant record and/or field(s) are known by the user. Thus, in an accounting application, for

---

† 'Dan n. From ~ to Beersheba, over the whole extent [~ in Palestine, f. name of a tribe of Israel]', *The Concise Oxford Dictionary of Current English,* sixth edition.

example, knowing a client's invoice number, or their name and address, may allow easy access to the relevant record. However, there are many simple data base search applications in the real world where the field descriptors are not known. For example, many academics now use automated library or abstract search facilities. In such applications there may be tens of thousands, if not millions, of records and generally the user wishes to extract a relevant subset, perhaps ten or so, from this enormous data base. This task requires the user to input field descriptors, usually keywords, in complex combinations of logical operators (AND, OR, NAND, NOR, etc.) and keyword synonym equivalents. The addition of even a single keyword can sometimes reduce the number of references (records) found in the data base by an order of magnitude. Furthermore, the keywords are not usually available and thus the user has to be highly creative in guessing the relevant, or even possible, keywords and their possible synonyms. Such a task therefore demands a considerable degree of intelligence on the part of the user and is most successfully carried out interactively, by altering the user's input to tune the search of the data base so as to provide a reasonable size of output. Even when finished, a conservative strategy is always advised as while not all the references provided by such systems are those the user wants, the user has no way of checking that the references produced are complete (i.e. that at least all the relevant references in the data base are included in the output list).

The field of computer science generally called Artificial Intelligence (AI) can almost be characterised as the investigation of automated search facilities that remove this burden from the user. AI has traditionally concentrated on problem games such as chess, missionaries and cannibals and the tower of Hanoi (Sell, 1985), where at each step of the game what is needed is to generate a set of possible future outcomes and to choose, usually only one, from this set. The generation of outcomes is analogous to data bases such as the ones described above, the only difference being their generation from a set of rules or other algorithmic methods, rather than those already existing, and the decision mechanism, which requires the searching of the data base tree, is equivalent to the intelligent human user of standard DP data bases. While in no way wishing to denigrate the field of AI, which has been one of the most successful research areas of interdisciplinary collaboration between computer scientists and cognitive psychologists, AI has generally failed to provide systems of commercial utility. Such a statement must, of course, be tempered by caution and the promises by those working with computer imaging systems or natural language processing, for example, are soon likely to bear commercial fruit, yet such applications generally are only promises at present. Notwithstanding the collaboration of the psychologists and computer scientists, the whole field of AI has, from a commercial point of view, failed because, at its core, it can be characterised as having been devoted to the production of genuinely intelligent machines. The psychometricians have long given up the attempt to define human intelligence (e.g. Butcher, 1968) and only the most foolish of undergraduates attempts anything more than an operational definition (i.e. intelligence is what intelligence tests measure). Perhaps then, when the concept of intelligence is itself undefined, it is hardly surprising that AI, as an attempt to provide true artificial intelligences, has also found the going difficult.

Without wishing to fall into the undergraduate trap outlined above, the term 'intelligence', as applied to machines, is used in this chapter to mean any machine that is able to deal with inputs that are incompletely specified. 'Incompletely specified' here includes inputs from both the user and the programmer. This sort of definition, while in many ways unsatisfactory, at least avoids the regressive definitional problem, such as that of Webber and Nilsson (1981), for example, who 'regard artificial intelligence (AI) as a branch of computer science whose objective is to endow machines with reasoning and perceptual abilities', and who, along with everyone else, cannot define either reasoning or perception even within this narrow context.

Expert systems and many current KBS provide a contrast to the, no doubt unfair, thumb-nail sketch of traditional AI described above. From the earliest development of DENDRAL in the mid-1960s (Buchanan and Feigenbaum, 1978), with MYCIN in 1972 (Sell, 1985) and PROSPECTOR in 1978 (Duda *et al.*, 1979) the emphasis has been on practical applications. DENDRAL was to provide a 'smart assistant' for chemists, PROSPECTOR was developed to assist field geologists and MYCIN to aid physicians in the diagnosis and treatment of infectious diseases (Alty and Coombs, 1983). It is essentially the case that expert systems are performance driven devices and their mode of operation, what goes on inside the box, is irrelevant to their success. It is certainly irrelevant whether they possess true intelligence or not and many vacuous debates have been held amongst the *cognoscenti* as to whether expert systems are, or are not, AI devices. Indeed, many still differentiate KBS from expert systems, yet the maintenance of such distinctions is only tenable where KBS takes on a generic cloak and covers the gamut of applications orientated machines so as to include, for example, imaging, robotic and natural language processing applications, as well as the knowledge manipulation and extraction applications that are central to expert systems. While most commercially available expert systems have been provided as stand alone machines there also exists an approach that incorporates expert systems into large DP environments. IBM, for example, are taking this approach and plan to develop expert systems that may intelligently organise inputs early in the DP stream prior to being incorporated into the main data base (Schorr, 1987). However, the software technology in these two approaches is hardly different, and it is questionable whether any useful purpose is served, given the history of the terminology, to calling only stand-alone systems expert systems and the integrated ones KBS.

Whether for good or bad, expert systems have come to dominate what is referred to as the fifth generation of computers. This description is confused and marks a break from the first four generations that are all defined by differences in hardware technology. The problem with this generational distinction is that expert systems are essentially software and many expert systems are designed to run, perfectly adequately, on stand-alone, third generation, desk-top microcomputers.

What crucially distinguishes expert systems from AI devices is their definition. Whereas the goal of AI has been to produce genuinely intelligent machines, expert systems are successful if they appear, from the users' point of view, to intelligently deal with the problems set them within their domain of expertise. At the heart of the history of expert systems is a beautifully clever, intellectual trick. Expert systems can be defined, and are throughout this chapter, as machines that are able to emulate some of the behaviours of a human domain expert. The important point here is that it is the behaviour of such experts that is emulated and not necessarily either the human experts' thought processes or knowledge. Such a definition, could, of course, lead to trivially calling nearly any tool that supplements or augments human performance an expert system. For example, a spade could be defined as an expert system as it emulates people's ability to dig holes in the ground with their hands. Such trivia is, at least in part, restricted by describing the person (or persons) emulated by an expert system as a domain expert, though such experts may be humble clerks or highly paid professional specialists, depending on the domain of application. Stand-alone expert systems have tended to concentrate on the latter type of experts whereas the IBM type of strategy of integrating expert systems/KBS technology within the mainframe DP environment is more likely to concentrate on the former. It is not denied that all humans are expert at many things, but the practical emphasis, for sound commercial reasons if for no other, is on expertise that is restricted to a relatively small, and valuable, sub-set of the human species. A vast range of expertise in medicine, finance, engineering, science, and 'non-benign' military (Pullum, 1987) applications, has been investigated for their suitability for emulation by expert systems and considerable effort has gone into identifying expert systems' range of applicability (e.g. Collins, 1987; Zack, 1987). A range of example applications within the general domain of construction are discussed in Chapter 6 and one particular example, in City finance, is described in Chapter 7 of this book.

It must be stressed that only a small sub-set of domain experts' behaviours are emulated by expert systems. Obviously, as most existing expert systems are operated via keyboard and screen, and all, perhaps desirably (Diaper, 1984, 1986a,b), lack full natural language interfaces, then the domain experts' linguistic behaviour, as well as the meta- and para-linguistic behaviours that may be crucial to some aspects of the experts' tasks, are not emulated. What has been successfully emulated by expert systems is the particular, specialist behaviours of the domain experts. As an aside, full natural language (i.e. the collection of sub-languages (Grishman and Kitteridge, 1986; Diaper and Shelton, 1987, 1988 — in press) possessed by the complete set of speakers of a language) may not be necessary, nor safe, for the users of expert systems who, in general, will not be highly expert in the relevant domain of expertise. Indeed, the one class of person who is unlikely to be an expert system user is the domain super-expert from whom the system was designed. There is the possibility that a language style too close to that employed between people may mislead users into believing that an expert system is more knowledgeable and intelligent than is actually the case. Also, the very restrictiveness of the domain of operation of any expert system suggests that only a fairly narrow sub-language, rather than full natural language, is required between user and expert system (Diaper, 1986a, 1988c).

All expert systems so far developed, and all those practically contemplated, thus excluding the science fiction like pronouncements that overwhelm many of the popularists in the area, some of whom should know better, are extremely restricted in their domain of expertise. At present there are theoretical issues associated with the possible size of expert systems such that systems that work more than adequately with modest sized knowledge and rule bases fail when attempts are made to increase their size by orders of magnitude. In essence, the traditional AI problem of combinatorial explosion, almost the problem of AI, and most graphically expressed by the chess type problems where looking ahead even one additional move requires enormous increases in computational capacity, is still not sufficiently well understood nor practically solved, available tree pruning methods notwithstanding, that it is no surprise that expert systems are highly domain restricted.

So far this introduction has stressed that expert systems emulate some aspects of the behaviour of human domain experts. This definition aside, it is hardly surprising that one solution to the problem of building expert systems has generally been to model the relevant knowledge of the domain expert or experts, though the limitations of this approach have been recognised (e.g. Slatter, 1987) and specifically include: the inefficiencies of human expert thinking; that the expertise of more than one domain expert may be desirable within a single expert system, and the fact that there are radically different underlying strengths and weaknesses to the implementation hardwares of human brains and electronic computers. On this latter point, Marr (1972), for example, was very clear that the effectiveness of the computational algorithms and conceptual representations in part depended on the hardware on which they were implemented. This point is discussed further by Johnson in Chapter 4. Confusion has arisen, however, when those working, particularly in academic research environments, have turned their backs on the practical, application orientated roots of expert systems and become embroiled in AI and/or psychological issues concerned with the modelling and emulation of knowledge. Expert systems need only behave as if they contain the knowledge of human experts and there is no requirement that they possess, in their internal architecture or processes, anything like the true psychological mechanisms of real people.

Perhaps one of the major reasons that the collaborative computer science and psychology venture of AI has, to date, generally failed, is that the psychologists are a very long way from elucidating even the most basic properties of information processing associated with human cognition. In fact, the computer science contribution to psychology far outweighs the contribution in the other direction and many of the psychological theories over the past few decades have borrowed, hand over fist, from the operation of digital computers. One thus finds, in the late 1960s models of cognitive psychology, suggestions that the human mind contains registers or buffers and that information is extracted from both long-term memory stores and from perceptual systems and placed in these before manipulation. Norman (1968), for example, says of buffers that 'Although these concepts can be criticized as being relevant solely to the computer technology from which they derive, it is more likely that the need for numerous types of temporary memory systems is a true general property of any large-scale system' and he borrows from the computer jargon of his time, admittedly with codicils, to talk of 'the address of the information' in human memory.

Gardner (1985) points to the limitations of this whole computer analogy approach and states, 'After all, information theory and computers are deliberately constituted content-blind', by which he means that their architectures are independent of their content. Gardner leans particularly on the work of Shepard (1981, 1982) who suggests that there may 'be a multiplicity of modes of metal representation, each tied to a particular content'. Further to this, Diaper (1984) has suggested that there are fundamental problems with the definition of information provided by information theory (Shannon, 1938; Gardner, 1985) in that the informational content of a stimulus is not at all a property of the stimulus but a property of the information processing perceiver. Similarly, the advent of possible, true parallel processors such as those proposed by Hinton (1981; Hinton and Sejnowski, 1983; Rumelhart et al., 1986) have perhaps placed the final nails in the coffin of the strong digital computer analogy when Rumelhart et al., for example, state that

> one important difference between our interpretation of schemata and the more conventional ones is that in the conventional story, schemata are stored in memory. Indeed, they are the major content of memory. In our case, nothing stored corresponds very closely to a schema. What is stored is a set of connection strengths which, when activated, have implicitly in them the ability to generate states that correspond very closely to a schema.

Whether the current vogue of Parallel Distributive Processing (Rumelhart and McClelland, 1986; McClelland and Rumelhart, 1986) which is perhaps a return to network models of human memory and cognition, if they ever left psychology, in the current language of AI, will suffer the same fate as the earlier serial computer-psychology analogies remains to be seen.

The point being made is that claims that expert systems emulate human cognition are misfounded, not surprisingly, given our ignorance of the operation of the human mind. The consequences of believing that expert systems can emulate thought, rather than behaviour, are catastrophic for both the building of expert systems themselves and for dealing with the major problems that exist with designing adequate interfaces between them and their human users. They lead Basdcn (1984), to take just one example, to suggest that an adequate interface to expert systems can be achieved by providing a 'human window' that lets the user directly inspect the internal operations of the expert system (i.e. the operations are transparent). Such an interfacing approach is doomed to failure unless the architecture and processes of both the user and expert system are at least compatible. If this is not the case, and it is extremely unlikely to be so given the radically different implementation architectures, let alone the differences in the breadth and depth of knowledge, then the human user is faced with the problem of translating the knowledge of the expert system into a form consistent with her or his own, unknown metal architecture and cognitions. While beliefs about transparency (e.g. Hayes-Roth *et al.,* 1983) may be convenient to expert system designers, they are bound to lead to expert systems that are either unusuable, or worse, likely to positively mislead their users.

Given that expert systems need to possess some sort of model of human domain experts' knowledge, thought this model need bear no resemblance to how such experts actually represent their knowledge within their own minds (i.e. it requires no psychological validity), then it is reasonable to ask what, if anything, is meant by the term knowledge. No technically adequate definition of knowledge exists that is not a tautology or oxymoron, which of these depends on one's philosophical background, or does not require some philosophically impossible test of external validity. The most plausible understanding of the term 'knowledge' is in its contrast with the use, in computer science terms, of either data or information. As characterised earlier in this chapter, data consists of things that are potentially available to a computer system, as records for example, and information can be characterised, at least here, as data that is accessed by a human user. Within this framework, it is the user who supplies the intelligence to the human–computer system such that it is the human–machine composite that could be called knowledgeable. It appears that the term knowledge has been coined to denote the importing of the intelligent manipulation of data into computers, no necessarily with any claim being made to psychological validity, so that they may be called knowledge based, rather than data based, systems. The dividing line between traditional DP environments and knowledge based ones is extremely narrow and is currently in danger, perhaps thankfully, of vanishing. The cynic, however, may gloomily predict that future intelligent systems may be called wisdom systems, a term already coined by Cooley (1987), in one more attempt to distinguish such technologies from their immediate precursors. Such a terminology is unlikely to be any better defined than the current state of affairs with regard to knowledge. Yet the whole field of expert systems is dominated by the term knowledge: expert systems are frequently referred to as a subset of KBS and the general field, to which this book contributes only a component, is most usually called knowledge engineering.

Central to expert system development is the requirement to be able to represent domain experts' behaviour and thus their knowledge in a form suitable for incorporation into expert systems. This enterprise is called 'knowledge acquisition' by Cordingley in Chapter 3 and those who carry it out are called knowledge engineers. Knowledge engineering is, of necessity, an interdisciplinary endeavour: the knowledge engineer must at least possess expertise of both psychology and computer science. The problem confronting the knowledge engineer is to be able to first extract and make explicit human domain experts' knowledge (knowledge elicitation) and then translate this into a form suitable for programming into an expert system (knowledge encoding). It is the knowledge elicitation stage of this process that has been frequently identified as the bottle-neck in knowledge engineering (Hayes-Roth *et al.*, 1983; Shaw and Gaines, 1986, etc.) and the major brake on the development of expert systems. There is no doubt that this is principally due to the already mentioned, apparently intractable problems associated with our ignorance of the real psychology of human knowledge representation. In addition, and discussed subsequently in this chapter and in several others (Chapters 2, 3, 4 and 5 in particular), are the issues associated with the methodological problems caused because human experts rarely, if ever, have access to how their own knowledge is structured or processed. Three radically different representations of knowledge need to be identified in knowledge acquisition, though this book, in general will concentrate on only the first two of these. The three are: (i) the implicit or tacit knowledge represented within the human expert(s); (ii) an intermediate representation or alternatively what Johnson calls a mediating representation (Chapter 4) which is an explicit, public representation of the elicited knowledge; and (iii) the representation that is encoded within the expert system. Johnson argues eloquently for the importance of mediating representations on a number of different grounds and their importance and rationale is left to a fuller treatment in her chapter, though their utility is also discussed further in the following section of this chapter.

This chapter has deliberately left out any description of the internal architecture of expert systems, as it is not an issue that is centrally relevant to the rest of this book, though it cannot be overlooked if knowledge engineering is to be successful. There is, after all, little point in being able to represent the relevant human knowledge explicitly if it cannot be subsequently used in the expert system. However, Gammack and Young (1985) do argue that knowledge that cannot yet be represented in expert systems deserves consideration now and there is considerable potential utility in knowing from the earlist stages of expert system design what the limitations of the system will be. At present, expert systems generally possess a bipartite architecture, the components being rather grandly called a knowledge base and an inference engine. A knowledge base is in fact the data base where the facts, represented declaratively, that the expert system possesses, are stored. The inference engine is supposed to provide the active intelligence to the expert system that allows it to search and manipulate its facts in response to its users' requirements. There are currently many different types of inference engine which use a range of techniques that include forward and backward chaining, fuzzy logics, Bayesian probabilities and so forth. The architecture of the knowledge base, at least in part, depends on which

of these inferencing techniques are employed and, not surprisingly, different methods are differentially suitable for different types of problem. Expert
systems were defined as possessing intelligence because of their ability to
deal with problems that are not fully specified. What needs to be clear is that
such a definition of intelligence, whilst it does usually involve inferencing of
one sort or another, is very different to that used to describe human
intelligence and that if its use is at all reasonable then it must be admitted
that expert systems possess only an extremely limited and narrow type of
intelligence.

This chapter will next deal with the general, current approach to expert
system development and then propose an alternative as a means of highlighting the inadequacies of current methods. The purpose of this section is
to set the specific topic of knowledge elicitation into its proper context as
only a part of the expert system design process. The chapter will then turn, in
its final section, to a discussion of the problems of eliciting knowledge from
human domain experts. Many of the particular elicitation techniques are
described in Chapter 3, so this final section will concentrate on the analogy
between the problems associated with user requirement specification within
the field of Human–Computer Interaction (HCI) and the problems associated with knowledge elicitation, in an attempt to place the fundamental
problems associated with knowledge elicitation in a historical context.

2.   DESIGNING EXPERT SYSTEMS

2.1   Rapid prototyping and first generation expert systems

The method one uses to design an expert system, hardly surprisingly,
depends on the type of expert system to be designed, its size and purpose,
and also on a host of factors concerned with practical issues such as the time
and financing available as well as on the prevailing ethos of the organisation
for whom it is being designed. There is no doubt that there exists a major
market for first, or even zero, generation expert systems, that can be built
easily and quickly using trial and error methods (more politely described as
using the designers' and knowledge engineers' personal expertise). A
number of systems built in this manner are described by Trimble in Chapter
6. In fact, the most common approach to expert system development, it can
hardly be called design, uses what is grandly called rapid prototyping. Rapid
prototyping involves first building, very quickly, a demonstration expert
system, and as Trimble points out, this is often an important factor in
convincing the purchasing organisation's management to proceed with the
project. The knowledge engineer then uses this first prototype to improve it
by repeatedly retesting the domain expert. In some expert system development projects this first prototype is almost the first thing that the domain
expert is presented with, though, of course, it is more common and certainly
preferable that the domain expert contributes to the building of the very first
prototype. The knowledge engineer in such projects is likely to use the
prototype as a focusing device (see Chapter 3, in particular) for interviewing
the domain expert and modifications may be made immediately, in the

presence of the expert, or more usually, immediately after each session. Such an approach can very quickly produce small working systems but it is certainly an error to believe that this is either a particularly satisfactory approach, nor one that warrants the title of a methodology.

The strength of this type of approach, however, lies with its saleability to the purchasing organisation and the speed at which it produces some results. From the outset of the project a working system can be convincingly demonstrated and the problems of specification creep minimised, or at least identified. Creep in a project is the shifting of the goals of the project and may involve changes, for example: in the domain, both in extent and in depth; in the tasks the system is to perform; and in the system's end user population. Without a well specified, early system specification, however, some creep is inevitable as, with growing familiarity, the purchasing organisation more clearly realises the potential of the developing expert system. This is by no means the worst of the problems associated with the rapid prototyping approach, though it must be stressed that if the final system must be delivered in a few months, or even weeks, then there is probably no alternative to rapid prototyping. However, in many commercial and industrial applications, a year is a more normal, and feasible time scale in which to develop an expert system, and Shackel (1986) has even suggested that with normal computer systems it can take between two and ten years from the initial 'study phase' to production! Of course, a rather better product is expected if resources are provided over such extended periods.

The problems with the rapid prototyping approach are first that it is rare for the end-user to be involved in the expert system's development. During most of the cycle it is the knowledge engineer and the domain expert who work with the growing system. As already commented on and discussed in detail in the final section of this chapter, the domain expert is usually, if not inevitably (depending on one's psychological model), poorly equipped to guess the requirements of the system's users. Yet the design of the user interface can consume half of the budget of an expert system project and is obviously crucial to the success of the delivered system as, if it is not liked, or is difficult to use, then, no matter how clever it is, it is likely to fail the ultimate test, that of being regularly used. The importance of good user interfacing is well recognised by those involved in commercial expert system development projects yet one suspects that this is lip service rather than a seriously undertaken aspect of a project when little is done in the early stages to discover user requirements and preferences. Oliver (1986, 1987a,b), for example, firmly places interface design at a very late stage in her rapid prototyping expert system development scheme and this can be contrasted with the emphasis placed on users by Bell and Hardiman (Chapter 2), in particular.

A second, and at least as important, problem with the rapid prototyping approach is the potential for uncontrolled growth in the knowledge base. Rapid prototyping, particularly in the expert system area, is a positive encouragement to poor software engineering proctice. It enourages elasto-plast solutions to each new instance that requires modification of the prototype by simply adding more knowledge or rules. These can quickly grow out of hand with the inevitable combinatorial explosion caused by the loss of any structure that may originally have been imposed on the expert system's internal architecture. Recovery can become impossible, or so expensive as to be prohibitive, and inevitably leads to difficult, if not impossible up-dating and maintenance problems. Schatz *et al.* (1987) clearly state from their real experience with commercial expert systems that 'planning for long-term maintenance when designing an expert system is critical for the system's continued success'. Systems that are not so designed are likely to have extremely brief, useful operating lives as the loss of either, or both, the knowledge engineer and domain expert will leave the organisation with an unmaintained and unmodifiable system that progressively fails to meet the changing requirements of the organisation. Thus one of the potential advantages to an organisation of possessing an expert system, that it retains the expertise of its domain experts, is abrogated. Of course, with small systems that are highly specific then this may be financially satisfactory and it could be cheaper to rebuild, from scratch, the essential core of an expert system every few years. However, if such a tactic is adopted it is not unreasonable to expect it to be made explicit to the organisation and not left as an unfortunate, unanticipated and possibly expensive result sometime after delivery of the system.

In most rapid prototyping projects, the delivered system is simply the final prototype, though it may be recoded and ported to a computer system different from that on which it was developed. Even when considerable recoding is involved, this is not usually carried out by the knowledge engineer and rarely results in any major restructuring of the knowledge base or inference engine. One of the solutions to the problem of combinatorial explosion and the elastoplast approach to software modification is the use of mediating representations, discussed by Johnson in Chapter 4. Such representations are able to provide a formal representation that can be explicitly mapped to the internal architecture and knowledge of an expert system and which is easily readable by those who were not involved in the original development programme. While potentially extremely useful, such mediating representations do, of course, have overheads during the rapid prototyping development cycle as both the mediating representation and the knowledge base and inference engine must be kept compatible. In the real world there is a problem, similar to that of documenting traditional software development, caused by the external demands on, and the human frailty of, the knowledge engineer, so that maintaining complete compatibility between the mediating representation and the expert system's knowledge representation is difficult to achieve. Once the slippage begins, in reality one suspects, it quickly becomes irrecoverable and positive harm may subsequently result from believing that the easily accessible mediating representation is a true model of the actual expert system. The use of such mediating representations is thus likely to be restricted to those expert system development programmes that use more sophisticated methods than the seat-of-the-pants rapid prototyping approach. Only if it becomes possible to automate the mapping between the mediating representation and the expert system is it thus likely to be usable within the rapid prototyping approach.

A final, and quite separate problem with the rapid prototyping approach is that it tends to mislead those involved with expert system development to underestimate the problems that still exist with this new technology. For a number of years now, there have been those, particularly those with experience of building real, commercially usable expert systems, who have claimed that all the main problems have been solved and that all that remains is the fine tuning of the methods and the expert system shells (e.g. Keen and Williams, 1985). Nancy Johnson (personal communication, 1987), with considerable insight, has dismissed such claims with the phrase 'that's just first generation talk' and all those who are, or who planned to become, involved in expert system or KBS development in the next few years should be careful of not being over impressed with the functioning of demonstration expert systems in very limited and narrow domains, particularly as many current examples of expert systems never make the transition from the development stage to that of fully functioning, regularly used systems in commerce or industry. Bramer (1985), for example, describes the current state of affairs 'as if aviation had now reached the era of the bi-plane' and in the few years since he wrote these words, we have done little more than put mono-plane like devices on the drawing-board.

2.2   A more formal approach to expert system design

This section makes no attempt to review the many, often partial, expert system design methods that have been recently suggested. Instead it will draw directly on the proposals of the author (Diaper, 1987a,b, 1988b) outlined in his speculative People Orientated Methodology for Expert System Specification (POMESS) to highlight the necessary stages that any sound expert system or KBS design methodology will have to possess and it is this complete process which might reasonably be called 'knowledge engineering'. The order of the eleven stages listed below may vary and there may be overlap, both in time and within the techniques variously employed, and there may also be considerable iteration between stages. They do, however, provide a fair list of the issues that must be dealt with in any expert system design method. Table 1.1 lists these eleven stages.

Each of the stages listed in Table 1.1 will be briefly dealt with so as to place the role of knowledge elicitation, the subject of this book, into its proper context within knowledge engineering for expert system or KBS design.

Excepting those few organisations who possess a considerable experience, usually in-house, of developing expert systems of practical utility, the expert system designer is usually in the position of having to educate the client expert system purchasing organisation (hereafter called the client). The reasons for the client wishing to buy into expert system or KBS technology are legion and unfortunately often misguided or even trivial. The client rarely has a sound understanding of either the advantages, and more importantly, the limitations of these technologies and, one suspects, that in

Table 1.1 — A list of necessary stages in expert system or KBS design

0.   Pre-project feasibility study
1.   Organisational modelling
2.   Personnel identification
3.   Knowledge elicitation   ⎫
4.   Knowledge representation   ⎬   Knowledge acquisition
5.   Knowledge encoding   ⎭
6.   User interface design
7.   Prototype testing
8.   Delivery system implementation
9.   Delivery system installation
10. Delivery system evaluation

many cases, the client has no more than a wish to possess the state-of-the-art technology for its kudos than for any well specified problem that only an expert system or KBS may solve. Obviously this is not always the case, but the pre-project feasibility study is marked within the list above as a common and vital first step in commencing an expert system or KBS development project.

The pre-project feasibility study often involves the expert system or KBS development manager having to deal with the client's senior management for a few hours, often without access to either the possible domain experts or the potential end-users of an expert system. The development manager is then required to pronounce on the feasibility of a possible expert system or KBS and to provide detailed project costs and cost–benefit analyses. Coopers and Lybrand, for example, who are one of the largest first generation expert system developers for external clients in both the USA and the UK, usually for financial applications, cost expert system development programmes by taking the worst (i.e. most expensive) estimate and they then add 40% to this to provide initial project costs (Church, 1988). It is now recognised that the development of formal methods, in the weak sense as opposed to meaning the logical proof of the properties of a computer system (Diaper, 1987b), for expert system design are urgently required so that, as is now possible with software engineering projects, accurate and complete project costs can be determined from the earliest stages of the project. Church admits that even his company's conservative algorithm does not prevent them 'getting their fingers burnt' occasionally. In a sane world such feasibility and cost analyses would be forced to wait on rather better information than that provided by senior management who are almost never either domain experts or potential users. To her credit, Oliver takes such real world considerations into account in her expert system development approach by providing a number of clearly identified points in a project where the client can be provided with up-dated information on the project's feasibility and costs so as to provide an opportunity for the client to bail out of a project with the minimum loss. This is, of course, a practical and desirable solution in the absence of good, complete design methods similar to those now available in commercial software engineering projects.

Fantastic though it may seem, most of those involved in designing expert systems make little attempt to properly analyse and model the client organisation for whom the system is being designed. Furthermore, management science, or perhaps more accurately, management art, has little to offer by way of general methods of organisational analysis and modelling that are suitable for defining the scope and possible application of expert systems, though a number of general models have been produced in the field of office automation (Bjorn-Andersen, 1986; Dawkins, 1987). In a serious expert system design method, one can make a strong case for starting the method by analysing the client organisation's structure. The author, for example, has suggested that, at least, an organisation should be analysed to establish the flow of power within it. Power is operationally defined as the flow of goods; services; responsibility; money; and information. No claims are made as to the exhaustiveness of this list. There are many uses to such organisational models. First, such an exercise allows the specification of what are the client's real problems, as opposed to what the client thinks they are, and thus allows a first specification of possible expert system applications. Such a model should naturally provide better project cost estimates. Furthermore, the introduction of radical technology needs to be assessed early in the project if the client is not to buy a 'pig in a poke'. Expert systems, like the generations of computers before them, are likely to require considerable restructuring of an organisation if their benefits are to be maximised. It needs to be borne in mind that there are always overheads to such reorganisations, both in financial and personnel terms, and that these, properly, should be costed into a project, at least by the client.

One likely consequence of many expert system applications is the distribution of some expertise throughout the organisation from it being centralised in one or small number of experts. This expertise distribution is thus likely to affect the job description of those who will become the direct users of the delivered expert system and also directly affect the tasks now undertaken by the domain experts. Furthermore, there is a class of personnel who can be thought of as indirect expert system users. Such people may never actually touch the expert system themselves but will be influenced by its introduction and use. It is therefore clearly sensible to attempt to identify such consequences as early as possible in the project so that appropriate plans can be made for the smooth and minimally painful transition in technology. At present, the palliative to such potential problems has been to introduce technologies such as expert systems, or indeed most new automated office systems, on a piecemeal basis and see how the personnel and organisation copes. Such an approach can be extremely expensive and lead, often for trivial and personal reasons on the part of a very small number of staff, in the new technology not gaining wide acceptance and use within the client organisation. In such circumstances the client has invested often considerable sums in a system that works, fulfils some organisational need, and yet is not used. Many of these issues are addressed by Bell and

Hardiman in Chapter 2 from the perspective of the role of the knowledge engineer, yet they need to gain wider currency within the knowledge engineering enterprise if future expert systems are to successfully fulfil a useful role in commercial organisations.

Perhaps the most important aspect of the organisational analysis is the identification of both the relevant domain experts and the end-users. This is so important that, for emphasis, it is marked as a separate stage in the scheme listed in Table 1.1. Shpilberg *et al.* (1986), for example, state that 'The task of identifying the professionals whose expertise should be tapped is significant.' and they identify, within the domain of corporate tax planning in the USA, four different types of experts who are expert: 'in the execution of the process'; in knowing 'what questions to ask and why, and what follow-up questions may be required to identify a relevant issue'; 'at summarising the results and presenting the information for analysis'; and at constructing 'viable alternative strategies, given the information presented to them'. Of course, in other domains, experts of other types are also likely to exist and one must be careful of assuming that all apparently equivalent experts are either equally expert at all aspects of a task, or that they tackle the same problems in a similar fashion. In general, the problem of incorporating knowledge from multiple experts into a single expert system has not been widely addressed, or even well understood. An exception to this is the work of Shaw and Gaines (1986) and Boose (1986) who provide a solution to what is likely to become a major problem, if it is not already one, by the use of repertory grids. The general application of Kelly's (1955) personal construct psychology and repertory grid techniques for knowledge elicitation is discussed by Cordingley in Chapter 3.

It is particularly important that experts, though there may only be one, are the true experts in their field and there is a sad history of some early expert systems being designed from the expertise of those available to the knowledge engineer, rather than with the inaccessible domain super-expert. Such cases have, in general, led to failed expert systems though Modesitt (1987) gallantly describes such expertless attempts as perhaps not making 'the undertaking impossible, but it undoubtedly makes it more challenging'. The organisational analysis which is bound to have included, amongst whatever other techniques it uses, interviews with the client's personnel, can obviously serve as a rich source of information so as to ensure that the appropriate domain expert or experts are identified.

Similarly, the potential direct users of the system need identifying. As already commented on in this chapter and emphasised by Bell and Hardiman in Chapter 2, such users are often excluded from the early stages of the design process when the crucially important decisions are made about both the applications and likely final implementation system. That they are not excluded from discussion of the likely consequences to themselves of introducing an expert system or KBS is only because these issues are rarely ever addressed at all in most, current expert system or KBS development projects because of the prevalence of the rapid prototyping approach already exposed. Such omissions border on the insane and are only understandable in the context of current software enginering practice. Methods such as the Jackson Structured Design (Cameron, 1983), while in common use, place surprisingly little emphasis on the analysis of either organisational or even user requirements. However, some attempts are being made to remedy this within the Jackson approach (e.g. Carver, 1988). At present there is a growing popularity with 'User Centred System Design' (Norman and Draper, 1986), though such ideas are made to apply principally to what has been identified as direct system users rather than to the wider organisational requirements, and generally, little attention is paid even to properly establishing detailed user requirements (i.e. using psychologically sound techniques). Task analysis, for example, does not even warrant an index entry in Norman and Draper, though Wilson *et al.* (1986) survey eleven different task analysis methods with claimed suitability for HCI applications, and many of these can be used for establishing user requirement specifications. However, an estimated 35% of operational software is devoted to the user–system interface in traditional computer applications (Smith and Mosier, 1984 — based on a survey carried out in 1980). Furthermore, the interfacing problems are likely to be even greater with expert systems than with traditional computer system applications (e.g. Diaper, 1984; 1986b) and one of the most expensive forms of project specification creep that can occur with the success of an expert system is the demand to extend the range of types of user who will use the system (Church, 1988). This form of creep can be particularly expensive because of the very considerable expense already involved in interface design. Identifying all the potential users of a system at the early stages can thus make the early system specifications very clear and the potentially exorbitant costs of changing interface specifications can be brought to the attention of the client. If the client does decide to make such specification changes during the project then the client might reasonably be expected to bear the cost of them.

A important point about identifying the direct end users early in the design process is that this can greatly aid the knowledge elicitation process by providing guidance as to the target users to whom the domain expert or experts should be targeting her/himself during the knowledge elecitation stages. Prior to other methods of knowledge elicitation, Diaper's POMESS methodology strongly advocates the application of proper task analysis techniques such as Moran's (1978; 1981) Command Language Grammar (CLG), Payne's (1984; 1985; Payne and Green, 1986) Task Action Grammar (TAG) or, as actually advocated in POMESS, Diaper and Johnson's (1989, Johnson *et al.*, 1984; 1985; Johnson, P. 1985; Diaper, 1988a) Task Analysis for Knowledge Descriptions (TAKD). The purpose of such task analyses, which can themselves be treated as knowledge elicitation methods and this is why they are not listed separately from other knowledge elicitation techniques in Table 1.1, is principally to establish the actual requirements of users and to formally identify the possible range of tasks and sub-tasks that the expert system or KBS may be expected to perform. The application of task analysis and its underlying rationale are exposed in the final section of this chapter where an analogy is drawn between the utility of task analysis in system design and the psycholgical problems attendant with the elicitation of knowledge from domain experts. Wilson in Chapter 5 discusses, in depth, the nature of domain experts' tasks and how these can aid the elicitation process and so will not be discussed further here. The use of task analysis as a knowledge elicitation technique in its own right is also discussed by Cordingley in Chapter 3 and briefly mentioned by Trimble in Chapter 6.

It perhaps needs pointing out in a book that is principally devoted to the elicitation of knowledge from human experts that they are not the only source of knowledge available to the knowledge engineer and a number of techniques suitable for eliciting knowledge from non-human sources are described by Cordingley in Chapter 3. In many domains there are vast data bases, usually on paper, that contain the established lore pertaining to a domain. To take just one example, Sharpe (1985) describes the production of an advisory expert system on UK Statutory Sick Pay (SSP) provisions where the only sources of knowledge was the 'Social Security and Housing Benefits Act (1982) and associated SSP regulations (1982)'. However, Sharpe concludes that an underlying conceptual framework is required, even within his relatively small application domain, and he states that

> We cannot assume that because the law is written down that there is no knowledge acquisition problem in representing it. This concep-tual framework will have to encompass both common world con-cepts, of time periods, events, etc., and as our system becomes more ambitious the soical context which gives the law its validity as a set of 'norms'.

Fairly obviously it must fall to the domain expert, rather than to the knowledge engineer, to provide such conceptual frameworks. Indeed, in many domains the elicitation of knowledge from non-human sources such as books, or on-line data bases, will be a necessary part of the knowledge engineer's task, yet for sound theoretical reasons it cannot be sufficient. Fundamentally, such passive repositories of knowledge, or data to be more accurate, are designed to be interpreted by an intelligent reader and it is the intelligent properties of the reader that must, along with the passively stored data, become incorporated together within the expert system. As an aside, it is, of course, for this reason that expert systems may represent a greater danger to the naive, or only poorly informed, user than do books as such users will not have to possess the domain expertise necessary to understand technical books to be able to use an expert system of similar technical scope. Thus expert systems have the potential to amplify the old problem that a little knowledge is a dangerous thing.

It has already been mentioned that the desirable product of whatever knowledge elicitation techniques that are employed should be a mediating representation. As knowledge elicitation is the topic of this book then no great discussion will be provided within this introductory chapter, which sets out to fill in the other aspects and properties concerning expert systems and their design. Mediating representations provide an important representational stage between human knowledge representation and the encoded expert system's or KBS's knowledge representation. The process of moving from such a mediating representation to an expert system or KBS is called, throughout this book, knowledge encoding, to distinguish it from knowledge elicitation and representation.

Mediating representations do need to be distinguished from intermediate ones, of which many alternatives have been proposed. For example, protocol English prose transcripts, systemic networks, diagrams of various sorts, semantic nets, influence diagrams, 2D or 3D layouts (Young and Gammack, 1987), are but a small sample of the total list of intermediate representations that have been suggested. It should be noted that these are a mixed bag in that they vary in how much analysis has been done on the expert's, or experts', behaviour. Far less, for example, on transcripts than with semantic nets. These intermediate representations are discussed in more detail by Johnson in Chapter 4. However, the fundamental difference between intermediate and mediating representations is that few of the former claim to represent or completely map onto an expert system's complete knowledge representation. Such intermediate representations are thus more clearly thought of as tools or aids for the knowledge engineer. In general they, by themselves, cannot form the basis of a fully automated method of producing an expert system, which can be thought of as a test of their ability and completeness to represent knowledge, as opposed to any claim being made for the probable desirability of such a process.

The utility of intermediate knowledge representations for helping the knowledge engineer represent knowledge within an expert system should not be underestimated. Knowledge Acquisition tools such as AQUINAS (Boose and Bradshaw, 1987a, b), which has been developed from Boose's (1984; 1986) work on the Expertise Transfer System (ETS), already shows some considerable success at automating the knowledge encoding processes. However, even though AQUINAS uses a intermediate representation, based on Kelly's Personal Construct Psychology, which does map reasonably well onto the expert system knowledge representation, it still requires the use of other tools and alternative intermediate representations in the construction of an expert system. Thus sophisticated modern tools like AQUINAS still represent a half-way house between manual knowledge encoding methods, which rely completely on the expertise and intelligence of the knowledge engineer, and possible future tools that will allow the full, automated production of expert systems directly from mediating representations. It is, of course, the case that the weakness lies more with the absence of adequate mediating representations than in any computational inadequacy of tools such AQUINAS.

At this point it is appropriate to issue a warning. The above discussion could be taken to imply that there is a simple linear transfer from the domain expert, by some knowledge elicitation technique, to either a mediating or intermediate representation(s) which is then encoded in the expert system or KBS. The processes of knowledge elicitation and encoding are not independent in that the knowledge encoded in the expert system is likely to influence subsequent elicitation processes. In any variant of the rapid prototyping approach, where the expert system or KBS is built quickly, then the inadequacies of the knowledge represented in the early prototype must drive the continuing elicitation process. The only exception would be where a mediating representation exists that directly maps onto the expert system's or KBS's knowledge representation. In such cases, since the content, but not the form, of the knowledge is the same then inadequacies in the mediating representation can directly influence knowledge elicitation and, of course, there will be no cycle, other than implicitly, between knowledge encoding and knowledge elicitation. In fact, if good mediating representations are developed in the future then there would be no need, in theory, to code the expert system representation until after the knowledge elicitation process is complete. However, such mediating representations are yet a long way off as the mapping between such representations and expert system representations would have to be formally proved (in the strong, logical sense of formal.

Following the knowledge acquisition processes should come the design of the direct end user interface. With the exception of techniques such as POMESS, where interface design is an integral part of these processes, interface design is sufficiently different that it needs to be clearly identified and so is a separate stage in the development scheme presented in Table 1.1. At the core of good interface design is the identification and modelling of the users and the tasks that they will perform on the new system. The early task analyses can provide a minimum requirements specification as they identify the functions that the users currently carry out. Such analyses, however, are less informative as to the type of interface that is required than one might hope. While there is one school of thought that believes that mimicry of the tasks performed on the old technology provides good interfaces to the new, this position is generally unsound, though its justification is that it minimises user retraining. It is unsound because many of the practices associated with a technology are caused by the nature of the technology (Diaper, 1987b; Diaper and Johnson, 1989). For example, the limitations of size and the expense of keeping multiple copies of documents is a major consideration in physical filing systems and limits the manner in which documents are stored and accessed. In contrast, quite different limitations are evident in computer data base systems, particularly those associated with data base navigation, because it is difficult to browse between computer-based files (e.g. Hammond and Allinson, 1987) which all superficially appear the same, unlike paper documents. It is unfortunately the case that, excluding the Wizard of Oz simulation technique explicitly tailored to solving this problem in POMESS, within the field of HCI there exists only a collection of guidelines and heuristics and not a method of designing interfaces, though, of course, once designed, there are many techniques for evaluating them. Furthermore, some of the popular beliefs within HCI are now under attack. For example, Fowler *et al.* (1987) state as a result of their experimental research that 'It would appear that menu selection in particular would not be suitable for the novice user'. in contrast to the opposite being widely believed (e.g. Kidd, 1982; Apperley and Field, 1984; Kaster and Widdel, 1984; Heppe *et al.*, 1985). At present, the design of good interfaces is a specialist task probably best carried out by an HCI expert and it is obvious that many knowledge engineers are not, perhaps unsurprisingly given their other skill requirements as described, for example, by Bell and Hardiman in Chapter 2, also HCI experts. Rather depressingly, Morris (1987) concludes her brief survey of expert system interface issues by stating 'that expert system interface design is a young and exciting area and one which is full of potential for enthusiastic researchers!'. This is rather like the Chinese curse concerning living in interesting times from the expert system or KBS builder's point of view.

The interface options for expert systems are enormous and range from menu driven systems that are principally system led (i.e. the system presents the options available at each stage) through command languages, which are user led, and dynamic graphical interfaces to those that are proposed to understand natural language and support rich, mixed initiative dialogues, a facility that users do take advantage of if it is available (Diaper, 1986a, 1988c). The move to adaptive and intelligent interfaces, which may themselves be expert systems (e.g. Totterdell and Cooper, 1986; Diaper, 1984; 1986a, b), is at present still an issue of research, rather than of practical application, and expert systems that are claimed to possess natural language processing interfaces in fact use extremely simple and highly non-natural methods, such as keyword searching, to achieve what is generally a very unrealistic language interface (e.g. Farris and Lucas, 1986; Trigano *et al.*, 1986). Such interfaces are almost certainly more difficult to build than the back-end expert systems they are supposed to service and until generic intelligent interfaces become available (e.g. Bundy, 1985; Diaper, 1986b) then they are beyond the range of the realistic commercial expert system builder.

However the expert system's interface is designed, and the point about employing HCI specialists warrants reiteration, at some stage a prototpye expert system must be built. The purpose of a prototype should be to test an expert system's or KBS's utility and usability, that is, before delivery real end users should be given access to it and proper evaluation methods employed (e.g. Hammond *et al.*, 1984; Fahnrich and Ziegler, 1984; Grudin and Maclean, 1984; Johnson *et al.*, 1986; Sharratt, 1987; and there are many more). This can be contrasted with the rapid prototyping approach where the main purpose of the prototyping is the testing and construction of the expert system itself. Ideally, usability evaluations should be carried out in the environment in which the delivered system will operate, though this is not always possible, and representative users should run the system on either real problems that they have in their normal work, or at least, example tasks that are known to be representative, in both range and style, of such real world tasks (Brooke, 1986). The quality and success of the efforts in the previous stages of the design process will determine how much modification is required to either the interface or the expert system's knowledge.

If the preceding stages have been done thoroughly then the prototype should be very close to the finally delivered system. Where the prototype fails there is a great temptation to apply what have been previously described as elastoplast solutions to the newly identified problems. In the real, resource limited world there may be no alternative to such software bodges, which is why getting the early design stages right is vital to the integrity and subsequent maintenance of the system. All of the well recognised good software practices that apply to traditional software also apply to expert systems (Partridge, 1986) and it is known that conceptual errors are orders of magnitude more expensive than bugs at the code level. Partridge, for example, states that 'Boehm (1984) suggested that 100 is a more precise number as a factor for the cost savings when an error is removed at the requirements analysis stage rather than when the system is in operation' and this estimate may be conservative.

Far too often the delivery of the system along with its documentation is seen as the end of the project from the knowledge engineers' and system builders' point of view. Such a state of affairs is highly unsatisfactory and can, for a number of reasons, lead to a well designed and potentially useful system not being used by the client organisation. While there is a certain commercial logic in taking the money and running, in the long term such an attitude must be bad for the expert system business generally. The organisational model described much earlier in this section can be extremely useful in providing a full and complete delivery system. Such a system should, at least, consist of the installed system itself, a proper set of documentation that is suitable for the identified range of users and which provides summaries, quick reference synopses and proper within and across documentation referencing. The complexity of the documentation problem should not be overlooked (Clement, 1984). The delivery package should also contain a training scheme as well as a proper plan for introducing the system to its users. Such a plan should consider the indirect as well as the direct system users and with expert systems, in particular, should also contain advice on the system's impact on the changed role of the domain expert, or experts, on whom the knowledge elicitation exercises were carried out. Commerce and industry has a particularly poor record, not only in the UK, of not providing proper training for staff with the introduction of new systems (Bjorn-Andersen, 1984; Fitter *et al.,* 1984), though there have been notable exceptions (e.g. Barber and Kempson, 1984).

Part of the problem with the rapid prototyping approach is that the last prototype winds up being the delivered system, though perhaps recoded and ported into a computer system different from that employed in development. Within this approach it is difficult to know when to halt prototyping and this is probably why what is usually delivered is the prototype that exists when either the project's time or money runs out. Without proper early requirements specifications, in fact, there can hardly be any other method as there are no independently established critera against which to evaluate the system. Honest suppliers of such systems do usually supply technical back-up, yet this can be extremely expensive on any system (e.g. Fitter *et al.,*

1984) and is likely to be even more so on expert systems that have suffered a long period of rapid prototyping, which is likely to make their knowledge maintenance and modification well nigh impossible. Such problems can be minimised by using variants of the approach suggested in this section, though it must be recognised that all customer support services are costly and need to be written into contracts at the beginning of projects. The client's management should be strongly dissuaded from believing that they will be able to manage without such support.

Finally, a good development approach should involve the full evaluation of the delivered system sometime after its installation. With any new technology there is bound to be a honeymoon period where the system is used because it is a new toy. Its real utility and success can only be properly measured after such a period when the system becomes another piece of office furniture that is used when it is useful, and not otherwise. There must be a suspicion that many delivered expert systems fail to pass this test and that they quietly slip away unnoticed and unloved as one more office automation failure (Bjorn-Andersen, 1986). The value of such post-delivery testing could benefit both the client and the system builder. For the client, recovery before the final whimper may be possible and an expensive investment, with suitable modification either to the system or to the client's organisational structure, given a second chance.

For the expert system builder, post-delivery evaluations provide the ultimate test of their product and, in the end, the only one that really matters. It is horrifying that within the field of HCI generally, formal, post-delivery evaluations are rare, and many system developers merely wait for customer complaints. This is common throughout the computer system industry and as Bjorn-Andersen's delightfully describes it:

> technological developments within office systems reminds us of a children's book about a negro boy going into the savanna where he met four tigers. They demand and got all his clothes, but they could not agree on sharing, and started chasing each other round a palm tree, having a firm bite in each others tails. It goes faster and faster until they all melt into tiger butter. Almost all computer manufacturers in the USA, Japan, and Europe are using the same philosophy in a frantic race to turn out new products which are only marginally better than the existing ones without allowing themselves to step back and contemplate whether a superior strategy is viable.

At present, expert systems are only starting their whizz around the palm tree, but the market is rapidly expanding. For example, Morris (1987) quotes the Ovum research groups estimates that 'expenditure on expert systems will leap from less than £40 million in 1986 to nearly £400 million in 1992'. and she continues by stating that 'Frost and Sullivan predict that in Europe the market for expert systems will grow to over £3 billion in 1990 (Jones, 1987)'. The precise accuracy of such estimates is immaterial to the point that there is a vast world market for expert system technology which, if only satisfied by badly designed systems that rapidly become unused and even detested, then the opportunity for both organisations and individuals to benefit from a technology ideally suited for removing much of the drudgery that current computer technology imposes on its workers will be lost. The solution must lie in good design that considers, early in the design process, the requirements of both the client organisation, the direct system user and all the other people who will be affected by the introduction of an expert system.

3.   HCI AND KNOWLEDGE ELICITATION

Knowledge elicitation is treated by many involved with it as if it was a new problem, unrelated to work in other fields. This sort of belief leads to the reinventing of wheels. In particular, the work of the ergonomists and applied psychologists have been confronting the central problem of know-ledge elicitation for decades. In essence the problem is that people either do not have, or have only poorly, depending on one's psychology, direct access to their mental architecture or mental processes. Furthermore, Bainbridge (1986) suggests that the more expert one is at a task the harder it is to access one's knowledge of the task for the purposes, for example, of describing what is involved in the task's performance. In addition, she identifies a problem that will be difficult to detect when she states of skilled people that 'When asked to report their knowledge they may revert to using inexper-ienced methods, which are slower, more verbal, and less integrated, so can be reported more easily'. This section will first examine the nature of expertise and knowledge and its relationship to both consciousness and behaviour, including verbalisation, and then point to the theoretical impli-cations of this for knowledge elicitation. Finally, this section will expose how the same problems have been tackled by those involved in the generation of user requirement specifications for computer systems.

A reasonable starting point would be to ask 'What is the nature of human knowledge representation?' However, our profound ignorance of the psy-chology of people, characterised in Section 1 of this chapter, suggests that any answer to such a question must be treated with extreme caution. It is also the case that it is necessary to distinguish models of human knowledge that are metaphors, from those that purport to have some validity. Of course, the solipsist position and that of the identity theorists (Fodor, 1981) is that all one can have is models or descriptions and that one selects a model appropriate for one's needs. Indeed, adopting this perspective makes meaningless any question about the correctness of different descriptions as the very existence of the real world is no more than a convenient and useful assumption. Descartes' claim, based on his introspections alone, that there was some knowledge about which he could not be misled, malevolent demons notwithstanding, is now widely recognised to be based on a faulty logic (Watling, 1964). Thus a sensible, alternative question to the one above would be 'What is a suitable model, or models, of human knowledge representation that will be useful for eliciting human knowledge?'. Of course, one rather simple-minded answer is to suggest that human knowledge representation can be described so that it is isomorphic with that employed by expert systems., This, however, rather puts the cart before the horse, and as a proposition it is demonstrably false and inadequate. If it were true then there would be no representational problem in knowledge acquisition, which is patently not the case. Thus we must turn to a psychology of people that, at least initially, ignores the purpose of the knowledge modelling enterprise and anticipate a two-stage process. First, expert human knowledge will need making explicit in a form consistent with its psychological representation. Second, this knowledge model will need transforming into a form suitable for expert system implementation. Thus we have the two processes of knowledge elicitation and knowledge encoding.

Before turning to statements concerning what little is known, or hypothesised, about human knowledge representation it is necessary to expose what is a fundamental problem and limitation in all psychological research. Cognitive psychology, the branch of psychology of principal interest here, like any science, is concerned with producing models of its object of study, in this case of the human mind. It uses as its major source of evidence the behaviour of human subjects, who are usually tested in laboratories where the stimuli and response constraints on subjects can be recorded and controlled. What distinguishes modern psychology from its history as a branch of philosophy is its emphasis on the observation of behaviours, rather than on the verbalisations, or other behaviours such as drawing, that purport to represent the contents of consciousness. There are basically two schools of thought that are distinguishable in psychology. The more extreme view, extreme in that it goes against the basic philosophical tenets of Western belief, is that the contents of consciousness never represent psychological processes but only the product of some, or a few, such processes (Miller, 1962; Neisser, 1967; Mandler, 1975; Diaper, 1982; 1987b). Furthermore, even those of the other school (e.g. LaBerge, 1974; 1981; Schneider and Shiffrin, 1977; Hilgard, 1980; Shiffrin *et al.*, 1981) who suggest that consciousness is involved in cognition as an active process, particularly in the allocation and control of mental processing resources (i.e. in attentional mechanisms) admit that only a small fraction of all the mental processes are represented in consciousness and that there are many automatic processes of which we are unaware, and which we therefore cannot introspect about.

In addition, there must be a range of automatic, unintrospectable processes that are involved in the translation of the contents of consciousness into observable behaviour such as verbal reporting. It is self-evident that much of the contents of consciousness are not represented linguistically and that massive corruption of the conscious representation occurs in its translation into behaviour. For example, very few, if any, people are able to reproduce externally, by drawing, the imagery that we all claim to experience, particularly if the normal acts of visual perception are included in the definition of imagery. It is irrelevant where this corruption arises for the argument in this chapter, but it is clear that is is not all caused by limitations in our physiological effectors alone. There is no reason to suppose that some sorts of knowledge do not suffer such corruption when self-evidently others do. Yet another problem was highlighted by Adrian (1966) who suggested that the contents of consciousness suffer a 'Heisenberg-type' effect in that the act of introspection itself changes the contents of consciousness.

Ignoring epistemological issues, psychology is clearly a science in its general approach and methodology. Thus, for example, in the same way that a biochemist must infer the composition of a molecule from indirect evidence, such as the gross changes in colour, opacity and so forth when a chemical reaction takes place, so the psychologist must infer the composition of the human mind from the observable, gross behaviour of people. It is vital to biochemists that their reagents are pure and their test-tubes uncontaminated by unknown substances. The problem with psychology is that the equivalent conditions cannot be met and there are no clean test-tubes or pure reagents in the science of the mind. Thus, apart from the philosphically unsolved problem of inference that all science requires, psychology is faced with a set of additional methodological problems which require considerable ingenuity to even partially overcome. Furthermore, the models of complex molecules in biochemistry are trivially simple compared with the required complexity of even the most inadequate, realistic model necessary in psychology. Indeed, the trial by fire that all good psychologists must pass, and on which many undergraduate and postgraduate students fail, is to recognise the incredible complexity and power of the human mind and to then solve the problem of how a science of psychology is possible at all. Kant (1781; Warnock, 1964) claimed that the enterprise of psychology was inherently impossible and, while now widely rejected (Gardner, 1985), the sheer complexity of the human mind may yet defeat the enterprise where Kant's philosophical objections have failed. Many people, including some eminent psychologists, have claimed that psychology has made little progress this century compared with other 'hard' sciences. Such a view depends on one's yardstick and one can plausibly argue (e.g. Diaper, 1987b) that the proper interpretation is that the 'hard', physical sciences such as chemistry, physics and physiology are actually the easy ones that study a subject matter of relative simplicity. At least with a Popperian (e.g. Popper, 1972) perspective it is clear that a great deal of negative knowledge is known in the science of psychology (i.e. we know what is not adequate). This section, having established the background complexity and difficulty with understanding the human mind, will briefly address some of the current views about human knowledge representation relevant to expert systems, before turning to a description of how applied psychologists and cognitive ergonomists have engineered practical, usable solutions to the problems that confront them.

Notwithstanding Marr's (1972) point about the relationship between implementation architectures and higher level representations, care must be taken to distinguish the way models represent the mind from the underlying substance of them. That networks, for example, provide a convenient representational format for many psychologists need in no way imply that memory is organised as a network and it is possible to re-represent network models in what appears to be radically different forms, say as production rules, without changing the substance of the model. The central distinction of substances with respect to human knowledge representation over the last decade or so is between knowledge that is represented declaratively from that which is represented procedurally. Declarative knowledge can be characterised as 'knowing that' whereas procedural knowledge is 'knowing how' (Winograd, 1975). While it is demonstrably possible to represent all procedural knowledge declaratively, and vice versa, with more or less ease, there are very considerable consequences of which representational form the human mind uses. Winograd summarises the advantages of declarative knowledge as being: that it is flexible and economic; that it is easy to understand and learn; and also that it is easy to communicate because, he says, 'Natural language is primarily declarative'. He claims that the advantages of procedural knowledge representations lies with: the ease with which they can represent processes; their ability to express second order logic (knowledge of what we know) outside of any specific context; and also their ability to integrate heuristic knowledge easily into processes such as deduction. However, Winograd's portrayal of declarative knowledge is at least questionable. He is tempted to represent declarative knowledge in the traditional logic of predicate calculus first formulated as syllogisms by Aristotle nearly two-and-a-half millennia ago. It is a well established empirical fact that people are awful at simple logic problems stripped of all context (Wasson and Shapiro, 1971; Johnson-Laird, 1983) and that the addition of logically irrelevant contextual information can radically improve performance. It had been assumed that to solve syllogisms people would have to possess logical inference rules, and this, in part, is what Winograd appears to have believed. However, Johnson-Laird (1980) produced a relatively simple AI program that solved syllogisms by testing their conclusions on generated, hypothetical worlds. The program succeeds without possessing logical inference rules and, intriguingly, it suffers from errors similar to those that people make when syllogism solving. It is also fairly obvious that logically irrelevant context would aid such a technique by facilitating the creation of hypothetical worlds on which to test a syllogism. A conclusion that might be drawn from such evidence is that people are incapable of treating any problem as simple, even when it is expressed in the context stripped form of traditional logic, and the reason for this is that they never use a knowledge representation at all similar to such logics. Why should this be? The quote by Rumelhart et al. (1986) in Section 1 of this chapter suggests a completely procedural representation for all human knowledge. People exhibit behaviours as if they possessed declarative knowledge but, in fact, they do so only by manipulating knowledge stored in some procedural form. Winograd's three advantages to declarative knowledge can be dismissed because:

(i) notions of economy are necessarily at least partly dependent on the implementation architecture, and it is plausible that the highly parallel processes of the mind are unsuited to the processing of the economic representations of traditional logic;

(ii) the ease of understanding and learnability may be tied to the lack of content in traditional logics, that is, there is just less to learn;

(iii) that the declarative properties of natural language are determined by the rather dull constraint that speech is distributed in time and that only one thing can be said at any one instant.

Furthermore, it is worth noting on this last point that both the sender and receiver of speech imply far more in the sequential language string than is carried in the formal aspects of its semantics and syntax. Thus the conclusion of the author is that while we may choose, at times, to represent human knowledge in a declarative form, its actual, psychological representation is always procedural.

If all human knowledge representation is procedural, then what, if anything, are the consequences for knowledge elicitation? In fact, the consequences are enormous. It is now widely recognised, and as Winograd suggested, that while statements in a declarative form are easy to express in natural language, it is difficult, if not impossible, to express procedures. Indeed, many tasks such as tying shoe-laces, riding a bicycle, skating, swimming and indeed even walking cannot be easily expressed verbally, if at all, in natural language1 (e.g. Bainbridge, 1986). This is like the party trick of asking someone to describe a spiral without using their hands, only someone with some expertise at geometry usually succeeds and even so it is difficult to do so in a non-procedural fashion (i.e. describing it as the curved path traced by a point about an origin with a constant or ever-increasing radius and with a constant linear translation of the origin on the remaining orthogonal axis is obviously procedural, as, of course, is the equation describing such spirals as, in both cases, the description embodies the actions that need to be carried out to generate a spiral). Thus it is not only tasks with a strong motor component that are obviously represented procedurally in people, but also what are primarily cognitive tasks. It should be noted that an inability to describe something does not mean it is not understood, obvious with the spiral example, even if we really do not understand walking. It is surely no surprise then, if all human knowledge is represented procedurally, that people have difficulty describing how they perform tasks. That some knowledge may appear to be expressed declaratively by the action of some procedures should not blind us to the fact that the psychological representation of the knowledge is procedural and that it is only for convenience that we choose to represent such knowledge declaratively. Such a position calls into question the reliability and validity of externally expressed knowledge in a declarative style. Given that these various arguments all suggest that verbal, natural language descriptions of thought are not to be trusted, then it opens the question of what alternatives are there to relying on experts' verbal behaviour in knowledge elicitation.

In the discussion below of possible alternatives to relying only on verbal descriptions, must first be injected a note of caution. It is at no point argued in this chapter that verbal protocols should not be used in knowledge elicitation or that valuable insights for the knowledge engineer will not result from the careful listening, and understanding, of comments made by domain experts and other personnel. Rather, what is argued is that this is likely not to be sufficient as the only technique employed in knowledge elicitation. However, many of these alternative methods are more time consuming than merely basing knowledge elicitation on domain experts' verbal commentary. Thus, in those expert system or KBS development projects where the expectations of the system are low and within a very narrow domain, and where the expert system must be produced in a very brief time, then collecting only verbal protocols from domain experts may be the only approach possible. Furthermore, the laboratory experiments of Burton and Shadbolt (1987; Burton *et al.,* 1987) appear to indicate, at least within the domain of geological rock identification that they used, that protocol analysis, which involves the domain expert attempting to express their thoughts as they perform the task, provides significantly less elicited knowledge than either using structured interviews, or non-verbal techniques such as card sorting or laddered grids. They have recently found similar results in at least one other domain, the identification of glacial landscape features from typical geographers' photographs (Burton and Shadbolt, 1988). Thus, even if external constraints force the use of verbally based knowledge elicitation procedures, then the evidence is that the popular, verbal protocol approach should not be used in preference to structured interviewing techniques.

Industrial psychologists and ergonomists, as well as psychometricians in quite a different field, have recognised this problem with verbal behaviour, even if it has not always been well articulated. Over the past fifty years methods of task analysis have been developed that emphasised the observation of what people do when performing a task, rather than what they say they do. It was not, however, until the early 1970s that task analysis techniques started to be developed that concentrated on the representation of tasks which were principally of a cognitive nature, rather than ones that were largely visio-motor. The impetus for developing these techniques comes from the information technology revolution and the original need was for the evaluation of user tasks on computer systems. Wilson *et al.* (1986) review eleven different task analysis techniques that have been developed for such purposes. A second application of at least some of these techniques is to allow the description of user requirement specifications in the early stages of design. This can be done by subjecting the potential future users of a system yet to be designed to task analyses of how they currently carry out their tasks. As mentioned in the previous section, this application of task analysis suffers a fundamental problem in that it can only provide a description of tasks using the current, old technology and that there is a gap between such specifications and how users will perform the analogous tasks on the new technology. The POMESS methodology (Diaper, 1987a, b-1988b) and its use of the Wizard of Oz simulation technique is a solution to this problem. It is not that simulation has not been done before, Shackel

(1986) lists a number of examples and advocates the approach himself, but only within POMESS has simulation been proposed as the main tool by which good ergonomics is brought into the design of computer systems at the very earliest stages. Also, it is not that task analysis does not often involve taking verbal protocols, either during a task or afterwards using a walk-through technique from a video record of the task being performed. However, when such protocols are taken it is quite common to find the behaviour of the person and even a concurrent verbal description are in contradiction. For example, in a video-tape of Peter Johnson (Queen Mary College, London) performing a word processing task while producing a concurrent verbal protocol, he can be seen placing the cursor, correctly for what he wishes to do, at the beginning of a word while saying 'I have now placed the cursor at the end of the word'. In other cases it is not possible to know which of two possible alternatives should be believed. Psychological theory, as portrayed in this chapter, suggests that it is safer to trust what people are seen to do, rather than what they say they do, which, after all, may not be such a bad philosophy for life in general.

There are also a number of other now well recognised problems of placing all of one's eggs in the verbal descriptive paradigms' basket (Bain-bridge, 1979; Diaper, 1987b). Firstly, the analyst not only ends up with incomplete descriptions because of the users' or experts' difficulty in accessing, in any form, most of her or his knowledge, but that they are incomplete because the verbal description is at a much higher, general level than that which can be obtained from the careful observation of behaviour. Thus some task details, usually unsystematically, are not available to the analyst, in contrast to the explicit decision made by a task observer not to record particular task details, such as the precise ballistics of the user's fingers operating a keyboard, or the inter-keystroke interval. Sometimes such a low level of detail is necessary to the understanding of task performance (e.g. Johnson *et al.*, 1986). Secondly, one tends to obtain a sanitised description of a task from using only the verbal modality. Particularly errors and error recovery procedures tend to be omitted and the author (Diaper, 1987b) has suggested that expert users are often unaware of even performing these. Anyone who has tried to teach novices how to use a computer program will recognise the difficulties in telling such students everything before they touch the keyboard, which is surely the same difficulty confronting the expert user being interviewed. Thirdly, people rarely describe tasks in a temporally linear fashion and they tend to jump around describing parts of the task out of sequence, even when prompted by the interviewer with comments such as 'Then what do you do next?'. Thus sequence information about the task is lost and, quite often, whole parts of the task are forgotten by the user who is describing a task while not carrying it out. Finally, as already commented on, a lot, if not all, verbal descriptions that purport to explain behaviour are *post hoc* and it is particularly worrying for the knowledge engineer that the verbal rationale provided to justify an expert's behaviour may have no bearing whatsoever on the real reason the expert behaved in a particular fashion.

It is surely clear that the problems confronting those using task analysis in HCI are identical to those confronting the knowledge engineer in knowledge elicitation and this point was made by Wilson (1987; and in Chapter 5). A great deal of effort in HCI has gone into the development of these techniques as a solution to the problem that people generally cannot describe what is involved in performing a task and that such descriptions are open to a range of types of distortion (Bainbridge, 1979; 1986). Furthermore, it should be clear from the arguments raised earlier in this section, and in contradiction to the hopes of Bainbridge, that there are fundamental problems associated with verbal descriptions and their relationship to human thought and knowledge representation. Thus the knowledge engineer is not tilling virgin soil and, in contrast to much current knowledge elicitation practice, a great deal can be learnt from the work of those that have preceded the knowledge engineer in a slightly different field. The ground has already been cleared and knowledge elicitation does not need another Locke, only a less blinkered perspective.

4. POSTSCRIPT

The purpose of this chapter has been to introduce the novice, and put into perspective for the expert, where knowledge elicitation resides in the processes of knowledge acquisition and knowledge engineering. The remaining chapters of this book concentrate exclusively on knowledge elicitation. This chapter has thus cast its net more widely than what follows and, I think, that it is not all uncontentious. The outstanding issue that has not been touched on in this chapter, for reasons of space if for no other, is that of the impact on society of expert systems becoming common. Like any tool expert systems will only be beneficial to people and society if used wisely and it needs recognising that the introduction of any new technology has, perhaps only temporarily, its down side as well. The present failure of many expert systems to make the transition from the research and development environment to the world of commerce and industry can still be brushed off as the teething troubles of a new technology. Like all new technologies expert systems are expensive and will only become cheaper by becoming common. It is possible that, with a few narrow exceptions, expert systems will suffer a backlash from those who hold the purse strings if the technology continues to fail to meet its promises. Furthermore, if better and more humane, people orientated methods of expert system development are not developed and used then, in the balance, the demise of expert systems may not be a bad thing for the general public.

Introduction to:
The third role — the naturalistic knowledge engineer

Having outlined the issues and problems of knowledge elicitation for expert systems design in the first chapter, this second chapter introduces the almost superhuman qualities of the ideal knowledge engineer. Bell and Hardiman refer to the knowledge engineer as having the 'third role' along with the first and second roles of the users and the domain experts and the chapter places this third role into its essential context within knowledge elicitation. They claim the knowledge engineer 'needs to be a psychologist, a diplomat, a researcher, an able politician, as well as having whatever technical skills are necessary'. Bell and Hardiman argue for a 'Naturalistic' knowledge engineering approach and by this they mean the 'new paradigm' of, for example, Lincoln and Guba (1984), or Heron (1981b) where, in contrast to the more traditional inquiry methods suitable for inanimate matter, it is possible to address the human subject of the inquiry and the naturalistic knowledge engineer 'will honour the humanity of the subject and researcher alike'. Furthermore, Bell and Hardiman are committed to a co-operative approach within a team and they identify and discuss the various roles of: the users; domain experts; users' managers; system maintainers; auditors; knowledge engineering managers; interviewers; notetakers; knowledge analysers; and system coders. Their naturalistic approach leads them to emphasise the importance of knowledge elicitation in its real world context or 'natural setting'. Thus the chapter addresses the nature of these roles as the context is at least as, if not more, importantly a social, rather than a physical, environment and their third role thus cannot be meaningfully divorced from these other roles. In particular, Bell and Hardiman emphasise the importance of the contribution that the users can make to the process of knowledge elicitation and they provide numerous examples of the importance of the dictum 'consult the user' from both 'live' knowledge engineering projects and from their extensive experience with running their course: 'The Human Side of Knowledge Engineering'. A valuable contrast can thus the drawn between the cynical portrayal of much real world knowledge engineering practices in Chapter 1 with the more human, and preferable approach advocated by Bell and Hardiman in Chapter 2.

2

The third role — the naturalistic knowledge engineer

Jill Bell
JB Associates, Winchester
and **R. J. (Bob) Hardiman**
Knowledge Based Systems Education, IBM United Kingdom,
Home Farm

There are three roles involved in the creation of an 'expert' or 'knowledge-based' system: the user, who will use the knowledge in his or her daily work; the expert, who is the source of the knowledge; and the knowledge engineer, who is the translator of the knowledge and mediator of the knowledge elicitation and acquisition process. This chapter addresses this third role and looks at the personal qualities and training necessary for anyone who wishes to undertake the task of knowledge engineering. Knowledge engineering, as outlined in Chapter 1, involves the elicitation of knowledge, changing it from the form in which it is supplied to a form that is comprehensible and usable to those who will be using the system. This chapter also describes the process of Naturalistic Knowledge Engineering (Bell, 1987a; Hardiman, 1987a; b) which provides a congruent framework to help the knowledge engineer to achieve the task in hand.

Naturalistic knowledge engineering will first be described within the context of the knowledge-engineer training course 'The Human Side of Knowledge Engineering'. It will then be described in detail and some justification for the use of the naturalistic paradigm will be offered, along with the approach's potential benefits for the knowledge engineer.

To remain consistent with the other chapters in this book we have reluctantly used the terms 'expert system', and 'user' throughout, rather than our preferred terms, 'knowledge-based system' and 'client'. We feel that the terms 'expert' and 'expert system' lay too much emphasis on *expertise*, when many useful and profitable systems have been developed using a combination of the appropriate computer technology and simple, heuristic knowledge that is certainly not 'expert'. Similarly, rather than 'experts' and 'users' we would prefer to talk of 'clients' and 'experts'. Clients are those who will make use of the knowledge in their daily work, and experts are those who supply the knowledge. Both the change of title as well as the change of order (clients before experts) reflect important considerations that we wish to draw out in this chapter. We would like to find an alternative term for 'expert', because expert is a loaded term and does not always accurately reflect the status of the source of the knowledge. However, 'source of the knowledge' is too clumsy, so, until a better term emerges, 'expert' will have to suffice.

Our experience with knowledge engineering projects and our experience with teaching the course have led us to realise that these terminological issues are important. We have observed marked changes in behaviour amongst various groups of people when they have been referred to as 'clients' rather than 'users'. Users tend to be unassertive and private with their views and thus end up with systems that do not fit their real needs. Clients, on the other hand, seem to react to the higher status that this term seems to confer, and are more readily able to state their needs in contrast to some of the ideas that may be held by the experts. However, we also appreciate the need for consistency of terminology; in Chapters 1 and 6 of this book the term 'client' has been used to denote the expert system purchasing organisation, rather than the direct users of the knowledge, thus we are forced to use the term 'user'.

This chapter differs from others in this book not only in matters of precise definition of terms, but also in the general style of writing. A word of explanation about why this is so seems in order. We are writing here of 'Naturalistic Knowledge Engineering'. In comments on an early draft of the chapter the editor (erroneously) referred to the 'Naturalistic Knowledge Engineering Paradigm'. What we are presenting here is knowledge engineering set in the context of a naturalistic paradigm of human inquiry. We see the activity of knowledge engineering as just another member of that set of acivities called human inquiry. This set includes such activities as sociological or psychological research, anthropology, detective work, journalism, and many more. Some of these activities have been pursued in the past in a strictly *ad hoc* fashion, others (for instance psychological or sociological research) have been carried out in accordance with well-defined methodological principles. These principles themselves are derived from a particular way of viewing the world — that of scientific inquiry based on an objectivist epistomology.

Recently there has been an upsurge of interest in looking at new ways of conducting human inquiry — of finding a new paradigm (Reason and Rowan, 1981; Schwartz and Ogilvy, 1979; Lincoln and Guba, 1984). This new paradigm pays heed to one fundamental difference between human inquiry and other forms of structured investigation — that both inquirer and inquiree are the same class of object (Heron, 1981b). If I am a chemist I am limited in the ways into which I can inquire into the nature of some substance — I can only observe the substance and its behaviour under controlled conditions. It makes no sense to inquire *of* the substance — only poets might attempt that ('Oh, Substance', they might begin, vocatively). However, as humans inquiring into human behaviour, the naturalistic inquirer realises that he or she *can* address the research subject. Further, the naturalistic inquirer finds that many of the more traditional inquiry methods, when applied to human inquiry, have an alienating and distancing effect. To be congruent with the ideas behind naturalistic inquiry, the conscientious enquirer will honour the humanity of subject and researcher alike, and will seek to be less alienating and less distancing. We, the authors of this chapter, work within this emergent naturalistic paradigm and are involved in the effort to map contours.

Part of this effort is an attempt to reduce the alienation that we feel results from a hard, objectivist view of the world. So when reporting our work, we tend not to talk of 'research subjects' or 'Ss', but of Fred or Joan or whoever. Similarly, we do not refer to 'the authors' but to 'We' and 'us'. This stance has caused our editor much heartache (here, he would prefer 'Editor'; we would prefer 'Dan'!) — we are grateful that he has allowed us the license to write in this style — one that we hope reflects the naturalistic paradigm that we are attempting to describe.

1. THE COURSE

The development of the NKE methodology has been influenced by a number of strands. In the first instance there was the work on research method, particularly co-operative inquiry, by Heron (Heron, 1981a; b; Reason and Rowan, 1981; Reason, 1988) and many others, and, in particular, Lincoln and Guba's *Naturalistic Inquiry* (1984), provided us with the impetus to address the problems of knowledge acquisition using adaptations of methods used by 'new paradigm human inquiry' researchers.

Subsequently we have used the Naturalistic Knowledge Engineering (NKE) methods in our own projects, have consulted in a range of other knowledge processing projects, and have run a knowledge engineer's training course called 'The Human Side of Knowledge Engineering'. At the time of writing (July 1988) the course has run 17 times, including twice in the USA (in New York and California) and once each in Germany, Singapore, and Brazil.

We have probably learnt more from the students of the course than from any other source (Bell, 1987a), although all our activities in this area have been fruitful sources of our own learning. It is relevant here to say a little about the structure of the course as we will refer to it several times during this chapter in order to illustrate a variety of points.

The course currently lasts for four days and is highly experential. On the first two days we introduce the structure of the NKE methodology and an outline of the process and then rapidly move into a series of exercises designed to introduce class members to the processes of interviewing, listening, data gathering (including using audio and video recording), notetaking, transcribing, and many other skills.

On the third day class members do a case study, in groups, based on non-vocational expertise of volunteer experts within the class. Over the 18 months that the class has run so far have had expertise ranging from building your own house in England to building your own touring bicycle in Japan, from playing the game of Risk in Holland (where, apparently the rules differ from the English version — it took the team nearly half a day, and almost created an international incident to discover this difference) to dancing the jitterbug in California.

We have stuck to non-vocational expertise in order to focus on the process of knowledge elicitation rather than on creating a working knowledge-based system. Indeed, we specify that the case study should stop short of actually implementing a system — a paper model is satisfactory.

On the final day of the course the case study teams present a summary of their system, of the processes that they went through, and the learning that developed during the day. The course ends with a theoretical review of the Lincoln and Guba 14-point naturalistic inquiry methodology, and how that maps onto the NKE process.

During the lifetime of the course so far some common themes have emerged, which are generally instructive to the student of NKE. They are:

- Telling people to consult users is not good enough; positive steps must be taken to ensure that it happens, that it happens before the experts are consulted, and that the user's need are considered throughout the project. If such positive steps are not taken then people will willingly give lip-service to the importance of consulting users, but much to their surprise, and despite their good intentions, when they come to review their process they will discover that they have ignored the users.
- The quantity of knowledge collected from an expert, even in an entirely trivial area of expertise, even when the 'expert' denies having any expertise, is usually completely overwhelming for everyone else concerned. A common feeling amongst NKEs is a feeling of depression and panic at the quantity of material produced, with a concomitant feeling of 'whatever will I do with all of this?'

  It is our experience that if experts are interviewed before users then the NKE team will continue to be depressed. During the case study they usually call us in around 3 p.m., point to a mass of information written up on flip-charts or 'Post Its' and ask us what to do next. When users are interviewed *first* the users' needs form a framework or structure for the system, on which the detail supplied by the expert can be hung.

2.   THE TASK OF THE NATURALISTIC KNOWLEDGE ENGINEER

An analogy can be made between knowledge and a natural, mineral resource. In this analogy, knowledge can be thought of as a natural resource, but, like many other natural resources, it is not always easy to extract. Like surface-mined coal, some knowledge is easily picked up. You need do no more than collect and read the appropriate book, procedures manual, or training package. Collection of this knowledge, while still valuable, is not the task that we are considering here.

To continue with this mining metaphor: some knowledge is not easily available on the surface; it has to be dug out. However, when a vein is hit, out comes whole, shiny nuggets. Knowledge in this form is half-remembered, but the expert can refer to old case records to jog his memory, in order to produce the information we need. This collection process whilst also important, is also not the main theme of this chapter.

So just what is the concern of the naturalistic knowledge engineer? It is the recovery of the 'expert' knowledge that has, paradoxically, both become so much second-nature to the expert that it is inaccessible. It is what Polanyi (1966) calls 'tacit knowledge'. This is also dealt with in Chapter 1, and by Bainbridge (1986), Diaper (1987b).

Consider for a moment a few common skills that are usually 'tacit'. For example the knitter who can turn out a garment in an evening, whilst watching TV and holding a conversation at the same time, but who cannot teach you how to knit. To her the skill of knitting is tacit knowledge. And the skill of driving is tacit knowledge to drivers who are perfectly competent at getting from 'a' to 'b' safely, but who are unable to teach their teenagers to drive. Expert maintenance engineers are also using tacit knowledge when they fix a box in a tenth of the time allowed in the manual, but are unable to articulate how they do it. Tacit expert knowledge is frequently a valuable resource in the company, a resource that has not been developed by conventional education, but which has been built up by years of experience. It is difficult to articulate, often because it has never been articulated before and also (as argued in Chapter 1) because procedural styles of knowledge are difficult to articulate than declarative styles. Finding, transforming, and disseminating this knowledge, through the process of building and installing an expert system, can often give companies significant competitive advantage. This is the task of the naturalistic knowledge engineer.

In describing the process of retrieving and transforming this tacit knowledge the mining metaphor still holds, but we are no longer scratching the surface or digging holes for nuggets — we are now searching for ores that will need considerable processing before they yield the material that we value. The naturalistic knowledge engineer has not only to *find* the knowledge, but also to process it into a form that is understandable by the expert, so that it can be verified. The form of the knowledge should be understandable and also be *usable* by the user. If the knowledge is not in a form that is usable, then users will apply the ultimate sanction to the system — they will not use it, or will not use it efficiently.

In the process of teaching knowledge engineering and consulting on knowledge acquisition projects around the world, we have encountered many knowledge-based systems that are demonstrated proudly by their authors, but which are ignored by the users for whom the systems were designed (see also, Chapters 1 and 6).

We even have one example of a highly successful knowledge-based system which is saving its owners many millions of dollars a year. The designers consulted some of the potential users of the system when the system was being built, but as the designers only worked from 9 am to 5 pm they only consulted the first- and second-shift users. When the system went live, the night-shift workers refused to have anything to do with it: the system was only being used by two-thirds of the work-force.

So the naturalistic KE needs to be able to elicit the tacit knowledge, and to transform it into a form that is acceptable to both the users and the expert. And in order to do that the KE needs to be a psychologist, a counsellor, a diplomat, a researcher, an able politician, as well as having whatever technical skills may be necessary.

3. NATURALISTIC KNOWLEDGE ENGINEERING

3.1 The process

The process of Naturalistic Knowledge Engineer involves recognising some basic principles:

- It is a co-operative process, involving users, experts, the KE, and management.
- It takes place primarily in the natural setting; the setting in which the knowledge is customarily used.
- It is essentially a process of research, or exploration, with people.
- It is about finding tacit knowledge and transforming that knowledge into useful knowledge capable of being articulated.
- It is an iterative process, following the *Experiential Learning Cycle* (Kolb, 1984) describe later in this chapter.
- It is a process which needs auditing.
- It is a process which produces context sensitive results.

We will take these one by one and discuss them below.

3.1.1 *A co-operative process*

Naturalistic Knowledge Engineering (NKE) is as much a philosophy as a process. A part of this philosophy says that working co-operatively with people is the way to achieve a useful and usable system. This may seem obvious. However, during our experience of teaching NKE, and acting as consultants for ES development projects, we have encountered many occasions where the users had not only not been consulted; they had not even been identified. In one memorable project in the USA we were told, 'That's all very well, but it doesn't apply to us — we don't have any users'.

It is not the case that all ES projects are staffed by loners who refuse to have anything to do with one another. The problem is more subtle than that. The NKE is faced with both experts and users who are very busy and do not have time to co-operate — they barely have time to be interviewed. And, as the system that is being built is often called an 'expert system', it is easy to be seduced by the presence of the expert, and to forget the needs of the people who are supposed to use the system.

Frequently, when you do find some users, and ask them what they want, they do not know (see also Chapters 1 and 6). The easy way then is to go off quietly into a corner and write the system, and tell them that is what they are going to get. If they complain, you can rightly point out that you did ask them what they wanted, but that they did not know.

Co-operation must be worked for. The NKE must insist on adequate involvement of the users and experts. If users do not know what they want, then they must be educated so that they know what is available. For example, they can be shown prototypes, be allowed to play with those prototypes, and be encouraged to develop ideas about what ESs could do for them. Then they will soon be able to say what they want. For example, if you were to ask a typist who had never seen a computer, what facilities she would like in a word-processor, she would probably not be able to tell you. If, however, you were to demonstrate a program, she would soon begin to have ideas of the possibilities available. If you were then to teach her how to use that program, and went away, she would soon be on the phone with suggestions of how she would like it changed.

Even amongst the most easy-going of experts, there is often a strong sense of 'owning' the knowledge. In our KE class we set simple exercises — interviewing 'experts' on how to get to their homes. Several have reported feeling very protective towards even this trivial level of expertise when users were interviewed first, and in the presence of the expert. We ourselves found strong feelings emerging when it was suggested that someone should 'ghost write' a book about naturalistic knowledge engineering and should start by identifying a user group of potential readers and interviewing them before talking to us. We became anxious that those interviewed would impose some sort of advance censorship; that their requirements would not be met by the book we wanted to write; that they would ask for something we were not interested in writing.

In order to ensure that the effects of such emotions do not interfere with the smooth progress of the project, much diplomacy is needed. We suggest that the users are, indeed, interviewed first, and not in the presence of the experts. Furthermore it is also important to explain the process to all involved, to seek their agreement, and to explain why the process is as it is. When people believe that they understand what is happening, they are much more likely to co-operate.

Another related phenomenon is the rejection of what people feel is an 'alien' system that is being imposed upon them. People refer to the 'Not Invented Here' or NIH syndrome — it is an effect of the feelings of alienation that can develop when outside solutions are imposed on people who have yet to recognise a problem. When experts, users, and management are all involved co-operatively with the NKE in the project a strong feeling of 'our' system emerges, and people feel pride of ownership, rather than alienation and rejection.

Another constant problem that can be alleviated by fostering a spirit of co-operation is the issue of status that arises. It is frequently the case that the experts are more senior in the organisation than the users, and may sometimes question the users' ability to understand the full extent of their skill and ability. Even when the higher-status experts are sensitive to the differences in position, just the labels used — 'expert' and 'user' — can shape people's behaviour.

We have noticed a surprising and recurring phenomenon in the class. We arbitrarily divide the class into groups for excises, and then ask them to allocate roles within the groups — expert, user, interviewer, notetaker, and so on. Having warned the class of the importance of first consulting the users, we then ask them to conduct interviews on some trivial subject. After the interview we ask the class to re-form, this time into 'role' groups — all the experts together, all the users together and so on, to discuss their experiences. Finally a representative from each role group is asked to present a summary of the experiences of that group to the whole class. The users always complain that they were not asked what they required of the system during the exericise. Even when we repeat the exercise with new people taking the roles, the new set of users *still* complain that they were not consulted. Somehow the label 'user' seems to drain people of any assertiveness that they ever had.

More recently we specifically charge certain groups with the task of conducting two interviews, some starting with the users, some with the experts. The groups who interview the users first report much greater understanding of the problems involved, but also report needing to understand the difficulties that the experts have with their sense of ownership of the knowledge. It is vital that each project group takes care of its members and attends to each of these points, checking out that people are being heard, and are being consulted.

The users and the experts are not the only members of the team to be beset by troublesome emotions. Probably the most powerful emotion to disturb the NKE is a feeling of needing to be in control. When interviewing anyone the prime skill required is the ability to keep quiet and to listen. This is especially true when the interviewee is having to think carefully about what is being asked. Long silences often ensue — the expert or user is thinking hard.

Frequently when this happens the KE feels inadequate — feels a strong need to *do* something. It is important for the NKE to realise that people should be encouraged to solve their own problems. That way there is no sense of the system being imposed upon them. NKEs should understand that their role is essentially that of catalyst and that the best NKEs say very little and seem to do even less. But like chemical catalysts, the process would not proceed without them.

Co-operation does not imply that everyone is equal or that each task within the project is done by committee. Instead it should be understood what roles need to be specified. These roles should be allocated (preferably volunteered or bid for) where they are not implicit in a person's job in the organisation, and everyone should understand that, within the team, each role has equal status and that each person has equal value. Managing, or facilitating, this co-operation is the task of the NKE.

Some of the roles that need to be filled are:

- Representative(s) of the users.
- Supplier(s) of the knowledge — experts.
- Management of the target function (users' manager).
- System maintainer — to keep the system up-to-date once it is in use.

- Auditor — whose concern is the trustworthiness c therefore the validity of the resulting system.
- Management of the KE process.
- Primary interviewer — normally one of the knowle may occasionally be the user or the expert interview facilitated by the NKE.
- Notetaker, or back-up interviewer — a function which needs filling in any interview and is best rotated between two NKEs.
- Knowledge analyser — primarily the task of the NKEs, but experts and users can do it to the advantage of themselves and the NKEs.
- System coder — the knowledge engineer again if he or she has the skill. Otherwise it can be delegated. The knowledge engineer should not be selected merely for programming skill.

The last five roles may well fall to one over-burdened knowledge engineer, which illustrates why we stress the importance of a partnership of two people for this job, preferably with complementary skills.

The team approach originated to some extent, with the course case study, where it is convenient to achieve team working, and, indeed, quite difficult to avoid it. However, it received such universal support, and so many claims that the work could not be done any other way, that we have strongly advocated it when doing consultancy in organisations. Case-study teams who adopt the co-operative approach achieve more than those who do not, and this applies also to organisations where the project manager has followed our advice to set up such a team.

3.1.2 *The natural setting*

Lincoln and Guba (1984) set out their 14-point plan for carrying out 'naturalistic inquiry'. The seond point in their system is that research should be carried out in 'the natural setting'. By this term Lincoln and Guba mean the setting that is natural to the activity being studied. They point out that the mere fact that research is now taking place compromises the naturalness of the setting, but this in no way suggests that the research should be carried out other than in the natural setting, only that it behoves the researchers to both minimise the effects of the presence, and to take steps to anticipate those effects, and to take them into consideration. The major reason that they give for insisting on the natural setting is that activity is context bound and that to study any human activity divorced of its context is to study it divorced of its meaning.

It is vital that any system that is produced be usable. In order to ensure the usability of the system it is important that the builders understand the context in which the system will be used. This context cannot be fully understood by verbal reports gathered from experts and users. The NKE must understand the natural setting in which they work — the environment in which the system will be used. If this setting is noisy or public then the verbal reports will need to be gathered away from it. Similarly, tha analysis and representation of the collected knowledge needs to take place in peace and quiet. However, at some stage in the collection process, the NKE should try, wherever possible, to join in the action. That is to say, the NKE should at the very least observe the process going on in as near normal conditions as possible. Complete normality is not possible — in the true natural setting the NKE would not be present. Nevertheless, it is important to come as close as possible to achieving natural settings.

It is even more helpful if the NKE can actually participate in the process that the system is supposed to be handling. Frequently we have found that, when NKEs actually immerse themselves in the natural setting to a considerable extent, they come away with a much better understanding of what they are trying to achieve. This ingredient has been conspicuously and necessarily lacking from the case-studies on the course, an omission which would have caused problems for the implementation of several of the systems in the real world. For example, one team worked on an expert system for flying a simple circuit in a glider. Some weeks later we went gliding and discovered a snag which had not emerged within the limitations of the classroom: that there is no room in a glider for any extra equipment — you are lucky to be able to move your knees more than half an inch in any direction. So that system could not have been used.

3.1.3 Research with people

The ideas behind NKE have been derived from the move by many anthropologists, sociologists and psychologists to find a new paradigm on which to base their research methodology (Reason and Rowan, 1981; Reason, 1988; Lincoln and Guba, 1984; Schwartz and Ogilvy, 1979). The thrust of this research is to acknowledge the essential difference between researching any other subject and researching people. This difference is twofold: first that the researcher and subject are the same class of being (Heron, 1981b), and secondly that the possibility exists when humans research humans that the researcher can *ask* the subject as opposed to just observing behaviour.

Furthermore, we (and many others) believe that there are also many moral and ethical questions that are more pertinent with research involving people as the subject matter, than with any other research area.

Perhaps the eventual conclusion of this methodological direction is the co-operative inquiry method developed by Heron and Reason (Heron, 1981b; Reason, 1988). In this process the distinctions between researcher and subject fade away as everyone involved becomes co-researcher and co-subject, equally involved in the thinking that drives the research, the analysis of the results and the drawing of conclusions, as well as the actual action of the research. Co-operative inquiry has been well documented in Reason and Rowan (1981).

Some work that followed on from Reason and Rowan's Human Inquiry was that of Lincoln and Guba (1984). Their work formed the basis for the naturalistic knowledge engineering process described by Hardiman (1987a, b). For more details of this process, and the mapping between Lincoln and Guba's naturalistic inquiry and Hardiman's naturalistic knowledge engineering, see Hardiman (1987b).

3.1.4 Tacit knowledge

As noted elsewhere, NKE is the process of uncovering and making plain tacit knowledge, as described by Polanyi (1966). There are many methods for gathering knowledge that seem naturally easy to represent in a propositional form. In particular, we can read it, write it, and listen to it from the lips of the knowledgeable by attending lectures and tutorials.

However, tacit knowledge has the property of seeming amorphous and being difficult to grasp. The process of NKE should be directed to giving form to this knowledge and is likely to result in as loud an 'Aha!' from the expert source of the knowledge as it does from the users or the NKE. The experts' cries of discovery are indeed frequently louder as they start to understand the subject in new ways. This is possibly because they do not expect to be surprised: they are exploring what they naturally think of as the known territory of their expertise and they discover unknown depths, new angles. This can be disconcerting, but it often provides useful material for considering how the job might be done differently or better. We have talked to a KE in California who seldom actually implements a knowledge processing system on a computer — he frequently finds that the process of structuring and clarifying the knowledge is sufficient for both his experts and users. And if analysis with a view to change and greater efficiency is all his clients want, then a paper system is usually adequate. However, if the expertise needs to be disseminated (either to teach newcomers or less skilled workers, or to standardise a procedure), then a paper system is not so flexible and portable, or so easy to maintain and update.

3.1.5 An iterative process

In processes that are repetitions of well-trodden routes it may be possible to plan the project meticulously from start to finish. The serving of complex equipment can be carefully scheduled with modern planning tools, as can the development of highly complex software systems, provided the entire process is well understood before the project begins.

With a system based on knowledge that is initially tacit this is not possible. Before we start we are in a state of 'meta-unknowing' — we do not know what it is that we do not know. At this meta-unknowing stage it is vital that all participants keep as open a mind as possible, suspending judgement and being open to whatever comes.

To people used to dealing with hard scientific facts this can be extremely difficult. In the course we encounter most resistance from students when we ask them to keep their minds quiet and open — they seem to be too used to thinking. When reading the original draft of this chapter, the editor took as much exception as the students usually do, and made some cutting comments about 'Zen' and 'Samurai'; we think that these comments were maybe more apt than the editor realised. The ability to quiet the mind and just 'be' is an essential part of many eastern philosophies, probably going to the extreme in Zen Buddhism. We believe that this is an essential attribute of a naturalistic knowledge engineer, and whilst we have not actually introduced Zen mediation into the course yet, the idea has definite appeal to us.

Brew (1988) proposes some guidelines for personal phenomenological inquiry which are relevant here:

(1) Entertain the hypothesis that everything is relevant.
(2) (After Husserl) When you think you know — look again.
(3) Act with unbending intent, without circumventing difficulties.

Let us examine these guidelines:

(1) As NKEs in a state of meta-unknowing we have to assume that everything is relevant. To do otherwise is either lazy, shortsighted, or arrogant, and risks losing valuable knowledge. Only during a later cycle of the process will we be in a position to judge which data falls outside the scope of the project. Even then it may be unwise to discard it in case the project should be extended to include that data area at a later stage.
(2) NKEs cannot assume that their understanding of the knowledge is the one intended by the expert or the user. NKEs may misinterpret because of a bias in their own experience or understanding of a word. Their understanding may be on the right track, but superficial. Only by constantly reflecting back to the expert or user for verification; by showing the expert or user their representation of the knowledge; and by working with their sources to create a mutually acceptable and understandable representation, can NKEs be sure of achieving an understanding which is as accurate as it is possible to be. Nothing can be taken for granted. The knowledge needs to be continually revisited, approaching it from different directions, and by different routes.
(3) The last item should be particularly borne in mind when faced with unavailable experts, systems that do not have users, and management who think that you can produce the entire system by yourself. It could be an exhortation to NKEs to have the courage of their convictions: to be assertive with managers who are obstructive about the availability of their staff; to insist on the importance of involving users; to persist in getting proper answers to questions, particularly of the sort 'who owns this problem?'; to insist they have proper support, whether that be equipment, a second NKE, or time allocated to do the job properly. This guideline could also be an encouragement to be disciplined with themselves: a warning against closing an interview prematurely just because the NKE feels overwhelmed and panic-striken by the seemingly endless flow of knowledge which is forthcoming from the expert.

Having collected some knowledge the NKE is in a position to retire from the fray and to consider what has been obtained. The NKE sits back and reflects and theorises. On the basis of these theories the NKE can plan the next stage of the investigation. Thus the project follows a cyclical process (Fig. 2.1) that is very akin to the experimental learning cycle of Kolb (1984). Such a cycle is also central to Lincoln and Guba's (1984) naturalistic inquiry process.

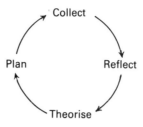

Fig. 2.1

(1) *Collect.* Before the NKE can begin to work on any part of the system there has to be some initial data. If, as NKE, you have pre-existent knowledge then maybe the first collection phase of the project has already, in effect, been completed, and all you have to do is record what you already know. We believe that there are two types of NKE; the specialist and the generalist. The specialist will be writing a system in an area where he already has considerable knowledge. The generalist, however, probably works in an expert systems department, and may be writing systems concerned with very different subjects on different days.

For the specialist the first collection phase of the project has been going on for years, and the start of the project perhaps all that is necessary is for the NKE to record his knowledge, the better to reflect on it at the next stage, and to make it available for others to check his assumptions. For the generalist, however, it is important to realise that there *is* no pre-existent knowledge, and thus the first phase of the project consists of open interviewing with the 'Zen-quiet mind' alluded to earlier. The collection can be by interview, reading or observation and should be as wide as possible — without prior knowledge of the subject the NKE has no knowledge that will serve to put boundaries on the collection process.

Lincoln and Guba label the first point in their cycle 'purposive sampling' and discuss the need for 'relevant' rather than 'representative' sampling. The distinction is, we believe, not so important for the NKE — it is seldom the case that one is presented with so many experts that one has to take a sample, but more work needs to be done on defining relevant samples of large user populations for expert systems.

(2) *Reflect.* When the first collection phase is over the NKE can spend some quiet time just thinking about what has been learned. We have believed for quite some time that it is important to sleep on the findings of an interview before coming to major conclusions. Recently we have altered the structure of the course so that the one-day case study starts and ends mid-day, in order to allow people a chance to sleep and reflect on their findings. We have had feedback from the students to the effect that this reflection time is most valuable. In Lincoln and Guba's cycle this point is labelled 'Inductive Data Analaysis'. In the course we include a rapid overview of the difference between inductive and deductive reasoning

— induction starts from the data and looks for patterns, deductions starts from the generalised patterns (which might be logic rules, or theories, or hypotheses, or even production rules) to generate data. We believe that the process of perceiving the patterns in the data works better after a period of reflection, and the application of some of the knowledge analysis techniques mentioned later in this chapter.

(3) *Theorise.* Record the patterns that have emerged from the previous reflections. These patterns are usually seen as theories or hypotheses about the way the expert or user may behave in certain situations. The theories have no pretence to being grand or universal truths. They are 'grounded theories' (Glaser and Strauss, 1967) which are grounded in the 'here and now' of what we are doing in this project. These theories have been drawn out of the data collected, refer to that particular context only, and make no assumptions about another time or another place.

(4) *Plan.* Well-known processes can be fully planned before they begin. Exploratory processes cannot. Until we have learned *something* we have no data to put into the planning process. But at the end of each iteration of the NKE process we have more data and greater knowledge than we had at the beginning. This data is input into the planning process for the next iteration of the cycle. On the basis of what we know now we can plan where we need to go next.

Of course, any computer scientist will look askance at a loop like this that does not come with a carefully described terminating condition. It is not only computer programs that go into infinite loops — many development projects exhibit the same propensity. Defining the terminal condition and monitoring whether or not it has been reached is another of the tasks of the NKE. The monitoring should also be done by the project auditor (of whom more, anon), on behalf of management.

3.1.6   The need for audit

We do not refer here to the process of financial audit, although there are strong parallels. The financial auditor looks to see whether well-known financial practices have been adhered to, and whether the financial accounts represent what they purport to represent. The audit process in an NKE project works in an analogous fashion. The auditor is someone who understands the process but is not involved in the project, and is someone whose responsibility is to monitor the process as a guard against 'malpractice', whether inadvertent or deliberate.

Validity is a tough issue to crack when NKEs, users and experts are immersed together in both the action and the thinking of the project, and when the subjectivity of everyone involved is a major part of the project. When reading the draft of this chapter the editor noted 'Validity needs defining' and went on to say 'Its normal usage is in the mapping of some theory, representation, postulate, etc., to the "real world"' (his emphasis on 'real world'). Those inverted commas around 'read world' summarise the difficulty, both for naturalistic knowledge engineers, and for natualistic inquirers, presented by the notion of validity. For when dealing with objective reality the *notion* of validity is easy to grasp, even if ensuring validity can cause methodological or experimental difficulties. However, when dealing with the subjective worlds of experts, users, managers (and NKEs!), the notion of an *objective reality* evaporates, and with it goes the notion of validity. But that still leaves us with the feeling that it is possible to create a system that is *wrong*, and hence we need to ensure that the system is not wrong, but is, in some sense, *right*.

In the same way, ensuring that a knowledge-based system is useful, usable and reasonably free of bias is also a difficult problem. The problem for the NKE is to manage the biases, and to ensure that those relevant to the success of the system are the ones that are included. The biases of the NKE probably have least relevance to the system, followed by those of the expert. The user should have the major say in what is included and what is not. But this method is over-simplistic — it may be that the user wants a system that does x, and is not interested in other possibilities. Is this because the extra facilities really are not relevant to the job that the user does, or is it that the user has some investment in excluding the other facilities — not wanting extensions to job responsibility, for instance? Conversely, are the extra facilities being put into the system because of biases of the expert (cover subjects that he is interested in) or of the NKE (demonstrates virtuosity as a programmer, for instance).

Whilst successful co-operative working has enormous benefits, it also introduces the problem of people not being able to see the wood for the trees, and of people colluding to avoid difficult or uncomfortable areas that need to be investigated.

To address this problem we suggest that the project should appoint an auditor. The audit process can be similar to the process of inspections or structured walkthroughs used by software developers — or, indeed, to the process of financial audit. During the audit an outsider, knowledgeable in the process but not necessarily in the task, reviews the progress of the task. He checks that it conforms to the process; that it is achieving what it purports to achieve; and the project objectives are being met. Clearly, this description is overly simple; we believe that much work remains to be done in defining the process of auditing a KE project.

3.1.7 Context sensitivity

One of the key points of Lincoln and Guba's naturalistic inquiry process is that it produces context sensitive results. By this they mean that inquiry findings should only be interpreted within the context of the inquiry — on these occasions and under these conditions these people acted, thought, behaved and felt in these ways. The implication behind the fact that inquiry findings are being written and published is that other people may find the findings interesting or useful, not that the inquiry findings have produced nomothetic laws applicable to all humankind. Similarly, knowledge-based systems also tend to be highly context sensitive: it is very rare that a knowledge-based system that is produced for one set of users will be usable by another set. Other potential user groups may admire the system, and see the potential benefits of having a *similar* system — but when it is suggested that they could use the same system, it is usually the case that 'that's not quite how we do things here'.

This attitude should be respected. If we have involved representatives of the first user group in developing their own system, then it is reasonable to suppose that other user groups will also want a system that is tailored to their own needs.

This doesn't mean that we have to continually re-invent wheels. A major part of the design work will have been done with the first system, and, provided that we are using knowledge processing software that capitalises on the ease of use that is possible with good quality products, we should be able to adapt the system to reflect the special needs of each user group, with a minimum of effort. In one major company we have encountered examples both of systems that have been widely used throughout the company, and other systems that have been widely described and discussed, but which have not been used other than in the original context. Careful inspection of these systems has revealed that the deciding factor in assessing the transferability of a system is the context of the system. A system that guides the manufacturing of a product is relevant wherever that product is manufactured, provided that consistency of the manufacturiong process is a prime requirement. Another system that provides guidance in interpreting tax legislation is also widely used — consistency in interpretation is expressed as a prime reason for using the system.

However, another system that helps users to use a complex computer system has been identified as potentially useful throughout the company, but has not been widely used in it original form. Potential users have been interested, but the 'not invented here' syndrome, local procedures, and local needs have all indicated the need for local systems. However, the original system frequently provides a useful model for the local system, or, at the very least, a starting point for discussion.

3.2   The methods
The fundamentals methods of NKE involve three major areas:

- Collecting the knowledge. This is commonly called 'elicitation', but attendences on the course have taken us to task for use of 'jargon', so we refer to 'collection' here, rather than 'elicitation'. We mean any or all methods of getting the knowledge.
- Analysing the knowledge, or making sense of the jumbled mass of information that is the usual result of any successful interview.
- Representing the knowledge in both an understandable and a usable form, in order to facilitate our own understanding as NKEs, to reflect back to the knowledge source for verification, and to encourage the production of more knowledge.

These areas are all inter-dependent and not separable in practice, but it makes sense to treat each separately when discussing NKE. We will now expand on each area in turn.

3.2.1 Knowledge collection

Collection consists of open and focussed interviews, reading manuals and other documents, observing current users and experts at work, analysing past cases and a host of other activities. In all these activities the naturalistic knowledge engineer is at pains to ensure that the knowledge being gathered is relevant, useful and as complete as possible. Furthermore all parties to the process should be left feeling that their involvement is of benefit to them as well as to the company or department sponsoring the creation of the knowledge system.

The term 'interview' is used in this chapter to cover all face-to-face interaction between team members. We then make the following distinctions between types of interview:

- Open
- Closed
- Focused
- Unfocused

We classify these interviews as

- Contextual and detailed
- Helpful and unhelpful

The contextual interview is intended to get an overview of the area in which the system under discussion is to be used. It is important to use the contextual interview to establish rapport and trust between team members, to expand the scope of limited thinking, to get the 'big picture'. A successful contextual interview is open — the interviewer says little, uses facilitative, catalytic interventions (Heron, 1986), and encourages the interviewee to do all the thinking. Facilitative interventions are those that help the process of encouraging the interviewee to talk.

Heron's Six category Intervention Analysis (Heron, 1986) is a categorisation of all the ways in which a 'practitioner' can 'intervene' in the process of the 'client'. This is a comprehensive analysis, covering a wide variety of situations. For the purpose of the NKE we can think of the NKE as the practitioner and the interviewee, whether expert or user, as the client. Heron's six categories are divided into the 'authoritative' interventions:

- Prescriptive
- Informative
- Conforming

and the 'facilitative interventions:

- Cathartic
- Catalytic
- Supportive

Of all these categories it seems to us important that the NKE avoids the authoritative interventions, with the exception that it is clearly important to inform those involved what it is that you are doing, how, and to what purpose. It seems unlikely to us that cathartic interventions will be appropriate (cathartic interventions are those that would enable a client to clear behavioural blocks by expressing the blocking emotions. We have heard of clients reduced to tears by the systems they are using, but we would not recommend this as a strategy for the aspiring NKE!). However, catalytic interventions do seem appropriate Heron describes catalytic interventions:

> They seek to enable the client to learn and develop by self-direction and self-discovery both within the context of the practitioner–client interaction but also beyond it. They facilitate the emergence of impeding client-generated change, never overstay their welcome, and are alive with active empathy. (Heron, 1986, p. 57).

Heron goes on to talk about the use of catalytic interventions in 'the facilitation of self-direction in learning'. It may, at first sight, seem strange to talk of facilitation of self-direction in learning, when it is our job, as NKEs, to learn, and the expert's or users' jobs to teach us. We believe, however, that when the task is the elicitation of tacit knowledge, that our task is one of facilitating meta-learning — that is, learning what we have already learnt — discovering what we know. Tacit knowledge is 'unconscious' knowledge — the task of the NKE is to help make this knowledge conscious, get it structured and into a propositional form, and to be a witness and recorder of the process and its outcomes.

To the uninitiated, the open interview appears deceptively simple — all you have to do is shut up and be encouraging. However, our experience is that very few interviewers have the ability to conduct an open interview until they have a lot of experience.

Focused interviewing follows open interviewing. Having established the context and understood the broad pattern of the project, it is time to start focusing on detail. Whereas the agenda for an open interview has a very few, broad items on it, the focused interview should have a clear agenda that spells out exactly what needs to be classified of discovered. The agenda may be written, and may be sent out before the interview — which is not the case with the agenda for an open interview. For example, here are two possible agendas for interviews, the first open, with the users, and the second focused, with the expert:

Interviewer's agenda for first open interview with users of XYZ Project
  Meet the users, introduce ourselves, check out what they know about us, and verify what we've been told about them.

  Establish rapport.

  Get a broad idea of what they do, and what problems they encounter.

Ask them to comment on the proposed system — get them to talk about how they feel about it.

Check whether they need an outline of what ES can do — have they ever seen one or heard of one. Sound out their feelings about ES.

And here is a possible agenda for a focused interview:

Interviewer's agenda for focused interview with expert of XYZ Project
Verify that models XJ2Q and XJ3Q are the only models with high susceptibility to lightning damage.

Check that the major causes of failure are only those listed below, and find percentages:

> Faulty installation of the power module
> Lightning damage resulting in TR3 failure
> Lightning damage resulting in TR7 failure
> Component failure in the addressing circuits

Ask about repair strategies for XJ847s that have been damaged by mechanical mishandling.

Ask to accompany expert on next field call to fix an XP254I.

In our classes we usually find that the first interviewing exercise that people do is far too closed, when we have suggested that they conduct an open interview in order to establish content and ground rules. Subsequently they realise that they have not learnt much from the open interview, and then try to conduct an open interview at the time when they are being asked to do a focused interview. The confusion is usually spectacular, but instructive! It is interesting to note that subsequent interviews are much more open in the early stages. There is also much debate as to whether it is a good thing to interview experts first, or users first. The debate gets quite vigorous in most classes, with most people holding strong views one way of another. From straw polls conducted in recent classes opinion seems to be split about 50-50. Our own experience suggests that a useful strategy at the start of the project goes

* Open, user
* Open, expert
* Focused, expert
* Focused, user

Subsequently, it very much depends on the project and the personalities involved.

There are also what Heron calls 'degenerate' forms of the contextual and detailed interviews. The degenerate form of the contextual interview, we call 'closed' — implying that participants have decided before the interview what will take place, opportunities for learning and discovery are lost, that the context uncovered is small, that rapport is not established, that the interview is not 'user centred' and that the interviewer does most of the talking. Closed interviews are usually the result of nervousness and a reluctance to be 'laid back' on the part of the interviewer. The degenerate form of the focused interview we call unfocused, or fuzzy. The interview turns up with no clear idea of where the project has got to, what he needs to find out. He has no agenda, and the inteview turns out to be a waste of time.

	Helpful	Unhelpful
Contextual	Open	Closed
Detailed	Focused	Unfocused

Fig. 2.2 — Types of interview

Actually recording the knowledge during the interviews is an important and difficult task. Our suggestion for a 'best possible' interview is:

- Have two interviewers. They should be equals, and should alternate the role of 'interviewer' and 'notetaker'.
- Record the interview. If *any* mechanical skills are involved, then record using video. If video is inappropriate then use audio recording. The ideal is to always use both.
- Transcribe the interview verbatim — and do it yourself rather than asking a typist to do it.

These recommendations may seem extravagant, but our experience shows us that they are justified.

Two interviewers. It is extremely difficult to listen well and to take notes at the same time. The primary interviewer should be a listener, should be attending 100% to what the interviewee is saying and doing. If you have your head buried in your notes you will miss at least half of what is said, and will probably put your users 'off their stroke' by your inattention. If there are two interviewers, one can pay attention to the interviewee whilst the second takes notes, pays attention to the equipment, and is free of the pressure of being 'the interviewer' and is thus more able to note points mentioned but not subsequently expanded upon, changes of subject, and points that need clarification or explanation. When the interview reaches a 'natural break point' the primary interviewer can invite her colleague to take over, 'Do you have any questions that you wish to ask?' At this point it is important to notice that the roles of primary and secondary interviewer have reversed, and the erstwhile primary interviewer is now responsible for taking notes and tending to the equipment.

Having a tape recorder helps enormously, but there are drawbacks to having a single interviewer with a tape recorder (and these are strong arguments for having two interviewers):

- You have to attend to the machine as well as to the person being interviewed — all your attention should be with the person.

- Clearly you cannot listen to the tape until the interview is over. When you do listen to the tape there will be many occasions where you realise that you have forgotten to ask something important.
- You cannot take time to reflect on what is being said if you are giving 100% of your attention to the speaker.

The implication is that the second interviwer (or notetaker) can handle the recording equipment, check that you are not getting too far from the point, that you are covering the agenda, can take some notes for use *during* the interview and can reflect on what is being said and ask for some clarifications. This is the point where the interviewers swap roles.

Record the interview. We have frequently been accused of being too profligate with resources during the knowledge collection phase of the project — 'We can't afford two knowledge engineers', and 'We can't afford video equipment', and 'We can't afford the time taken to do a verbatim transcript' are the three most common complaints from course students as well as ES project clients. In answer to these challenges we usually suggest a simple experiment. Interview a friend or colleague, by yourself, for about 20 minutes on some trivial subject — what you did last weekend, for instance. Tape the interview, but take notes during the interview as if your notes were your only record of the occasion. After the interview, write a summary from your notes, and then sit down and transcribe the recording verbatim. Check your summary against the transcript. Unless your shorthand is around 200 words per minute, and your recall almost perfect, you will be surprised at the difference between your verbatim transcript and your summary made from your notes and your memory.

When reading the draft of this chapter the editor commented 'Do you really suggest this to the managing director?' It is not that usual to encounter the managing director, but yes, we do suggest it to client management. Knowledge elicitation is not an easy thing to do, and it is our experience that it is also not easy to persuade people that it is not an easy thing to do. But it *is* vital that clients understand what they are getting into before starting a project; if they do not have this understanding the project will be under-funded, under-resourced and will be set fair to founder. If people, be they knowledge engineers or managing directors, doubt what we say, we have no problem suggesting that they try a simple, 20-minute experiment which will give them some experience of what is involved. If suggesting this experiment to the managing director is necessary to get the project taken seriously, then we are certainly not shy of making the suggestion. How many take it up is altogether a different question!

Transcribe the interview yourself. There are two main reasons here. One is to ensure that the transcription is indeed verbatim (we have experienced many transcriptions done by typists where the transcription turns out to be a paraphrase of what was said, rather than what was actually said). The other reason is to do with the NKEs own understanding of the material. Listening in detail is a difficult thing to do. A 'Catch-22' occurs. If you are listening to me and I say something that is interesting, and which catches your attention, then you are likely to think about that for a while, and miss what I say next. On the other hand, if I get boring, you are likely to doze off — and miss what I say next. Either way, the 'listening' is patchy. If you have a transcript and you read the transcript this effect is reduced — you can stop, think and go back, but our experience is that there will still be bits that are missed. But if you transcribe the interview, verbatim, yourself, you are forced to listen to every word. We find that our understanding of what has been said in an interview is greatly enhanced having done the verbatim transcription ourselves.

Clearly, if you are a one-fingered typist and you have a two-hour interview to transcribe you will need professional typing help. However, once the typing is finished, try checking the transcription carefully — the effect is nearly as good.

It is important not to see the contextual interview as a one-off at the start of the project. One purpose of the open interview is to establish rapport and that should only be necessary once in the life of the project. But the open interview is also for seeing wider perspectives, for examining the context of the project. It is important to keep checking the details that you are gathering with the wider context, to ensure that they do indeed fit where you think they fit. We have come across cases of projects that examined certain subjects in great depth, and where the participants became so involved with the detail that they lost sight of the fact that the company did not in fact have the problem that they were solving. They had 'lost sight of the wood for the trees'. It is also possible for the context to change. Maybe changes in business practice, changes in the law, manufacturing process, etc., will change the context of the project. But it is also possible that the progress of the project itself will change the context. It may well be that part of the original context of the problem was that the subject-area was not well understood in a structured manner. It may be that this will change as the project progresses, and maybe the knowledge elicitation process will become an end in itself, rather than just a means to an end. Not only because of outside factors, but also because being involved in the knowledge acquisition process frequently gives people new perspectives that change the way they carry out their tasks — irrespective of whether you have produced a knowledge-based system to help them.

Thus we recommended that the collection should continually cycle between fine detail and re-establishing context, between high-level, general concepts, and lower, more detailed levels (e.g. Diaper, 1984).

We use a variety of structured methods to acquire detailed knowledge. There is insufficient space here to describe these methods in detail; we can but list them and say a few words about each here. A variety of methods are described by Cordingley, in Chapter 3.

- *Case analysis.* This involves asking people to comment on how past cases were dealt with. We usually start with case files, or fault dockets, or any records of past cases, and then ask both users and experts how they dealt with them (or would have dealt with them if the case were dealt with by someone else). We do not have our own criteria for selecting cases; this should be left to the experts and users. The experts will probably have more to say about the *interest* of individual cases, and what light particular cases throw on the process, whereas the users will usually have a better perspective on the *representativeness* of particular cases.

Additional light can sometimes be shed by asking different people to comment on the same cases, and comparing results. There is a tendency for people, when commenting on past cases that they have dealt with themselves, to produce *post-hoc* justifications, and to only mention the productive solution paths, ignoring the less- or non-productive paths (Bem, 1972; Nisbett and Wilson, 1977)

- *Protocol analysis.* This is normally meant to mean reading through transcripts and categorising and analysing what is said. We use the term to mean the analysis of specific behaviours — looking at what people actually do and in what circumstances. From this we develop 'Protocols' that we can describe and build directly into the system. For example:

Protocol: Mechanical Mishandling of XJ23
Explanation: XJ23s are awkward to hold and many people drop them. Mr S told us that upwards of 65% of all faults on XJ23s are due to people dropping them.
Cues: The unit is an XJ23
             Signs of physical damage on the case — usually on the corners
             Rattling noise
Diagnosis: Check the output of circuit 3: that's nearly always the one that fails
Repair: Replace the circuit 3 card and return the faulty card to dept Q

- *Critical incident analysis.* This involves asking people to discuss interesting, difficult, memorable, and funny cases. Critical incident analysis can often enliven a boring interview and frequently gives valuable insights that would otherwise be missed. Analysis of the results of discussing critical incidents frequently help to bound the scope of the system. However, we believe that critical incident analysis is relevant only as a levener to the more serious knowledge elicitation that happens elsewhere. Used by itself it can produce 'systems that are uneconomic, infrequently used and lack an appropriate core (i.e. all icing and little cake)' (Diaper, 1988, private commmunication).
- *Commentaries.* These involve asking people to give a running commentary of what they are doing. Most people find this difficult to do (Diaper, 1987b; Bainbridge, 1986); possible variations are:

— Video the action and get them to do a *post-facto* commentary (can result in *post-facto* justification, but at least all the action is recorded, so that not all of the unproductive paths will be lost.).

— Get someone else to do the commentary
— Get someone else to do the commentary of the video.

These last two are less likely to produce *post-hoc* justifications, but you are also unlikely to hear the actual *expert's* reasons for a particular action, be they *post-hoc* justifications or no.

● *Repertory grid.* This involves using the work of Kelly (1955) and Shaw and Gains (1986) to explore people's thinking around a subject. Boose (1987) has extended this work to produce semi-automatic knowledge acquisition and automatic production of expert system rules using the Aquinas system.

● *Conceptual graphs.* Eden *et al.* (1983) have described their approach to problem solving in their book *Messing About with Problems.* We have found their methods useful in getting people to explore their perceptions of their jobs and the problems involved.

● *Prototypes.* Working with a prototype of the system is the most powerful way of getting people to talk — provided that they understand that the system is not 'cast in concrete', but is easily changeable. We like to show people the latest prototype within days, or weeks at the most, of the last interview. If the knowledge-based system tools that you are using are easy to use it it may be possible to change the system *during* the interview. Fixing things during the interview certainly shows the users and experts that they have permission to make comments and get things changed, but the NKE should guard against confusing them with technical difficulties. See also the restrictions on rapid prototyping discussed in Chapter 1.

3.2.2 Knowledge analysis

When working with quantitative data one first collects lots of numbers, and is then faced with the task of making some sense of the data collected. Statistical analytic methods are applied to the morass of numbers in an attempt to 'reduce' the detail in order to be able to derive some meaning from the data. Much the same process takes place in knowledge acquisition. The immediate product of an open interview is a long transcript filled with 'messy' knowledge (Church, C.; interviewed on Alvey videotape 'Expert Systems in British Industry'). In order to be able to make sense of this data we must apply some process that will analyse it, or reduce it. This is the process that we term 'knowledge analysis'.

Analysing the knowledge consists, usually, of getting an intuitive feel for the subject and starting to find a workable structure. A wide variety of processes have evolved and a full discussion is beyond the scope of this chapter. However, the basic processes is one of 'unitisation' and 'categorisation' as Lincoln and Guba term it, or, to use our own terms 'chunking' and 'sorting'.

We recommend that analysis of a transcript is not attempted in committee, many potentially beautiful friendships have foundered on the rocks of trying to make joint sense of the meaning of an interview transcript. We recommend that the initial task is undertaken by whichever member of the

NKE team is most at home with solitary tasks. The rest of the team get their say when they are presented with the fruits of the analysis, and are invited to comment.

The process then consists of reading through the transcript and identifying chunks of meaning. Precisely what constitutes a chunk is a subject of great debate, some researchers arguing for sentences or even words as 'units of meaning'. Marshall (1981) suggests the units of meaning should be intuitive, and we agree with that. Whilst this does not produce uniformly agreeable definitions of chunks we feel that this debate is of relevance to experimental psychologists, but not germane to the essentially intuitive process faced by the NKE — that of making her own sense of the transcript data. We suggest reading through the transcript and making chunks of meaning with a highlighting pen. Recently we have programmed some modifications to a computer text editor to speed the process of chunking, but whilst we have insufficient experience with this tool to make recommendations, our early experience looks promising.

Each chunk should be recorded on some movable medium. If your word-processor will support it, you can use that — we have heard good reports of using hypertext programs to manipulate transcripts. We generally use 'PostIts' (those ubiquitous yellow semi-sticky rectangles of paper). With each chunk should be a note of where it came from — the transcript page and date, or the person who was talking. Sooner or later you will pick up a piece of paper and wonder what was the context in which the statement was made.

Subsequent to beaking the transcript into chunks comes the process of sorting or categorising those chunks. Sorting is the second phase of the process of understanding the data. Having produced the chunks we arrange them, categorise them, 'play' with them, look for apparent connections between the chunks and the categories — whatever seems to aid the process of understanding. These broad and fuzzy instructions for this intuitive process frequently offend the more objectively minded of our students, who are unhappy with our exhortations to 'engage with the data' and demand to be 'told what to do'. We have looked at other resarcher's methods of analysing data. The process has been discussed by Lincoln and Guba (1984), who refer to Glaser and Strauss's (1967) constant comparative method. Glaser and Strauss seem to start with pre-defined categories ('comparing incidents applicable to each category . . . integrating categories and their properties'). Marshall (1981), however, prefer to let the categories emerge from the data 'I let the categories build up . . . as I put things together that *go* together'. For this, Marshall is branded as 'cavalier' by Lincoln and Guba, but we would support this more intuitive approach. Basically, sorting is a very simple mechanical process that undoubtedly is a very complex psycological process. However, the underlying complexity need not concern the NKE — go through the simple process and watch the understanding emerge!

The process involves sorting through a pile of knowledge chunks and arranging them in categories. The process is iterative, as categories are refined, and then leads into the organisation of the categories into hierarchies, nets or other forms as seems appropriate. With knowledge that organises easily into a hierarchy, we have found a progam called 'Max-Think', that runs on an IBM PC, to be a valuable aid. It allows us to type in chunks, to sort them, rearrange them, categorise them, and then to print out the results. We have recently interfaced our modified text editor with MaxThink in order to allow us to extract chunks from transcripts and then to categorise them and sort them with MaxThink.

3.2.3   *Knowledge representation*

Representing the knowledge is probably the most difficult and important stage of the process. Considerable research has taken place in the field of AI to find ever more promising ways of representing knowledge in order to be able to compute with it. Barr and Feigenbaum (1981) list logic, procedural representations, semantic networks, production systems, direct (analogical) representations, semantic primitives, and frames and scripts. There are undoubtedly many other forms. These computable knowledge representation forms are not really our concern here, for the prime consideration of the natualistic knowledge engineer is that the representational form be *understandable*.

It is important that there is also a computable representational form; if there is not, then a system cannot be built. The tension is between highly computable but opaque representation methods, as opposed to methods that are simple to understand, but impossible to compute with. If it is not possible to find a KR method that is both computable and understandable then we would recommend representing the knowledge in a manner that both experts and users understand. It becomes the task of the KE to translate that representation into a computable form. If there is not a one-to-one mapping, that is unfortunate. The loss of knowledge due to this translation should be documented and both experts and users should be consulted about the importance of this loss.

Our first concern is always to build a model of the knowledge that user, expert, and KE can all understand. We have found that formal representations tend to be less useful than informal ones. When we have used some formal system of knowledge representation we find that people get hung up on the precise rules of the formalism and that interferes with the natural process of understanding and representing the knowledge. Similarly, a visual representation, if drawn too tidily, can also seem too formal. We have found that if we produce a hierarchical diagram on a word-processor, with a nice typeface, maybe with a graphics package, than people will admire it. If we present the same data, scribbled onto a flipchart with a felt-tip pen, they have no problem about grabbing a pen themselves and scrawling all over the picture. You are more likely to get a structure that reflects the thinking of the expert or user it they had a hand in devloping that structure.

4.   EMPHASISING THE HUMAN SIDE

All the expertise, techniques, and methodologies in the world will not help you to produce a knowledge-based system if you do not take into account the way human beings in general behave, and the way the project team members in particular, are reacting. ESs are still new enough that there are many people around who have not heard of them or who do not know what they are — including large numbers of managers who realise that they ought to know about them, but do not.

Many people consider expert systems to be a part of Artificial Intelligence, with an association with machines that can think. That link, together with the commonly used name 'expert system', makes them seem a very different and very awe-inspiring sort of computer program.

When expert systems can be programmed in langauges which are accessible to people who are not computer programmers, people who have never before encountered computers can become involved in developing and maintaining their own systems. This will mean a different way of working, often involving interacting with a machine for the first time and learning new skills. It may mean less human contact — for the experts, less contact with people seeking answers; people who also happen to make them feel needed and important.

For the users it may bring more responsibility. They are now alone with the machine; solving the problem and carrying the can without the expert to turn to for reassurance and advice.

For the experts even more change is in prospect when the system is in place. Instead of the boredom of routine work or the excitement and stress of firefighting, they are free to explore the more creative side of their work. Depending on the expert, reported reactions include relief, anxiety, disappointment, and a sense of loss.

The prospect of change often invokes strong emotions in people.

Some find it exhilarating and challenging — the NKE can pray that there is at least one of these in the team — ideally the user.

Some restless people are addicted to change and need a constant shift of scene to avoid becoming bored and stale. Here there is a danger of new technology being espoused for its novelty value with little sensitivity to the effect on other people, and little attention to whether it is genuinely useful.

Many other people find change threatening and react with anxiety or hostility to significant changes in the status quo. They need reassurance that they will not suffer in the new situation. The key point is that people who feel threatened *may* be reacting badly to change *per se*, rather than to any specific effects of that change. This means that if the mystery and the dread can be removed from this prospect of 'change', then they may be well able to accept its particular effects. When people are co-operatively involved in the development of a system then it never becomes a mystery; the change is exciting because the team are the owners of the change process, rather than its victims.

So people's emotional needs may be threatened by the change implied by a knowledge processing system. The penalty for neglecting them could be the failure of the project, because people may, either deliberately or quite unconsciously, sabotage it in order to protect themselves. One of us (Bell,

1987a) has taken John Heron's model of emotional needs and adapted it to the working environment to illustrate how this might happen. This is discussed in the next section.

4.2 Emotions

Heron (1977) has postulated that human beings have three fundamental emotional needs (as opposed to the physical, intellectual and spiritual needs). These needs are:

- To love and be loved
- To understand and be understood
- To be free, living amongst other free people

Most people reserve the hope of being loved for their personal lives and do not extend that expectation to the work place. Bell suggests three parallel needs for the working environment:

- In place of love we expect appreciation and recognition of our worth.
- In place of understanding (or, maybe, in addition) we need good communication and clear objectives.
- An in place of complete freedom it seems reasonable to expect a degree of self-direction.

If we follow Heron's model (and look into our own life experience) we find that non-fulfilment of our needs for love, understanding, and freedom produce negative emotions. Heron suggests that frustration of the need for love produces grief, that of understanding produces fear, and that of freedom produces anger. Similarly if people at work (and in a knowledge engineering project) are continually denied appreciation, good communication and self-direction, they will also experience similar negative emotions. Lack of recognition will engender apathy, poor communications result in anxiety, and lack of self-direction can produce hostility.

These negative emotions are likely to sabotage the project, often in indirect ways which may not be recognised by the knowledge engineer: people's interest may flag, they will become elusive and unavailable, and information will be withheld. Let us look at these needs in more detail.

4.2.1 Love/appreciation

Frustration of this need tends to lead to low energy, depression, and apathy. In our experience this results in absenteeism (maybe just from the project — 'Sorry I couldn't make the meeting — rush job on') and a loss of interest in the quality of their contribution because nobody seems to care about it. There have been many examples of this on our course among the user groups in the exercises and on the case studies. Repeatedly users have reported back that they felt ignored, neglected and unimportant, and lost interest as a result. See below under the section on team members.

4.2.2   Understanding/clear objectives

Frustration of the need for clear objectives produces confusion and anxiety; people do not know what is expected of them and thus they feel insecure. These symptoms are common in new knowledge engineers especially during the open interview stage when the territory is not yet charted and they do not yet trust the process enough to feel in control. It was also particularly noticeable on the course before we had mastered the qualitiative knowledge analysis process sufficiently to give clear instructions to the students. The cry of despair went up: 'Yet, but what do we actually *do*?'

Having a defined structure within which to work allows people to move forward more confidently.

4.2.3   Freedom/autonomy and initiative within limits of role

Lack of autonomy leads to feelings of anger and a temptation to rock the boat or even shipwreck it in retaliation. We see this hostility expressed by the user who will not use the system simply because it is alien (the not-invented-here syndrome again). It has appeared on the course in people who have been pushed into roles they did not want. It is rare for them to say overtly that do not like the role and refuse it. More often they swallow their resentment and find themselves unable to function.

Giving autonomy allows people to feel in control of their task, able to make a full contribution by using their own ideas and imagination, and trusted to take responsibility appropriate to their role in the team.

NKEs who apply this model to the members of the knowledge engineering team may well be able to understand or anticipate problems.

It is important that the KE feels that giving time to feelings problems is as important a part of the KA process as collecting facts. This is the key to solving or lessening those problems.

- The first step is to give permission for the feelings, by not being surprised or critical about them.
- Next give time and space for people to sound off; to express the feelings — this may be all that is necessary.
- Help people to identify their needs and clarify how they want them met.
- Help them to renegotiate their work contract with colleagues and/or their manager to make sure that their needs are met — this may often be simply a question of facilitating communication between the two parties.

It is also important that *naturalistic* KEs remember to include themselves when taking into account the feelings of team members. They will need to acknowledge and deal with their own feelings if they are to be able to cope with other team members expressing theirs.

4.3   Perception

The well-known effects of selective attention have been clearly demonstrated on the knowledge engineering course — that we tend to see and hear things which we are interested in, understand, feel good about, and tend to screen out things which have no relevance, which we have blocks about or which remind us of uncomfortable experiences. Course members repeatedly reported with surprise 'I only heard what I was interested in'' 'I didn't notice that because I was bored'. In the feedback to one case study the team reported that they had assigned one member the role of 'process observer' and had forbidden him to take part, or even talk, all day. They were as interested as we to hear what he had to say. And they were embarrassed when he reported that at 9.20 am on the previous day they had all made a decision *not* to examine a particular area of the expert's knowledge, as it was not relevant. And then for the rest of the day they had discussed pretty much nothing else, because several team members found that area by far the most interesting aspect of the subject.

We have also had the experience, in a live project in which we were involved, of conducting a 20-minute interview and then nearly coming to blows when transcribing the tape, because we had both heard the expert saying different things. A tape recorder only records sound and silence. Probably we were arguing about our remembered sense of what had been said, gathered and interpreted from other, non-verbal cues.

Just having awareness of how complex a process perception is, and of our tendency to bias, guards against the problem to some extent. And the careful use of recording equipment can also help as the above story illustrates. If feelings are acknowledged and given space this is also likely to reduce this bias in perception: if we are allowed to criticise the bad points about a scheme we are much more likely to notice the good ones too. If we are obliged to keep quiet we tend to hang on to the resentment indefinitely.

Again it is vital for NKEs to be aware of their own bias which could affect both the collection and analysis of the data — which brings us to issues of validity.

4.4   Project monitoring

The issues discussed above demonstrate the need for some sort of monitoring process. As we have discussed earlier, an audit process can ensure that the sort of bias we have described is reduced to a minimum.

The auditor needs to be someone who understands the process of NKE but has no vested interest in the project either directly or indirectly. The auditors will work directly with the NKE and should not be a manager, but preferably a peer of the NKE. The auditor's authority should derive from his understanding of the NKE process rather than from his position in the organisation. In general terms the task of the auditor is to monitor the methods used and the time taken, and to retain the ability to see the wood for the trees. We have produced a checklist which breaks the ingredients of the audit process down into seven sections:

(1) *Preliminaries.* Ensuring that the NKE knows what the problem is, who owns it, who the users are; and that the users know what the project is about.

(2) *Interviews.* Questions about who has been interviewed, how often and

under what circumstances. Checking whether interviews have been recorded, and whether tapes have been transcribed.

(3) *User requirements.* Aimed at making sure that users are being properly listened to and fully considered.

(4) *Interviewing experts.* Offering suggestions and reminders about techniques, particularly concerning tacit knowledge, and acting as devil's advocate and asking awkward questions about what the NKE has done or left undone and why.

(5) *Feelings, personalities and politics.* This might include listening to the NKE's anxieties and frustrations; drawing it to their attention when their personal motives seem to be getting in the way of the project; role playing difficult encounters, for example, negotiating for more of the users' time, with a manager who is being obstructive.

(6) *Handling data.* Is the NKE being swamped and does he or she need help with that; are there enough resources (time, space, equipment) available; and are knowledge representations understandable?

(7) *Schedules, management reviews and checkpoint meetings.* Involves nagging about keeping to schedule, reviewing the schedule, and checking that management are being kept involved or at least informed.

The checklist is intended as a set of guidelines which auditors can adapt to their own style of working.

A schedule of regular meetings between the NKE and the auditor should be drawn up. What happens at those meetings will vary according to the personalities involved, how their relationship develops, and what ways of working they are confortable with.

4.5   Team members
Before looking at the qualities and skills the NKE needs, let as look in turn at the team members and the problems we have encountered with each of them.

4.5.1   The user
The backbone of our NKE methodology, and of course, is the dictum 'consult the user' (or, more recently, 'consult the client'). It is easier said than done, but vital: the user has the ultimate sanction — that of not using the system, or not using it effectively.

However, as we have said before, telling people to ask the user is not enough. To get course members to actually do it we have had to be very dictatorial. There is a reluctance to talk to users which is not easily overcome, and with which the user, wittingly or unwittingly, seems to collude. We think there are associations about the word 'user' which make it easy to regard users as of low status, and to neglect them; especially when contrasted with the distinguished 'expert'. It is also the case, of course, that there are more users than experts; the users may have the feeling that they are 'two-a-penny'; of no account, whereas the expert is unique and valued.

Even on the course, where people come as peers, and are strangers, often from different parts of the world and from different companies, people who role-play users consistently report being ignored, neglected, and feeling left out. These people are not allocated the user role: they choose it within their groups, and the role is swapped around during the course. They are not typically mouse-like people in other roles, but seem to take on this submissive acceptance when they are in the user role.

For example, typical comments from users after KE course exercises might be:

- 'Nobody asked us.'
- 'We felt inferior.'
- 'Lip-service was paid.'
- 'What about the interface?'
- 'We felt ignored and neglected.'
- 'How could we know what to want?'
- 'We didn't know what there was to want.'
- 'The expert had a totally different way of thinking.'

And, if, as NKEs, we do ask the users, what do we discover? Often that management are asking for a system which will solve problems that the users do not have. This is not to say that there is no problem to solve, but that it is important to be clear who has the problem, and whether the system will *solve* the problem, or merely move it to someone else.

For instance, if an expert is snowed under with routine enquiries, it may be the expert who is complaining because there is no time for the more rewarding aspects of his job. Or it may be the expert's manager who needs the expert's skill elsewhere.

As NKEs we need to identify who owns the problem. Only then can we begin to understand precisely what the problem is. The owners of the problem, together with their managers, need to sell the idea to the other people involved (users, experts or managers), and enlist their co-operation. In practice it is often the knowledge engineer's task to make this happen, particularly where consulting and informing users is concerned. Unless managers understand the importance of involving users, and are convinced that they have a contribution to make, they will be reluctant to make the users' time available to the project.

Even when users do have a problem, or can be persuaded that they have, they may not know how it can be solved — it is not, that they do not know what they want; they do not know what there is to want. And when users do know what they want they may find it difficult to articulate those needs; either because they are not good with words; or because those needs may be tacit, like the expert's knowledge described above.

Our impression is that if the expert's knowledge is tacit, everyone respects and understands; but if the *users'* needs are tacit people lose patience, give up quickly and write them off as not knowing what they want.

The users are often lower down the organisation's hierarchy than the expert, the KE, or the managers involved. This may mean that even if they do have a problem, do know what they want *and* can articulate it, they may not dare to assert it in a way which gets heard. If this is the case it is the job of the NKE to make sure that the user is heard — first of all in a separate interview and maybe later, with support, in a session with the expert.

It is usually the case that users have a totally different perspective from the expert. This is often seen as a problem by the knowledge engineer, the expert, and even the users themselves. We believe that this is an asset and a valuable key to the building of the system. The user's view is usually less complex, less sophisticated and more practical than the expert's. If NKEs understand this, they not only have the key to the complexity of the knowledge, but also a simple structure to hang it on, derived from the user's view of the world.

4.5.2 The domain expert

The first problem that experts may have is that they do not think of themselves as expert. This is usually a good sign and it is up to the NKE to reassure them and make them feel special and appreciated. Some are already prima donnas and already feel special, hopefully they are also genuine experts. We would define a real expert as someone who has:

- skills which have been developed and built from complex experience, not based on mere repetition.
- idiosyncratic ways of working — probably involving tacit knowledge.
- a reputation as an authority with colleagues.

Key points about experts are:

- Their time is precious and likely to cost more than anyone else's.
- They are likely to enjoy the attention.
- They will welcome the rare chance to stop and think about their work and their methods. They may benefit from the process and may even improve their ways of working as a result.
- They may need permission and encouragement to keep talking, for, in spite of the official agenda that that is what they are there for, social conventions about boring an audience creep in to inhibit the process.
- At other times they may get bored and impatient and need to be kept interested.
- Sometimes they *cannot* articulate the knowledge:

  — Either because they are not articulate
  — Or because the knowledge is tacit

- Sometimes they *will not* articulate the knowledge because they:

  — Feel possessive of the knowledge they have acquired and nurtured over the years.
  — Do not trust the knowledge engineer or management and are anxious about what might be done with their knowledge.
  — Fear redundancy or change of job.

Fear the loss of a firefighting role and fear being lonely.

— Resent or fear the user's input which may mean compromising in some areas.
— Fear technology.
— Fear exposure of their unorthodox methods or of being a real or imagined fraud.

Successful knowledge elicitation depends upon these issues being handled. In order to do this the NKE needs to establish a relationship of trust with the expert. This consists partly of personal rapport, trust of motives, and mutual respect; and partly of a full understanding of the planned system — the benefits and the limitations.

4.5.3   Management
The failure to involve management fully in the development of knowledge-based systems is probably the second most common reason for their failure (the first being the failure to involve users). Without management, for example, it is unlikely that there will be provision for maintaining and updating the system after the developers have moved on, or that issues of responsibility will be resolved, or that people's time will be made available. If these, and other issues important to the success of the project, are to be resolved, it is vital that management be closely involved at all stages.

Some common human frailties of managers that may cause the NKE problems are:

• Pre-occupation with time and budget.
• Wanting everything tomorrow.
• Expecting a cut and dried, procedural approach with a precise schedule.
• Being misled by expert system 'hype' into thinking not only that the ES will be the answer to all their problems but also that it will be up and running tomorrow.
• Preoccupation with status (and aiming to enhance their status with the ES).
• Wanting the solution (ES) but having no problem.
• Technophobia.
• And fear of being found out!

Managers have the formal power in the team, but if they are ignorant of the NKE process, may not use that power to the best advantage of the project. The NKE should ensure that everyone involved understands the process; educating the managers may need more diplomacy than is needed when educating the other team members.

4.5.4   The naturalistic knowledge engineer
The job of the NKE is to co-ordinate the team in such a way that each member can make their contribution and feel valued. The problems that beset NKEs typically fall into three broad categories: problems with their own abilities; problems with other people; problems with the process.

- Problems with their own abilities.

    — Being overawed by the status and expertise of the expert.
    — Forgetting they are experts themselves — in NKE.
    — Getting over-confident and forgetting that they are not expert in the expert's field.
    — Feeling panic-striken and overwhelmed by the volume of data collected.
    — Forgetting that they do not have to understand all the data.
    — Feeling silly asking so-called 'foolish' questions and needing repeated explanations.
    — Finding it hard to trust to intuition because it is not 'scientific'.
    — Finding it hard to cope with their own feelings of anxiety and frustration, let alone listen to other people's.
    — Impatience with the process.
    — Feeling guilty not having all the answers.

- Problems with other people:

    — Being seduced by the expert's aura into neglecting the user.
    — Having difficulty gaining co-operation.

        ■ from experts whose jobs make them clusive,
        ■ from users whose managers will not make them available,
        ■ from managers who are resistant to putting resources into the project.

    — Antagonising the expert by 'becoming expert' in their field.
    — Being overwhelmed by other people's worries and feeling responsible.

- Problems with the process:

    — Not believing it will work.
    — Impatience with the time-comsuming elements of the process.

        ■ open interviews,
        ■ transcription,
        ■ knowledge analysis.

    — Feeling threatened by the audit process.
    — Fearing technology/feeling paranoid about the tape recording.
    — Being unable to see the wood for the trees.
    — Not trusting intuition.
    — Not coping with open interview.

This last is probably the most universally reported problem on the course, and I rarely see a well-managed open interview in any situation. Most of the problem stems from the need to be in control: the interviewer feels uncomfortable without a structured agenda because he or she cannot predict what will happen; the need for good listening further precludes the directing of the interview and is a rare skill. Silence is another necessary part of a thoughtful and productive interview which causes discomfort to many interviewers. And some are so eager to contribute their own opinions that they fail to even notice the pause which could have grown into a productive silence.

5.   QUALITIES OF THE NKE

This section considers what qualities a knowledge engineer needs to cope with all this? The NKE needs to have a friendly, outgoing, and reasonably confident personality. This is not to say that shy or overbearing knowledge engineers cannot learn the techniques: they simply start with a handicap. When choosing an NKE on the basis of prior skills and experience we feel that human experience is more important than technical ability — we would choose a psychologist over a programmer. If your knowledge engineer has both abilities, that is fine; but our ideal is to have two knowledge engineers with complementary skills (technical and social) who can give each other both moral and practical support throughout the project. Chas Church endorsed this view in his early days of knowledge engineering with British Telecom when he spoke of himself and his partner, a psychologist and a logic programmer, as an ideal marriage.

We would also recommend two knowledge engineers when interviewing. The interchange of roles of primary interviewer and back-up interviewer is a key to getting the most out of an interview, and allows the primary interview to give all his or her attention to the interviewee. The back-up interviewer can manage recording equipment, time-keeping and keep track of points which need to be checked back on. The back-up interviewer is not in the line of fire and has time to note key points and give them some thought. For this arrangement to work well the pair must develop a working partnership and learn to manage the role switch smoothly.

Here is a list of skills or qualities we would like to see in all naturalistic knowledge engineers:

- *Friendly and outgoing personality.* The sort of person whom people readily talk to, who has the knack of making people feel relaxed, and who enjoys meeting new people.
- *Interview skills.* Being able to set up and manage an interview; having the skill of enabling an open interview to happen, as well as being able to pursue relevant points in a focused interview.
- *Facilitator skills.* These are partly about encouraging people to talk about things they do not usually readily talk about; and partly about achieving successful interaction between the members of the team, with particular reference to communication between the expert and the user.
- *Listening skills.* An obvious, but difficult and quite rare skill for the interviewer. It is an important ingredient in making the interviewee's enjoyment and sense of being valued, as well as being vital to a true understanding of the material.

- *Counselling skills.* These may be useful when the NKE is aware of tensions, and senses that people have hidden agendas. He or she may need to give people the opportunity to express their worries and anxieties.
- *Tolerance of chaos.* This involves the skill of surviving the enevitable panic of being presented with an overwhelming volume of data which seems, not only limitless, but also amorphous and incomprehensible very often.
- *Empathy.* This is a quality which is part of the skill of being outgoing and a good listener.
- *Diplomacy.* Very necessary for the NKE to negotiate a way round the interpersonal relationships and political manoeuvring which tends to go on in most departments.
- *Assertive skills.* A very necessary part of the diplomacy and essential for standing up to managers, and for championing the cause of unassertive users.
- *Handling technology.* This does not refer to the computer end of the process, but to the use of recording equipment in interviews. We know that everyone can turn a tape recorder on and off, but our experience is that there is a world of difference between knowing how and actually doing it efficiently when the pressure is on. Over and over again red-faced knowledge engineers, both on the course and in life, report forgetting to switch on the microphone, failing to check the batteries or running out of tape. The message is — know your equipment, practice until it's second nature, and prepare for all eventualities.

This list serves to emphasise the difference between writing a computer program and undertaking a knowledge engineering project. It shows that the NKE needs training in order to understand the task and process fully, to learn to make best use of existing skills and qualities, and to learn and cultivate new skills and techniques. On the course neophyte NKEs have the opportunity to stand in both the expert's and the user's shoes. This gives them a grasp of the richness of the task, and better equips them to recognise and deal with the complex and varied problems they are likely to encounter.

6. CONCLUSION

The impetus for the development of NKE and the course came from noticing that very little attention was being paid to the human skills of knowledge engineering. Our starting point was noticing some very obvious mistakes being made which were leading to the failure of projects. Our impression is that the gap around human issues still exists in the literature and at exhibitions and conferences, but that is balanced by many success stories in companies who have recognised the value of the NKE approach, whether through experience, enlightened management, or determined individuals.

We still find our course students the richest source of learning about this subject, and hope that this process will continue with the new five-day course, which was due to run for the first time in the autumn of 1988.

Introduction to:
Knowledge elicitation techniques for knowledge-based systems

Betsy Cordingley's chapter is without doubt the central core around which the rest of this book is based. It has provided a definition of knowledge elicitation that has been used by the other authors and there is a vital contrast to be drawn between knowledge elicitation, which involves the two related stages of eliciting knowledge from human experts and representing that knowledge in a public form, and that of knowledge acquisition. Knowledge elicitation is a stage or component of knowledge acquisition which also involves the initial specification of the system and also the encoding of the elicited knowledge in an expert system or KBS. Before describing a host of knowledge elicitation techniques the chapter introduces the general issues associated with dealing with the personnel involved in knowledge elicitation and the general issues involved with the selection and recording of material during knowledge elicitation. The major portion of the chapter reviews knowledge elicitation techniques appropriate for use with human experts (knowledge providers) and deals first, in some considerable detail, with interview techniques. Other methods such as focused discussion and teachback, that are similar to interviews in that the data they elicit is of a principally verbal nature, are then reviewed. A considerable range of other techniques are reviewed. First, the numerous and popular methods associated with Kelly's Personal Construct Theory are discussed in detail before techniques such as sorting tasks, laddering, 20 questions, matrix generation, critiquing, protocols, role play and simulations are introduced. The next section then deals in a similar way with methods for eliciting knowledge from other, non-human sources and reviews the issues associated with getting knowledge from existing systems, from the physical and social environment and from documents. Techniques reviewed include: observation; object tracing; listening; and the collecting of artefacts. Tools such as FACTFINDER, ETHNOGRAPH and the OXFORD CONCORDANCE PACKAGE are also introduced. The chapter finishes with a discussion of the selection and use of techniques and how these may vary according to the current state of the knowledge elicitation programme, the personality and/ or nature of the knowledge elicitor, the knowledge provider or other knowledge sources and also the nature of the domain and the constraints of encoding elicited knowledge in an expert system or KBS.

3

Knowledge elicitation techniques for knowledge-based systems

Elizabeth S. (Betsy) Cordingley
Department of Sociology, University of Surrey

1. INTRODUCTION

This chapter is both modest and ambitious in its aims. Modestly, it does not attempt to resolve current debates about the nature and proper conduct of knowledge elicitation (KEL), nor does it claim to present an exhaustive catalogue of techniques that could be used in the elicitation process. In particular, it does not cover techniques for working with groups in one location (Douglas *et al.*, 1988 is recommended for those interested) nor collections of people spread across different locations whose views are to be utilised as a whole as in the Delphi Technique (e.g. currently being used by Michael Adler and Roy Sainsbury of the Department of Social Policy and Social Work of the University of Edinburgh). Ambitiously it takes a broader than usual view of KEL and aims to provide sufficient detail for the reader to judge which techniques are appropriate for a particular elicitation task and know where to find more detailed treatment of pivotal issues. The chapter is intended to widen the repertoire and deepen the understanding elicitors have of techniques they might use themselves. Although some computer aids for the elicitor are included in the chapter, automated knowledge acquisition software is not discussed except as a means of providing a focus for discussion, as there is no particular role for a human elicitor in a fully automated knowledge acquisition process itself.

Techniques included in the chapter are found in various forms in the literature of the fields from which Knowledge-based Systems' (KBS) practitioners are drawn. Descriptions can be found, for example, in publications on artificial intelligence, social or psychological research methods, social anthropology, computer science, operational research, and management studies. The characterisations of the techniques described in this chapter are an amalgam from many sources. The book by Hart (1986) which sets knowledge engineering in the context of systems design and systems analysis, the collection of papers edited by Kidd (1987) each of which provides guidelines for knowledge engineers and in which Kidd provides an interesting four class framework for characterising domains, Wright and

Ayton's paper (1987) and the article by Neal (forthcoming) which includes a review of machine aids for knowledge acquisition are particularly recommended as additional overviews. Welbank's Insight Study (1987d), an update of her 1983 report, is currently restricted solely to Insight members and so is not cited here. A summary of her update is contained in the paper she contributed to the SERC Workshop (Welbank, 1987b) which is cited.

In the chapter a working definition of KEL is developed (Section 2); comments general to the elicitation process are made (Section 3); techniques for getting material from human knowledge providers (Section 4) and those for getting material from other sources (Section 5) are discussed; factors affecting the selection of techniques (Section 6) are outlined; and finally the chapter is summarised, outstanding differences of view are argued and an approach to elicitation is recommended (Section 7).

2.   A WORKING DEFINITION OF KNOWLEDGE ELICITATION

The building of knowledge-based computer systems is still a young enterprise. It can be characterised as: pre-scientific, in that laws and theories of knowledge have yet to be formalised sufficiently to be tested and widely accepted; pre-engineering, in that principles of construction have yet to be formulated and interactions between knowledge components have yet to be made predictable; and pre-disciplinary, in that commonality of meaning, approach and valuation in the field has yet to be achieved, the numerous disciplines from which its practitioners are drawn all contribute concepts, techniques, and suggest bases for judging accomplishments to the field. The foundations are multidisciplinary, the language in flux. It is not surprising, therefore, that there is ambiguity about the meaning and inconsistency in the use of two terms particularly relevant here, 'Knowledge Elicitation' (KEL as distinguished from KE which is often used to mean Knowledge Engineer) and 'Knowledge Acquisition' (KA). Until recently they have been largely used interchangeably. Now it is more typical for them to be distinguished from one another. But neither has an undisputed single meaning. Dillon (1987), for example, uses KA to mean the knowledge *of the system* which a user acquires through using the system, whereas knowledge engineers usually take KA to mean the acquisition of knowledge *needed by the system*. We take KA to mean the latter.

2.1   Knowledge acquisition
Classically, systems development was seen as a linear sequence of stages from problem definition and feasibility study, systems analysis and specification, design, implementation (in the computer world sense of writing programs), testing, transfer to user (this is implementation in the user's world) and maintenance which might include further developments. In KBS developments, the KA process was primarily associated with implementation, getting the knowledge into the computer. Breuker and Weilinga (1983a) started with a largely linear model of this sort, made up in their case of five stages: analysis, specification, design, implementation, testing and

validation, although they did note then that 'The implementation and testing phases will probably show a cyclical and incremental development of the knowledge base' (Breuker and Weilinga, 1983a, p. 17). Increasingly the previously dominant linear view of a system's life cycle is being superseded. For example, 'It is widely accepted that one does not build an expert system in a simple linear manner; first eliciting knowledge then implementing it' (Burton *et al.*, 1988, p. 144). The 'single-pass' characterisation of development has been replaced by models of development which have cycles across stages — as where prototypes are designed, built and tested and then revised versions are designed, built and tested. There are also models of development such as that incorporated in the KADS methodology which have the same steps — consideration of the environment, the task, and the static knowledge of the domain — used within each of several stages of KA, orientation, problem identification and problem analysis (e.g. Breuker *et al.*, 1986, p. 4) creating 'cycles' of changing focus within each stage. In addition it is now recognised that even 'in the conventional LCMs [Life Cycle Models]. . .the acquisition of data about the domain is implicit in the early analysis activities' (Hayward, 1987, p. 8). KA is recognised as prevading development. It begins when a development is first mooted and may continue beyond evaluation of a delivered system into the period of use in its final setting and its further development. With the coming of this realisation has departed the strict compartmentalisation of the KA process in terms of its location in the development cycle and the personnel who undertake it. Initial analysis to determine the feasibility of adopting a KBS solution to a problem which has been identified may involve the same people using the same techniques as is later employed during what has 'traditionally' been regarded as the KA phase and yet later after transfer to the user setting to consider the need for enhancements. This has implications for our understanding of KEL as well.

2.2 Knowledge elicitation

Kel has been thought of as a stage of KA. The KA process is usually divided into the three stages: deciding what knowledge is needed, variously referred to as the definition stage or initial analysis; getting knowledge predominantly characterised as coming from human expert(s) and interpreting it, usually called elicitation; and 'writing' the knowledge in the internal language of the system, encoding it, usually called representation.

Seeing elicitation as a stage of KA has both advantages and disadvantages. Doing so has particular appeal among software engineers. It is consistent with the engineering paradigm of successive decomposition of difficult problems in solvable ones and large tasks into manageable chunks. It promises the advantages of modularity. The underlying assumptions, it should be remembered though, are that the components are independent of one another, that the whole can eventually be assembled from the parts, and the division into subtasks or stages makes sense in human terms. For much KBS work the decomposition strategy is appropriate, makes conceptual sense and is helpful for managing development. Separation of elicitation from encoding often works well because the activities require different skills and are often performed by different people. But there are difficulties, especially for the purposes of this chapter, in separating elicitation from definition. The skills required are very similar; they may be, and often are, undertaken by the same person or team; and many of the techniques are useful for both initial analysis and elicitation. Therefore, the notion of KEL will not be confined to the second stage of KA here. Tools and techniques normally associated with initial analysis will also be included.

Though the stages are not independent of one another, a decomposition of KEL into three constituent stages — getting knowledge, interpreting and analysing it, and putting it into a pre-encoded form — is as helpful here as it is for Johnson (Chapter 4) and Wilson (Chapter 5).

2.3   Knowledge sources

In the expert systems literature KEL is usually discussed in terms of getting and using the knowledge from human experts. But, as Frost asserts explicitly (1986, p. 6) and Diaper makes clear in his characterisation of expert systems in Chapter 1, not all KBS are expert systems, and knowledge is required for all KBS.

Even for expert systems it is unhelpful to confine the notion of KEL to elicitation from experts or even from humans. Knowledge may have to be elicited from non-expert humans. There may be no expert performing the task, as for example is the case in systems for the containment of rare disasters. As emphasised by Bell and Hardiman in Chapter 2, they also require knowledge of, and from, end-users who may be skilled practitioners, administrators, novices, other experts or members of the public rather than the experts whose expertise may be the basis of the system. As the KBS team is likely to need to gather knowledge from end-users as well as from experts, it is helpful to treat the techniques as though they might be used with non-experts as well as with experts. In addition knowledge from sources such as documents, artefacts and settings is usually necessary for expert systems as well as other kinds of KBS. The performance of available experts may not conform to the behaviour the system intends to promote and another model of the ideal must be used. For example, a system designed to critique user performance against guidelines laid down by regulatory bodies, guidelines which do not reflect the heuristics of experts, will certainly use the guideline document as a major source of knowledge. Burton and Shadbolt suggest that 'For many types of expert system, the whole set of domain knowledge may be found in documentation, books or in-house training manuals. For expert systems which are expected to perform 'slave-like' chores and jobs which are very well-defined the knowledge engineer may have to look no further than such documents' (Burton and Shadbolt, forthcoming, p. 2). The examples given are systems for writing school timetables or keeping track of one's finances. Although many would argue that it is inappropriate to use the term expert system to label these systems, the point that some KBS rely heavily, even entirely, on non-human knowledge sources make elicitation from those sources worth including in this chapter.

2.4 The working definition
So, taking advantage of the fact that terminology is not cast in concrete a working definition of KEL is proposed. It applies to all KBS but is confined to elicitation involving human elicitors so that divisions of activities must make sense in human terms.

Knowledge elicitation is those activities undertaken by a person, the knowledge elicitor, to

— *obtain material from any relevant source,*
— *analyse and interpret that material, and*
— *put in a pre-encoded form which, while useful to those who will encode the knowledge in the KBS language, also allows it to be scrutinised by all parties interested in KBS development.*

3. GENERAL COMMENTS ON THE KNOWLEDGE ELICITATION PROCESS

There are certain general remarks about the conduct of elicitation that are worth making before the techniques are treated in detail as they apply to several techniques. These include relations with domain personnel, qualities elicitors should have to cultivate, what should drive the elicitation process, the selection and recording of material, and confusions between the terms *focused, structured,* and *systematic*. Other issues, specific to particular groups of techniques, are presented in appropriate sections below.

3.1 Relations with domain personnel
Once the KBS team has settled on the domain of interest, they will need to gain access to appropriate settings and identify the personnel whose knowledge and activities will be useful in building the system. The KBS team will have to secure the co-operation of these people, and their immediate superiors. The co-operation of groups, such as trade unions, who represent the interests of potential knowledge providers and end users will also have to be secured.

As emphasised by Bell and Hardiman in Chapter 2, promoting a shared view of the KBS is crucial to elicitation. Participants from the domain will need to know what kind of development they are contributing to. In Chapter 1, Diaper suggests that the client organisation should be modelled early in the design process so as to provide a specification of the possible role of an expert system in the organisation. A concept of this role and the nature of the system designed to fill it should be made clear to all interested parties and an agreed version negotiated not just with the paymasters, but also with those whose participation in the development and acceptance of the 'final product' is vital. The KBS development team will have to have or, in concert with people representing domain interests, arrive at a clear idea of the aims of the KBS, what it will be like and how the knowledge which is being sought will contribute to the enterprise.

Demonstrations or hands-on-experience with appropriate KBS or prototypes may be useful in clarifying the nature of the system towards whose development people will be contributing. But warnings in the literature about overselling systems and about premature unveiling of prototypes should be heeded. It is all too easy to foster unrealistic expectations, and for prototypes with serious shortcomings to undermine confidence in all similar systems. There is also the danger of contaminating people's views of what the final system should be like if an appropriate system is demonstrated.

Whatever the difficulties of conveying this clear idea of the KBS-to-be, it is well to remember that whoever knows about the development will have some expectations about its nature and effect. Fruitful co-operation and eventual credibility is likely to depend on the elicitor and the persons from whom knowledge will be elicited having similar notions of the system; as Trimble points out in Chapter 6, successful completion is likely to depend upon the support and fulfilling the expectations of the clients' senior management; and acceptance depends on end-users trusting the system and feeling it fills a need without harming their positions.

The development team will, in particular, have to establish its credibility in the eyes of domain personnel. Knowledge elicitors will have to establish that they have the technical competence to elicit and analyse knowledge, and the professionalism to do it without putting the interests of people or groups in the domain who co-operate in jeopardy. The first contact with a person from whom knowledge is needed can significantly enhance or reduce the team's credibility, so it is important to take some care with it. Whether the style is formal or informal, in person by telephone or by letter, the first contact should be clear, appear well thought out and competent. It should display a respect for the person's concerns including: wanting to be clear about the KBS and whether it will have adverse effects on their job or that of others; how much of their time and effort will be required; what will be expected of them and will they be able to provide it; will it be unpleasant; will their shortcomings or weaknesses become apparent; whether confidentiality is appropriate and, if so, that it will be respected; what use will be made of any audio or video-tape recordings of the elicitation; what will become of the activities they would otherwise have been doing; how will co-operating with the development affect their relations with their colleagues and friends and paymasters; who will pay expenses or lost wages for time off work; and finally whether they have any real choice in whether to co-operate or not.

Details of the occasion itself will largely be determined by the elicitor's view of what kind of knowledge is needed and the elicitor's expectations about the knowledge provider, for example: what kind of knowledge can be provided; what techniques will be fruitful and possible in different venues; how long can sessions be before the people involved become stale and/or co-operative; how many sessions the elicitor is likely to need; and for how many sessions the knowledge source will be available. The human knowledge provider's expectations are affected by what is arranged and how the details are presented.

Decisions about venue are not trivial. The knowledge elicitor will have to decide, possibly on the advice of the client organisation, whether to conduct interviews in the normal work setting or away from it. The elicitor will have to see that the necessary arrangements for space and any recording equipment are made in time to give the other participants adequate notice of the location and time.

Elicitation conducted in the normal work setting can be more naturalistic than that conducted elsewhere, and it allows the elicitor to make observations of the work environment itself as well as getting knowledge from people. It reduces the time domain staff must devote to KEL and may allow the elicitor to get knowledge from a number of people in rapid succession. However, it increases the amount of time the elicitor must commit to non-productive activities as it is the elicitor who must do the travelling and make the arrangements for using an unfamiliar place which can be time consuming and problematic. Noise levels may be too high to use tape recorders or even to hear well enough to take written notes. Although it may be possible to arrange for the knowledge elicitation to take place in a quiet room near the setting, this should not (and often cannot) be arranged at the last minute. The equipment and elicitation aids the elicitor intends to use may be difficult or impossible to transport or operate in or near the setting. *In situ* KEL is also prone to interruption, and the person whose knowledge is being elicited may feel self-conscious about being overheard answering questions and talking about their work or being seen doing non-verbal knowledge elicitation tasks.

Elicitation away from the setting means that artefacts and information used by the person in the domain may not be available, but the elicitor is likely to have greater control over the KEL environment. It can be made conducive to the conduct and recording of the KEL process. It can provide a standardised setting for KEL activities. People from the domain may welcome the opportunity of a 'day out', and an opportunity to meet the development team and see the work that is going on in the development environment. Making KEL an 'outing' may be valuable in maintaining the interest and commitment of certain domain personnel over a lengthy KEL process.

Even the name given to the elicitation occasion may be important to its success. When eliciting knowledge from domain personnel, the occasions are usually called interviews even though techniques other than the interview may be employed. The name given to the occasion is not really important to experienced elicitors. Calling it an interview does not prevent their employing additional techniques, when appropriate. The inexperienced elicitor, however, may not think to use other techniques in what is called an interview. For domain personnel, the term interview may have unhelpful connotations or be an unfamiliar, untypical style of interaction. One team of KBS practitioners, for example, found it more helpful to refer all knowledge elicitation occasions as meetings, an unthreatening and familiar style of interaction which staff could clear through their line managers without the need for lengthy explanations. In many domains everyone attends meetings in the course of their normal work, but interviews are for appraising, disciplining, firing, or job seeking. In this chapter the term interview will be used to describe a technique for eliciting knowledge rather than the occasion during which it is done.

Agreeing objectives (Hart, 1986, p. 32), and providing advance indication of the focus and intent of a particular session is usually to be recommended (e.g. Waldron, 1986, p. 32). It prevents misunderstandings. The elicitor is less likely to be regarded as coming to 'poke around the office and all my folders' (Hart, 1986, p. 31) and more likely to be seen as having a legitimate interest in how activities in the domain are documented. Advance notice also allows domain personnel time to collect their thoughts; gives them a chance to undertake whatever preparation they think appropriate, including a chance to gather together whatever material they feel might be necessary or useful. It allows them to judge whether their participation will be of value, preventing the elicitor going to an inappropriate venue or spending time with a person who does not have the knowledge the elicitor needs. It requires and therefore is evidence of pre-planning, and may be useful to reassure participants that the elicitation will not stray into taboo areas. It may be taken as evidence of respect for their concerns.

Some elicitors feel it unnecessary, and even unhelpful, to go into detail about the programme for the KEL occasion. One danger with doing so is that the knowledge provider may misunderstand the depth or breadth of what is sought and wrongly decide she/he does not have the requisite knowledge. Advance notice may also be taken as an indication that the participant needs to prepare for the occasion and thereby cause additional stress and unnecessary effort on the part of domain personnel. But practitioners involved in fully participative development strategies find it invaluable to keep participants fully informed of the elicitation process. In that style of development, domain personnel contribute to decisions about KEL and their agreement about methods is sought in advance and again at the beginning of each KEL occasion. They begin to take 'ownership', as strongly recommended by Bell and Hardiman in Chapter 2, of the development and the knowledge-base from the very earliest stages of the process.

Whatever level of detail is provided in advance, the knowledge provider should arrive with a fair idea of what the occasion is about and how it fits in with the KBS development. Nonetheless going over some of that ground is a useful ice-breaker and gives the participant an opportunity to confirm or clarify his/her understanding.

Although presented as applying to a particular kind of elicitation, that of interviews with experts, there are canons of good practice, such as Killin's (1987) guidelines which are paraphrased below. These guidelines are as applicable to any type of elicitation occasion as they are to interviews and are as applicable to eliciting knowledge from non-experts as they are to eliciting knowledge from experts. It should be noted, however, they are neither universally endorsed nor universally practiced.

— not more than one KEL occasion with the same expert in any one week
— an occasion should not last more than three hours

— sessions should be subdivided into periods consisting of 2/3 elicitation and 1/3 rest
— no session more than 40 minutes
— pre-process (e.g. transcribe or code) and initially analyse results of one phase of elicitation (i.e. occasions in which a particular knowledge acquisition objective is being met) before beginning the next phase, even better if possible would be to transcribe and initially analyse the material from one occasion before the next elicitation occasion takes place
— beware of inadvertently cross-fertilising experts
— always use the same techniques in the same order for different experts
— assure consistency and suitability of environment

The importance of these guidelines is not in their actual strictures but their echo of the importance attached to 'hygiene' factors (cf. Herzberg, 1968) and the recognition of how draining the elicitation process can be for all participants.

It is also well to remember that breaks can be rich in useful knowledge, so elicitors would do well to keep their ears open and make brief notes of discussions over lunch, coffee or tea. Although it is best not to take notes during these breaks the fact that they are useful need not be hidden, making notes need not be covert. The elicitor may find it helpful in a subsequent session to refer explicitly to 'leads' picked up informally — 'You mentioned . . . at lunch. I wonder if you could tell me a bit more about it.'

Most of the advice above applies in any dealings with domain personnel. Liaison staff and other non-experts may not be as imposing as experts, their value is not apparent, but if their efforts are sought by the KBS team they will all need to know that their time and contribution is valued. They should be granted the same courtesies and consideration accorded to experts. It is usually less experienced elicitors who make the assumption that experts will be difficult to relate to and that non-experts can be handled in a cavalier fashion. In work with either, the elicitor will have to have: a clear idea of what needs to be accomplished during the elicitation; the ability to convey this idea to other participants, and secure and maintain their cooperation in the enterprise; the perceptiveness to monitor the knowledge provider's mood; and the flexibility to adapt the elicitation process so as to get the best out of each knowledge provider.

3.2   Qualities elicitors should have or cultivate
Killin (1987) is among those who assume or strongly recommend that the knowledge provider be an expert.

> Basically, it is up to the [elicitors] to insist upon the best. . . . The expert(s) that you require are the ones who are least available, have spent the longest time working in the domain and command the highest fees. This set will be so small, typically ≤ 1, that the aesthetic criteria, i.e. Is he motivated to cooperate on the project? Is he easy to relate with? Can he communicate his thoughts? become super-

fluous. The skills to balance this will be required from the KEL team. (Killin, 1987, p. 1).

Even when the knowledge provider is not an expert in Killin's sense, it is the elicitors who must exert themselves to gain an understanding of how to get the best out of the knowledge provider and adjust their interactions with him/her accordingly. In either case, 'The main qualities required for the task are PATIENCE, an ability to COMMUNICATE with the expert (and with end users at later stages of the development),' a relegation not endorsed here, 'an ability to RELATE to the expert's objectives and behaviour, and an ability to EMPATHISE with his qualms and misgivings. The member of the team who is responsible for interviewing must be FIRM in his handling of the expert, must be able to think on his feet, must appear INTERESTED in the expert's domain, and must be able to MOTIVATE the expert into giving up his expertise.' (Killin, 1987, p. 2).

Hart (citing Feigenbaum and McCorduck, 1984; and Welbank, 1983) creates a rather similar wish list of qualities for the knowledge engineer, the person she sees is likely to take prime responsibility for eliciting knowledge:

Good communication skills	Logicality
Tact and diplomacy	Persistence
Empathy and patience	Self-confidence
Versatility and inventiveness	Programming knowledge
Intelligence	Domain knowledge

A similar list of such desirable personality traits are discussed in Chapter 2 by Bell and Hardiman.

3.3 What should drive the elicitation?

There is a debate, as yet unresolved, about the relative merits of the elicitation being driven by requirements of the particular system and its implementation, models of good system development, a model of 'generic tasks' as suggested by Wilson in Chapter 5, the domain, or a theory.

The perspective that the system should, or of necessity will, be driven by the implementation of the particular system is sometimes supported on the grounds of efficiency, sometimes on the grounds of practical necessity. The first argument is that efficient KEL is only possible of decisions about what knowledge the system needs, and how it will be represented in and used by the system are taken in advance of elicitation. The second is in recognition that if the client organisation has made the decision to use a shell or some other particular implementation, that is what will be used and the elicitor will have to obtain knowledge and provide it to encoders in a form which is compatible with the implementation. In these cases, decisions about the system its implementation will affect, among other things, what material is collected, how it should be recorded, analysed and interpreted, and finally presented.

Hart takes an intermediate position, seeing elicitation as both system and domain driven. She sees the system influence as a distinguishing feature of a knowledge engineering approach to elicitation. '. . . the knowledge engineer is almost bound to anticipate how a particular inference method or knowledge base can be represented, and tailor questions accordingly. So the objectives of questioning depend on both the knowledge domain and the possible representation' (Hart, 1986, p. 52).

In contrast, Grover's recommendations (1983, pp. 436–7) are driven by the needs of the development process. It provides a framework for determining what material is relevant and what form it might usefully take. He suggests the creation of a *KA Document Series* to include *domain definition material* presented as a Domain Definition Handbook, and *fundamental knowledge*, i.e. the most nominal, the most expected, the most important, the most archetypal, the best understood situations, written in English and providing a baseline.

Domain definition material includes:

General problem description
Bibliography of reference documents
Glossary of terms, acronyms and symbols
Identification of authoritative 'experts'
Definition of appropriate and realistic performance measures and
Description of example reasoning scenarios

Fundamental knowledge includes:
An ontology of domain entities; object relationships (classes) and object descriptions
A selected lexicon (vernacular)
A definition of input sources and formats
An initial state description including 'background' knowledge
A fundamental set of reasoning and analysis rules
A list of human strategies (meta-rules) which may be considered by system designers for possible inclusion as control rules

Breuker *et al.*, ESPRIT projects 12 and 1098, have adopted a modelling view of KBS. There is a model of the KBS development process upon which they have based a methodology, KADS (Knowledge Acquisition and Structuring), for knowledge acquisition some aspects of which were described briefly in Section 2.1. KADS provides model-driven support especially for analysis. One of the analysis tasks is to identify an *interpretation model*, one of the 'generic models of the problem solving processes in classes of tasks and types of domains' (Breuker *et al.*, 1986, p. 31) such as the generic task model discussed by Wilson in Chapter 5. These are domain-independent abstractions of domain-dependent conceptual models, onto which domain knowledge can be mapped. 'An interpretation model is a kind of catalogue of types of ingredients the knowledge engineer can look for in the data, and thus serves as an organiser that provides coherence to these data' (Breuker *et al.*, 1986, p. 31). Thus, although far from ignoring the domain, this approach can be characterised as driven by models which apply across domains.

Those who take a more domain dependent position argue that systems decisions must follow analysis of the knowledge gathered during elicitation, and elicitation must be guided by the domain, its knowledge sources and end-users. There is the added advantage, Burton and Shadbolt argue in conference discussions, that the system independent material gathered during elicitation can be used for different implementations, alternative or enhanced systems. Johnson, in Chapter 4 outlines the advantages of system representations which she calls 'mediating representations'.

Yet others take their lead, at least in part, from theories such as: Guttman's Facet Theory (e.g. Canter, 1983; Canter, 1985; Brown, 1985), or Conversation Theory (e.g. Johnson and Johnson, 1987a), or Personal Construct Theory (e.g. Kelly, 1955, 1964, 1970, 1977; Fransella and Bannister, 1977; Shaw and Gaines, 1987b) collecting and recording their material within its framework so as to exploit its potential. It would be a distraction to rehearse these theories as it is not the content of the theory which makes the point valid, but the fact of the theory provides the framework if not the driving force for elicitation.

3.4   Selection and recording of material elicited

There are three main issues related to the selection and recording of material: what to record, when to record it, and what form should the record take. The first of these depends on factors described above; the second depends on elicitation and development strategies; it is primarily the last which is considered here at a very practical level. Although comments seem obvious when one thinks about it, they highlight the rocks upon which many otherwise well thoughtout elicitations flounder.

Although the effort in making full use of audio and video records is considerable, one should budget at least eight times the length of the tape for simply transcribing the verbal data if this is going to be done at all. It is wise to record elicitations on tape as a check and to make results credible even if full transcriptions are not envisaged.

3.4.1   *Audio recording*

The straightforward precautionary advice which applies to the use of any electrical equipment certainly applies. Be certain that there is an electrical supply with enough sockets for all the equipment or that it has batteries which are likely to last for the length of the recording session. Recharged batteries will not last as long as they did new, even though they were fully charged at the beginning of a session. Whatever arrangements have been made, a spare set of new batteries is good insurance. The mains outlet socket must be compatible with the plug for non-battery operated recording equipment or an adapter will be needed. Be sure the flexes and leads are long enough to allow the equipment to be placed where it will be most useful without creating an obstacle of trailing electrical spaghetti. Lengths of rubber-backed carpet may be useful for covering wires which must be placed across pathways, but they can also be a hazard. Be sure all the leads are there and actually do fit the equipment. Whoever is to set up and operate the equipment should be thoroughly familiar with it and confident about doing so.

Second, quality can be improved with planning. Microphones must be properly placed and sensitive enough to pick up the required sounds. Decide whether a directional or all around microphone is more appropriate. Be aware of extraneous noises. Heating, air-conditioning and lighting devices are much louder than might be expected, as are street noises in some settings.

3.4.2   Video recording

A decision to usee a video-recorder will depend on there being images of the setting and activities which take place there that need to be captured for later examination. The setting itself cannot be transported through time or space to be available for future or remote analysis. Events which are fleeting, the changing pattern of activities may need to be recorded on video, especially if non-verbal activity is important.

All the cautions about audio recording apply, and there are additional complexities. Do not forget the tripod. Different equipment requires different levels of lighting. Modern video cameras which operate well at the light levels normally found in offices are available. However, if the only camera at your disposal does not function well in this relatively low light, be sure to have the necessary additional lights and have taken into account the need for electrical outlets. Beware that strong lights increase stress on participants (Killin, 1987, p. 4) and make the environment hotter which can be significant in already warm rooms if filming takes place over an extended period. Killin also warns that softer lighting may have too relaxing an effect on the expert, but if the lighting is similar to that in the person's normal work environment that is unlikely to be a problem.

Use of a video camera in a natural setting has other hazards. Take account of human factors in the settings. It may seem less intrusive and a more effective use of the elicitor's time to leave the video camera running in one setting while she/he is interviewing or observing other settings in person, but if the video equipment is plugged into the socket which is usually used for the electric kettle someone is bound to unplug it just long enough to make the tea. If the video camera goes into pause on start-up, the pre-brew-up scene will be the last that is filmed until someone notices and restarts the camera. Allow for people's curiosity and the 'high spirits' which surface especially when they are nervous of 'being watched'.

Video cameras are less flexible than human observers. The amount of the scene they take in — determined by their angle of view, zoom and sweep capabilities — is restricted and slower to change than the human eye. Unless a portable camera with its own power pack is used, they are static and cannot follow the action into other settings. Even if someone operates the video camera continuously, this will not usually solve the problem of restricted camera angles, as the operator will still have the difficulty of selecting from instant to instant what should be recorded.

Many practitioners prefer to use video equipment only in a setting which has been specially prepared and found in trials to allow recordings of good quality to be made. The setting becomes the 'studio' for the purposes of the project even though in reality it may be an office or some other quiet corner. The elicitor will need to ensure that all the necessary 'props' are available to allow knowledge providers to fully express their knowledge in front of the camera. If a 'studio' is used instead of the normal work setting, many (anticipated) everyday activities, most artificial tasks, role plays and interviews can be recorded, but some naturally occurring activities will not be recorded. Unexpected everyday events cannot be scripted. There will also be a limit to the number of people who can be brought into the 'studio'. The knowledge elicitor will have to weigh up the advantages of having a fixed recording environment into which the action must be brought against recording in the environment in which activities usually take place with all its difficulties and distractions.

3.4.3   Other methods of recording
Records can also be made as 'documents' such as field notes or interview forms. They can be held in an electronic form, as files on a computer, or on paper. The literature on social research field methods (e.g. Fielding and Fielding, 1986), anthropolgy and ethnography (e.g. Spradley, 1979; 1980; Agar, 1986) provide useful models for making and keeping these records. The main difference is that these records, unless they are the result of a knowledge provider performing some activity, are less direct than the audio or video record. The person making the record is filtering the material in advance of its being recorded.

Recording styles associated with particular ways of 'getting material' are discussed in Sections 4 and 5 below when a technique is introduced.

3.5   Distinguishing between the terms *focused* and *structured* and *systematic*
There is some confusion in the way the terms *focused, structured* and *systematic* are used in describing elicitation techniques. Although it is not helpful to be pedantic about terminology, it is important to be aware of there being differences in usage and to be clear about how the terms are being employed in any particular discussion. Killin (1987) captures the difficulty rather well when differentiating between the *focused interview* and the *structured interview* in his discussion of interviewing techniques for knowledge elicitation teams:

> Mnemonically, focused interview should focus upon one aspect of problem solving, pursue it alone throughout the session, and not be sidetracked by other factors. Unfortunately, the name focused has been associated with a prepared set of topics, which are introduced to the expert in a 'normal conversational' style of interview. This association (Breuker and Wielinga [1984a]), has of course a counterpart. Their conception of a structured interview is very close to our conception of focused. These definitions, then will be

inverted [in Killin's paper], so that a structured interview means any interview prepared by the KEL team in advance, and designed to elicit general knowledge of the domain. . . . Focused interview can then be used as a specialised technique to elicit, in depth first fashion, all that the expert knows and has to say about a particular, single concept, operation, etc. . . . (Killin, 1987, pp. 7–8, citing Breuker and Weilinga, 1984a).

3.5.1   Focus

In the discussions below, as in Killin's usage, the focus continuum is reserved for characterising the scope of what is being elicited, although focused elicitations will not be confined to dealing with a single aspect of the problem or the domain. A focused elicitation could, for example, deal with several aspects in sequence. It is also possible to adopt a *funnelling* strategy, described for example in Waldron (1986, p. 34) in which unfocused questioning is followed by focused questioning (funnelling down or in) or focused questioning followed by unfocused questioning (funnelling up or out).

3.5.2   Structure

The structure continuum will be reserved, here, for characterising the extent to which the elicitation is designed to fit a preplanned format. This is consistent with the social research terminology, but differs from Killin's in an important way. It is not the fact of planning that distinguish structure from unstructured elicitations. All elicitation sessions require planning. What is different is the extent to which the elicitation follows a format laid down in advance.

Highly structured elicitations follow a predictable sequence and impose a consistency across sessions, across elicitors and across knowledge providers. They are most useful when the nature and range of the material being collected is well known, even though the exact content is not. The format can be so detailed as to have the wording as well as the order in which the elicitation proceeds laid down for the elicitor to use. Typically the records of these elicitations are made on prepared forms which have the anticipated responses pre-coded for quick recording. The record can resemble a questionnaire if the elicitation is an interview, or it can be a check-list or observation sheet if the elicitation is an observation.

Semi-structured elicitations conform to certain aspects of the prepared format. Typically the content to be covered is predetermined, but the order in which it is elicited and the way in which it is done, the wording of questions for example, can vary. The elicitor may have a guide or *aide-mémoire* to work from rather than a questionnaire. Interviews in this style can be more like 'natural conversation' than in structured interviews. Semi-structured observations may be planned, for example, to capture both the activities in a busy corner of a setting and activities in a quiet corner. It will be the pattern of activity, rather than an observation schedule which will determine where the observer looks, when each kind of activity is observed, and what is deemed to be noteworthy.

Unstructured elicitations have a purpose and will be planned as one part of the elicitation programme, but neither the precise content nor the order of elicitation need conform to a format prepared in advance. These are most useful when the elicitor wants to allow surprising, unexpected aspects of the domain to be revealed. They usually occur at an early stage of the elicitation process or when a new aspect of the domain is first being explored.

3.5.3   Systematic

A systematic elicitation process is taken to mean one in which the elicitor has devised some sytem for ensuring that all the relevant material is identified and gathered. Many different techniques can be used (e.g. observations, interviews and sorting tasks) and different styles of using a particular technique (e.g. unstructured unfocused interviews followed by, say, focused semi-structured interviews) can be used in a systematic elicitation. Use of particular technique and/or a particular style does not ensure that the elicitation will be systematic. Waldron (1986, p. 34) recommends, for example, that in any one elicitation occasion the elicitor exhausts one topic before moving on to another, and he provides suggestions for how to direct the elicitation to make this possible (see Section 4.1.6). There are almost as many systems as there are authors. The important thing is not so much which system is adopted, but that some system is adopted, and that it be made explicit in the documentation of the elicitation process. Documenting one's system, even if it is an evolving one, allows the elicitor, and others, to review it and reconsider its merits from time to time. It is available for the elicitor, and others, to see if they wish to check that it is being faithfully followed. It serves as a reminder for the structure and sequencing of elicitation occasions, and is available if the elicitor becomes unavailable through ill-health or change of post. Bell and Hardiman also argue in Chapter 2 for the need to audit the content and process of elicitation.

4.   GETTING MATERIAL FROM PEOPLE

Adopting the broad notion of knowledge elicitation means that a variety of sources must be considered within the province of the knowledge elicitor: not only people but also existing computer systems, documents, and the environment. This section considers techniques for eliciting material from human knowledge sources, typically a veteran, i.e. someone who is knowledgeable and skilled in the domain of interest, or an expert, sometimes characterised as a person with rare and 'world class' knowledge. The next section introduces techniques for getting material from other, non-human, sources.

Reiss (1986, p. 103) characteristics the kind of elicitation process considered in this section as an interface between the knowledge source and the elicitor, and like any interface it needs careful design. When the knowledge source is a human, the activity is essentially a social undertaking requiring co-operation between knowledge provider(s) and elicitor(s), each of whom brings expectations to the occasion and each of whom has some rationale for taking part. All participants interpret the occasion as it develops and adjust their responses to one another in ways which seem to become appropriate. Social skills are high on the list of desirable qualities for elicitors.

Guidelines

There are a number of guidelines for elicitors which apply to all techniques involving human knowledge sources (e.g. Davis, 1983; Hart, 1986, pp. 49–52, cf. Welbank, 1983; Waldron, 1986, p. 34). The elicitor should:

— be as specific about what is wanted as possible, keeping in mind that different stages in the elicitation will require/allow different levels of specificity;
— devise and use an appropriate system for covering all relevant knowledge;
— retain the 'capacity' for surprise', i.e. be open to learning something unexpected;
— allow the person to provide material in the way which is most natural. From this it follows that unless there is a good reason, one which can be made clear to the knowledge provider, alien tools should not be imposed;
— not interrupt to correct inconsistencies and contradictions as they can be tactfully checked later;
— remember that 'An interview is not a contest', which implies that the elicitor should
    — avoid attacks,
    — avoid excessive use of jargon,
    — conduct an interview, not a 'snow job'. Talk to people, not up to them, down to them, or at them (Davis, 1983);
— remember that 'an interview is not a trial' which implies the elicitor
    — can ask probing questions,
    — should not cross-examine (Davis, 1983);
— use the person's body language clues to monitor when the person seems to become hesitant or confused and take appropriate helpful steps to keep the session productive;
— listen to how the person uses and partitions knowledge, noting boundaries, sequences, and patterns and use the person's natural demarcations of the domain to structure elicitation sessions;
— be aware that learning will take place on both sides, but that it is almost always more important for the elicitor to learn about the domain than for the knowledge provider to learn about knowledge engineering or computers;
— be aware when the person is using the elicitation session to try out new ideas and should check the prevalence and stability of material within and across sessions;

— be conscious of time. If a person has agreed to be available for an hour and the elicitation looks as though it will not be complete within that time either the elicitor should wind it up without completing everything or check with the person to see if they will be able to stay longer to complete the session giving a realistic estimate of how long it will take;
— not let the furniture and 'props' reduce rapport. The elicitor may find it useful to rearrange seating so that the knowledge provider can see the notes and diagrams the elicitor draws. Thus, putting papers on a flat surface rather than holding them up makes the elicitor seem more approachable and less secretive;
— make audio and/or video recordings of as much of the elicitation as possible, as well as taking sufficient notes to navigate through the tapes later. One can not always predict in the early stages of elicitation what may turn out to be vital material. Not all tapes need to be transcribed;
— not let note taking get in the way of elicitation. Working in pairs eases recording difficulties, a point also made by Bell and Hardiman in Chapter 2;
— plan for there to be time, and energy, after each elicitation session to review and supplement the record made during the session with notes which flesh features of the context, such as interruptions and where the knowledge provider seemed confident and where tentative;
— provide feedback and an opportunity to check the accuracy of the material elicited.

Techniques for getting material from people
The techniques considered here show the variety, but do not fully exhaust the range, of possible elicitation techniques. Twelve types of techniques are described below with some of their more prominent variants to illustrate the multidisciplinary inheritance of knowledge elicitation. The twelve groups are:

— Interviewing.
— Focused talk.
— Teach back.
— Construct elicitation which includes a discussion of Kelly's Personal Construct Theory and the Repertory Grid technique.
— Sorting tasks.
— Laddering.
— '20 questions'.
— Matrix generation.
— Critiquing.
— Protocols.
— Role play.
— Simulations.

Devices and 'props'

The main use of devices and 'props' in knowledge elicitation is to supply what the knowledge provider requires to perform or describe a domain task. These are typically artefacts used in the domain such as a microscope to examine a rock sample in the case of elicitation from geological experts. They can also be used to facilitate an elicitation task, for example serving as the focus for discussion (see Section 4.2) or the cards which are sorted in a sorting task (see Section 4.5).

One which is not discussed elsewhere in this chapter is a device used to facilitate quantification. In particular, if the KBS uses measures of uncertainty elicitors will have to design elicitation to get various probability judgements. The 'probability wheel' (e.g. Welbank, 1983, p. 35; Wright and Ayton, 1987, p. 22) can be used to help knowledge providers make direct probability estimates without having to express the estimate in terms of a number. Typically it is a cardboard disk with a 'cover' of a different colour. When the 'cover' is rotated about the centre of the disk of a larger or smaller pie-shaped portion of the disk is revealed. The knowledge provider is asked, for example, 'How probable' an event or an outcome is by revealing an appropriate portion of the disk. A '1 in 6' chance, i.e. a probability of 0.167, would be indicated by revealing a sixth of the disk, i.e. a 'pie slice' whose edges made an angle of 60 degrees at the centre of the disk. People seem to be able to make visual estimate with which they are happy when they would be reluctant to supply a numerical estimate. The probability wheel can also be used for quantifying confidence in a judgement. Complete confidence would be represented by the complete disk being revealed, complete lack of confidence by the disk being fully 'covered' so no 'slice of the pie' was indicated. Similarly with strength of belief.

4.1 Interview

The term interview is used here to indicate a specific technique not, as is common in the literature, as an occasion. This is not an effort to redefine the term interview permanently, but the distinction is useful in the context of this chapter because it allows the unpacking of elicitation features. Most discussions of interviewing treat it as an occasion during which it is typical for several different techniques to be used. In this way very different elicitation techniques are lumped together as interviewing and their differing requirements and possibilities are glossed over. Here 'interviewing' is confined to a bi-partite activity, the interaction between people where the elicitor is the *interviewer* and the human knowledge source is the *interviewee*. The term *questioning*, was considered as alternative to *interviewing* as a title for this section but questioning which can be accomplished via self-completion questionnaires or interactions between a person and a computer, is not what this section is intended to be about.

A simplistic, because it ignores all that goes on to maintain this social interaction, but useful view is that the main kind of interaction in the 'interview' involves the interviewer asking *questions* to which the interviewee reponds with *answers*. This narrow conception of the term 'interview' is taken as a starting point for considering more complex elicitation interactions in later sections. This is why topics often included in discussions of interviewing are not covered in this section.

It is as well to be reminded that KE interviewing involves the elicitor asking a person with domain knowledge questions about topics to get material which will be of use to the knowledge elicitator for developing a KBS. The use of the question–answer strategy is, most often implicitly, based on the assumptions that the interviewee has access to the knowledge and can put that knowledge into words. Both accessibility and verbalisability are important if verbal answers are to be of value, but for reasons hinted at below and discussed by Diaper in Chapter 1, much human knowledge is difficult, if not impossible to verbalise.

4.1.1 Answers as verbal data

To have access to knowledge, the person answering the direct question must 'know' the answer, i.e. must have had the general experience necessary for knowing. For example, the experience of seeing is necessary for a description of what something looks alike. Knowing also requires that the person is neither ignorant of, nor has forgotten, the specific knowledge such as what a particular machine part looks like. Having access also means that the 'knowing' is mentally accessible. This criteria of mental accessibility means that the knowledge is neither unconscious, as for example how to breathe; nor so compiled as to be unavailable, as for example how to shift gears in a car. Being able to put the knowledge into words means that verbal reports of essentially non-verbal activities, such as how to ride a bicycle or what chocolate tastes like, are to be treated with great caution if elicited at all. Diaper discusses these psychological issues in more detail in Chapter 1.

The expectation that knowledge can be verbalised implies that there is a vocabulary for that knowledge, and that there is a body of cognoscenti who have a shared understanding of that vocabulary. One of the major requirements of the knowledge elicitor is to have, or develop, an appreciation of the vocabulary of the domain so she/he can utilise the knowledge couched in those terms. However, there are some domains where there is no established vocabulary. Kidd identifies this as one of the main factors in making certain domains, e.g. her Class 3 domains, difficult or impossible for KBS applications. An example she gives is that of electronic mail in which there is a lack of agreed language and underlying theory. When constructing systems in these domains the elicitor is among those who are creating 'a "new" language (and therefore an implicit theory) that will adequately support reasoning within the domain. This new language is likely to be the subject of continuous negotiation with both experts and users even when the expert system is developed' (Kidd, 1987, p. 4). The lack of a common vocabulary may undermine the elicitor's faith in the value of verbal reports. At the very least, awareness of the problem should guide questioning strategy and cause the elicitor to take even greater care in how verbal reports are interpreted and what use is made of them.

The appropriateness and value of verbal reports is discussed in detail by

Ericsson and Simon (1985), who point out among other things that using verbal reports does not mean taking them at face value. The person can be misinformed, unwilling to convey a faithful characterisation though well informed, or unable to do so. There are occasions when an elicitor will elicit verbal reports, in spite of being aware that the assumptions are being violated, as additional supporting evidence or as one of a battery of ways of getting at related knowledge. In these situations direct questions are being used as an indirect, and problematic, way of accessing otherwise unavailable knowledge.

4.1.2   Kinds of questions

Direct/indirect

Questions can be *direct*, e.g. 'What evidence leads you to that decision?', when the elicitor has a clear idea of what knowledge she/he needs and it is thought that the interviewee will recognise and be able to put that knowledge into words. *Indirect* questions, such as 'Tell me how you go about deciding what to do', are useful when an elicitor wants to leave the interviewee free to suggest categories of knowledge of which the elicitor is not yet aware, e.g. new taxonomies. They are also useful when the elicitor wants to access knowledge which is analytically important but which either the interviewee would find difficult to recognise or which if asked about directly, would lead the interviewee into perhaps artificially utilising categories which would otherwise not be used, e.g. whether welfare advisors predominantly categorise benefits in terms of the source of funds or the administering agency.

Explicit/implied

The questions can be *explicit*, i.e. in the form of a question such as 'What do you do first?'. They can also be *implied*, i.e. in the form of a statement such as 'The first thing you do?' or a phrase such as 'And first?'. Interviews consisting entirely of explicit questions from the elicitor and answers from the interviewee will feel stilted to both. This can be useful in a small range of elicitations, e.g. where a more natural interaction would be interpreted by the interviewee as sloppy and unbusiness-like, but generally occurs when an inexperienced elicitor wants to give the impression of being well prepared or needs a question list for support or to establish and maintain control of the elicitation. Experienced interviewers will be able to establish a business-like, professional atmosphere and retain the appropriate level of control without the interview seeming stilted.

Good question design

There is no shortage of advice available about good question design (e.g. Moser and Kalton, 1978; CSO, 1976; Stacey, 1969). Among the pitfalls to avoid are:

— phrasing questions in the negative;
— making them so vague that there is both no suitable answer and many possible answers, e.g. 'To what extent do you . . . ?';
— using jargon which is not usually used by the person;
— using pretentious language;
— phrasing questions so they are threatening or embarrasing;
— asking *leading questions*, sometimes called *directive* or *loaded* questions, i.e. ones which 'designate a particular response' (Waldron, 1986, p. 33);
— asking *double-barrelled* questions (i.e. questions with two or more parts to them);
— asking questions which presume something about the person which may not be true, e.g. 'How do you process . . . [something the person may not process at all]?';
— asking *hypothetical* questions; and asking very long-winded questions.

There are special techniques for assisting recall with which the elicitor should become familiar. Retrospective studies may design questions to: work back through time; suggesting the person check appropriate records before answering; help them place the events in relation to other memorable events (e.g. was that before or after you last. . .); and, as recognition is easier than recall, showing them appropriate lists or collections from which to select what they would otherwise be asked to remember. Alternatively it may be possible to adopt a prospective strategy and have the knowledge provider keep a diary of activities as they happen. The phrasing of questions for finding out about periodic behaviour can be crucial as different forms are likely to produce different responses (Moser and Kalton, 1978, p. 150).

As already discussed when defining terms above, questions can be more of less *focused* (see Section 3.5.1) and more or less *structured* (see Section 3.5.2). In addition the elicitor's role can be more or less *directive*, and interviews can be made to feel more or less natural to the interviewee. The requirements of the knowledge elicitation process 'drive' the KEL interview, even for those interviews which may seem to the interviewee to be free flowing and where the elicitor does not seem to be exercising control. Unlike observations, there is no such thing as a non-participant, passive interview. The elicitor always takes an active part, even if, as in interviews where the aim is to 'generate talk' about the domain, the elicitor needs to ask few questions and seems to the interviewee to be undirected.

Complementary questions
Although it might not be surprising that different kinds of questions are needed to elicit different kinds of knowledge, elicitors do not always ask as many kinds of questions and they could in order to gather well-rounded material. LaFrance (1987) has developed a manual 'tool', the *Knowledge Acquisition Grid* to enlarge the questioning repertoire of elicitors, to improve the targeting of questions, and to help elicitors avoid falling into the trap of thinking that a single question can elicit all the information required in a particular, even small, area of knowledge.

4.1.3 LaFrance's six question types

The grid, which is a matrix of five *forms of knowledge* by six *Question types*, provides a framework for knowledge elicitation. '... each dimension is intended to provide the knowledge engineer with a wide-angled lens to see more of the relevant expertise. ... the categories within each dimension overlap to some degree' (LaFrance, 1987, p. 253). Appendix B contains a discussion of the Forms of Knowledge dimension and strategies for using the grid. Question types are considered here.

The question type dimension of the grid is a recognition that different questions elicit different information and that a pluralistic questioning strategy is needed to elicit all that is relevant. The theoretical foundation of this dimension is that a persons's

> memory trace is composed of several features and hence the effectiveness of a question or retrieval cue is related to the amount of feature overlap with the event being reported. In other words, some questions pick up elements that are neglected when other kinds of questions are asked. A second outcome of this research is the recognition that there are probably several retrieval paths to the encoded event, so that information that is not readily accessible by one retrieval cue might be available with a different cue (Tulving, 1974). (LaFrance, 1987, p. 252).

There are six question types included in the grid. She characterises them as:

— Grand tour questions.
— Cataloguing the categories.
— Ascertaining the attributes.
— Determining the interconnections.
— Seeking advice.
— Cross-checking questions.

Although she recognises that they do not exhaust possible question types, together they are designed to collect 'full and valid' information,

> producing a comprehensive survey of the expert's knowledge. ... The six types of questions also vary in their level of specificity which, in combination, have the advantage of pulling out material varying in detail and composition. [Use of more than one type] should counteract the tendency of knowledge engineers to favour one type of question over another at the expense of a more comprehensive grasp of the relevant expertise [and] guards against unwarranted assumptions by both the knowledge engineer and expert. (LaFrance, 1987, pp. 252–3).

The descriptions below, beginning with the question type that elicits the most general material and ending with the one that elicits the most specific material, closely follow LaFrance's presentation (unless otherwise indicated the quotations are taken from pp. 250–51).

Grand tour questions, e.g. 'Could you describe the kinds of things that schedulers do? Please do not edit things out of your description, even things that you think may not be important.' Thus they seek an overview and elicit material about the boundaries of the area under discussion, and the knowledge provider's 'perspective, goals, organisation, and classification'.

Cataloguing the categories, e.g. 'When you gave me an overview of your job, you talked about schedulers. Are schedulers a subtype of some other kind of job?' These are attempting to elicit 'an organised taxonomy of the expert's terms and concepts'. It is a question format which would be usefully employed, for example, in the laddering technique discussed in Section 4.6 of this chapter.

Ascertaining the attributes, e.g. 'You've described a number of types of scheduling situation that you've encountered. I wonder whether you could now take the first two that you mentioned, and describe some ways in which these two are similar to each other but different from the third example that you gave.' These are aiming 'to discover the distinguishing features and range of possible values of the expert's concepts.' This type of question could be used in the elicitation of constructs which is discussed in Section 4.4 of this chapter.

Determining the interconnections, e.g. 'In describing the routine set of steps for scheduling an order you said that checking the request date occurs before anything else. Why is this the case?' These aim at 'uncovering the relations among concepts in the domain. Of particular interest is the existence of a causal model for the whole domain or parts of it.'

Seeking advice, e.g. 'You've compared scheduling to playing a board game; from your experience with playing board games what advice could you give on doing scheduling?' These aim to 'reveal the expert's recommendations and hence strategies for how to deal with a variety of conditions such as how to determine current conditions and which conditions warrant which actions'.

Cross-checking questions, 'are designed to validate and examine the limits on previously obtained information. [They] actually consist of five subtypes [which are] the *Naive question, Playing Devil's Advocate, Posing Hypothetical Situations*, asking *How Sure Are You?*, and *Seeking the Exception.*'

4.1.4   Preparation and strategic decisions

Interviews are usually arranged in advance, and can take place where the interviewee works or away from that environment. But there may be occasions when the elicitor unexpectedly has an opportunity to conduct an interview 'on the spot' and it seems unwise, or impossible, to make a future arrangement. If the occasion is to be an interview rather than a conversation, it will be planned, however quickly and however broadly. The elicitor will have to make almost instantaneous decisions drawing on general, rather than specific, preparation. The elicitor will have to adopt an interview style and formulate the purpose before even a 'spur of the moment' interview begins. Thus, all KEL interviews, 'spur of the moment' notwithstanding, involve preparation and planning and are conducted for some purpose.

Althought there are some general principles which may be of use, it is neither possible to identify, nor profitable to seek, a single KEL interview scenario to recommend to all KBS teams. Decisions about purpose, style, environment and recording method for interviews are all affected by the nature and ethos of the domain, the roles and personal styles of participants in the interview, how well the domain is understood by the knowledge elicitor, and the ethos of the development team. Once an elicitor knows the range of possibilities and requirements, an appropriate interview scenario can be selected. Sometimes it will be decided that similarity across interviews is desirable. Sometimes it will be decided that different scenarios will be more effective. In either case a decision will have to be made and a scenario adopted for each interview.

At the beginning of a project it is useful to conduct interviews which allow unexpected perspectives to emerge. They are typically wide ranging (broad), and do not explore issues to any great depth (shallow). The knowledge elicitor should have become familiar enough with the domain to broadly grasp its terminology and main features, but this understanding should not be paraded more than is necessary for maintaining rapport with the interviewee. The elicitor must know how enough to question effectively and to appreciate the value of the answers and to note the gaps in them. But there is still room especially in the early interviews for 'creative ignorance', the elicitor asking for elaborations of terms and comments which the elicitor feels are already understood is a way of determining how closely the background sources reflect the perspective of the interviewee. Although the elicitor must not lose credibility as an elicitor of knowledge, this credibility should not be based on being knowledgeable about the domain, but on an ability to grasp what it said, check it with others in the domain, and to interpret it in ways which are useful for building the KBS. Having said that, for better or worse the elicitor will learn about the domain as the elicitation process proceeds. Some practitioners even argue that experience of the domain is an invaluable asset in an elicitor, but this is debatable. The more the elicitor knows about the domain, the harder it is for the elicitor to keep an open mind.

Typically, later interviews are more focused and may be more structured. The perspective and function of the KBS will have been selected, general knowledge will have been gathered and the elicitor will pursue selected topics in greater detail. Later still, certain specific kinds of knowledge may be required, knowledge which people find it difficult to express in response to even skilled and imaginative questioning. It is then that techniques other than interviewing may be adopted during the session.

Contrary to a widely held view, it is not the case that more structured interviews are necessarily better planned and more effective than less structured interviews. But it is true that in structured interviews both the interviewer and the questions are more constrained.

4.1.5   Structured interviews

Structured interviews are interviews in which the interviewer asks the same questions in the same words and in the same order for each interview. Many of the questions used are closed questions, ones where the expected answers are short, with few surprises, so likely answers can have been formulated in advance and responses precoded. For this reason they are sometimes referred to as closed interviews.

Structured interviews are useful when there is specific material required and features of the topic and responses can be anticipated. They are also used when the wording and order of questioning is felt to be important and where consistency across a number of interviews is desirable. These conditions are more likely to apply in a large scale survey than in a knowledge elicitation process where there are few knowledge providers and where multiple interviews are more likely to be conducted in an effort to fill gaps in the knowledge base and check accuracy of information rather than to test consistency of response to a series of questions.

Elicitors conducting a structured interview are likely to have the questions and expected answers on a form so the interviewer can tick or circle the answer. There may also be small spaces for writing comments or unexpected responses to closed questions and larger spaces for briefly noting responses to any open questions, those where longer answers are expected, where the variety is great enough that they cannot be precoded, or where the differences in the details given is important enough to note.

It is important to the design of structured interviews that the range of likely responses is adequately covered. The interviewer does not usually show the interviewee the list of precoded answers, nor are they usually read out, so it is important that the interviewer is familiar enough with the precoded answers to be consistent in categorising the answers. It is also important that the questions are properly worded as there may not be enough discussion for the interviewer to realise when an interviewee has misinterpreted a phrase or term. As with general question design (Section 4.1.2), the issue of question wording is well documented (e.g. Labaw, 1980) and this work should be consulted before designing questions for structured interviews.

4.1.6   Semi-structured interviews

Semi-structured interviews are those where there is a list of questions to be asked, but the order in which they are covered and the words used to express them may vary from interview to interview. This flexibility allows the interviewer to adopt the vocabulary of the interviewee where appropriate, and to note answers to questions when they are offered, even if they arise in answer to a different question. This style of interviewing is likely to seem less stilted to the interviewee and can flow more smoothly than a structured interview. It puts more demands on the interviewer who has to jump around the interview schedule and take care not to repeat questions to which answers have already been given. It allows a knowledge elicitor to note the interviewee's associations between topics that are likely to be unavailable from a structured interview.

4.1.7 Unstructured interviews

Unstructured interviews are designed to allow interviewees to cover topics in largely their own way. They provide 'capacity for surprise' for interviewers who have an idea of the kind of information that is needed and are prepared with a set of seed questions, prompts and probes. Nancy Johnson used a elegant starter question in her VLSI knowledge elicitation work: 'Imagine you went into a bookshop and saw the book you wish you had had when you first started working in the field. What would it have had in it?' (Johnson and Johnson, 1987a). Another starter might be 'When I read the documentation for this system, I had some trouble with (mention a part or section). Can you explain to me?' (Davis, 1983).

Probes

In addition to the starter question, the interviewer will, use probes, which 'must not in any way affect the nature of the subsequent response' (Babbie, 1979, p. 176). This stricture is primarily intended to distinguish probes from prompts for interviewers conducting structured interviews as part of surveys in which efforts are made to ensure comparability between interviewers. Probes tend to elicit more information on the current topic, enouraging the interviewee to elaborate on a detail of interest so as to give a more complete answer. Probes include comments such as 'Tell me a bit more about that'; 'Anything more?'; 'And then?'; 'Yes?'. Waldron (1986, p. 33) characterises 'probes' as being of one of two kinds. There are *reflective probes*, i.e. those which paraphrase what the knowledge provider has said in such a tone as to imply there might be more to add. These have the added function of providing feedback and allowing the knowledge provider to hear what he has said. The externalisation of his words gives them a new dimension which may cause the interviewee to consider them afresh. Reflective probes provide an opportunity to correct misconceptions as well as encouraging the provision of additional information. Waldron also speaks of *request probes*, i.e. those such as 'Oh?' and 'Please go on' that are requests for more information. Silence is also a powerful probe in some western cultures such as North America, but less so with people from cultures such as those in the Middle East where silence is a comfortable part of conversation.

Prompts

There are other short phrases which are useful for allowing the elicitor to change the course of the interview. These include what Killin calls *directive probes* which 'get the expert back on the track' and include comments such as 'Can we return to ...'; and *change-of-mode probes* which change from 'What' questions to 'Why' and 'How' questions (Killin, 1987, p. 9). They might more properly be called prompts as they do not meet Babbie's criteria of being neutral to the response. The distinction between prompts and probes is not very important except on highly structured interviews where consistency is of great importance and where probes would be allowed but prompts would not. The interviewer can also prompt with comments such as 'And what about . . .?' 'Who handles that?' to explore additional features or a related topic.

The content of unstructured interviewing is unpredictable and it requires a confident and skilled interviewer to remember the many clues and follow them up in a productive way. The interviewer must listen very carefully and make fine judgements about whether apparent ramblings will unearth material of value. Although there is little apparent control, the elicitor will have to exercise some if the interview is to be effective. It is, however, a difficult kind of interview to control, especially if the interviewee is used to being in command and has a firm, though not necessarily correct, idea of what the elicitor will want to know. The interviewer can acknowledge the importance of what the interviewee wants to say, and suggest they return to it later e.g. 'I want to make sure we discuss the oil pressure today, but first I'd like to really understand how the electrical system could be part of the problem' (Waldron, 1986, p. 33).

4.1.8 *Recording data*
Material elicited during interviews is typically recorded on audio tape and/or on paper records of the occasion. Paper records of the interview may include an interview may include an interview schedule on which there are questions, the interviewee's answers and written comments made by the elicitor. Free form notes may be made during the interview. Audio tapes may be fully or partially transcribed. Some elicitors prefer to work directly from the tape, only noting the tape recorder counter number at topic shifts or when particularly interesting material emerges. In some cases the audio tape is considered to be the main record with the notes made during the interview being used only as supplementary material, e.g. notations of features of the office, shifts of attention, level of certainty expressed through non-verbal cues, and noting what the interviewee was referring to but did not name. In other cases the notes are the main record with the tapes made as a back-up, a way to check the accuracy of notes or to fill in gaps. In all cases the material should be viewed as data which needs to be interpreted, not nuggets of ready-to-use knowledge mined from the mind of the inter-viewee (Kidd, 1987, p. 3), a notion also rejected by Bell and Hardiman (Chapter 2) and by Johnson (Chapter 4).

4.2 Focused discussion
An elicitation activity closely akin to the question and answer strategy of the interview is the focused discussion. It is similar to interviewing in that it is primarily designed to elicit verbal reports rather than some other behaviour such as the physical performance of some task. It can be characterised as 'introspective' rather than 'behaviourist' in nature if, unlike Ericsson and Simon (1985, p. 2), one wishes to make such a distinction. They argue that such a distinction disregards the fact that verbalisation is itself a kind of

behaviour, but the distinction may still be useful to non-pursuits as a reminder that eliciting verbal reports through interviewing or focused discussion is rather different from setting the knowledge provider another kind of task to perform.

In all introspective techniques the knowledge provider is asked to think about or imagine something of interest to the knowledge elicitor, such as the steps necessary to perform a particular piece of work. Killin (1987) identifies four associated introspective strategies:

— Retrospective case description.
— Critical incident strategy (e.g. Hart, 1986).
— Forward scenario simulation.
— '20 questions'.

Each of these will be discussed as separate techniques below. Its useful to have the techniques brought to one's attention, but they neither exhaust the collection of introspective techniques nor, in the case of '20 questions' is it clear that the label 'introspective' is entirely apt. The linking of them to introspection is not pursued by Killin, nor particularly helpful, except as a warning that the doubts attached to the value of introspective data may apply to knowledge elicited using these techniques. For a discussion of the dangers and justifications for using introspective techniques and the verbal data they elicit, see Ericsson and Simon (1985, pp. 1–61). The general warnings concerning the validity of verbalised data already mentioned in this chapter, and by Diaper in Chapter 1, are also, of course, germane.

The focused discussion can be distinguished from interviewing in that it introduces a third element, the focus, into the interaction between the elicitor and the human knowledge source. It can therefore be considered a tripartate activity. The presence of the third element reduces the intensity of the interaction as it allows the elicitor and the knowledge provider, together or separately, to consider the third element rather than only one another. This can reduce the stress for both of them.

The focus for the discussion can be any of many kinds of items, for example:

— *cases* the person is working on, e.g. 'Tell me what did you do on the case you finished this morning';
— *artefacts* of the domain, e.g. 'What was involved in getting this leaflet out';
— *intermediate representations* (intermediate either in the sense of being stages along the road to a final system or in the sense of being between the domain and the system builders), e.g. 'These are the things that we agree the users need help with. Could you go through them and tell me what you need to know about the situation to help with each one?';
— *lists* such as checklists, agenda items, personnel lists, customer lists, or activity cycles, e.g. 'Could you go through each of these in turn and tell me ...?' or 'Let's start with the hardest to prepare. What are the problems involved with that?';

— *domain concepts*, e.g. 'I've noticed that you talk about repairs in terms of being . . ., . . . or . . . . Could you tell me how they are different?'.

The focus can serve to *mediate* the knowledge being provided in the sense that the verbal data is expressed in terms which are relevant to the focus. But the focus is not synonymous with Johnson's 'mediating representation' Chapter 4 (also Johnson, 1987b). The presence of the focus may, as Johnson describes, serve to reconcile the elicitor's understanding and that of the human knowledge source, but it serves other purposes as well. It stimulates, reminds, highlights gaps and may structure the verbal data which suggests the term 'mediating representation' is too restricted to apply here.

4.2.1   Setting the task

Like an interview a focused discussion is, in a sense, a task setting and task performance interaction. The elicitor sets the knowledge provider a verbalisation task and the knowledge provider responds by producing a verbal report and perhaps artefacts such as diagrams, graphs, or sketches. The knowledge provider will want to perform the task well, so it is important to select an appropriate focus, such as two cases being worked on at present, and set appropriate tasks such as, say how they are different. For persons whose expertise lies in verbalisation rather than physical manipulation, talking is usually a comfortable task. This sort of person may prefer to talk about their work, rather than be observed doing it, or be asked to try out a prototype system. The focus can not only serve the purpose of stimulating, directing and structuring the talk but may lead to a willingness to take part in a 'hands on' exercise. On the other hand, for persons whose expertise lies in physical manipulation rather than verbalisation, question answering and discussion can be stressful. It is made easier by having a concrete focus to talk around, but this sort of person may prefer to demonstrate how something is done rather than describe how she/he does it.

Task setting can be accomplished by a way of a question, a statement or instructions. The knowledge to do the task, must, as in the interview, be accessible to the person and the verbilisation requested by the elicitor must be appropriate to the task. The main advice about task setting is that the elicitor should make it clear, as simply as possible, what is being requested. Lengthy preambles about the reason for the discussion or how it would be helpful for the person to provide the verbal report should be separate from the setting of the specific task. If the verbal report is expected in a form which is unusual for the person, not usually advisable, but occasionally appropriate, an example or two as *training* may be helpful. It is discouraging for the knowledge provider to launch into a verbal report only to be interrupted with a request to do it differently, or be told at the end that it was not quite what the elicitor had in mind. Forethought may help the elicitor avoid such situations which then require the exercise of considerable tact to repair.

There is a range of verbalisation tasks from which the elicitor can select in designing a session of 'focused discussion'. These include Case Study tasks of *forward scenario simulation* and *retrospective case description*, which can have as their focus either: a representative selection of cases; only typical cases; only interesting cases such as rare or difficult ones, or only critical incidents. There are goal related tasks such as *dividing the domain, reclassification, distinguishing goals*, and *goal decomposition*. List related tasks such as the form of *decision analysis* make up yet another group. These types of task are described below.

4.2.2 Case study tasks

In all case studies the knowledge provider focuses on particular cases. They may be real or imaginary. They may be devised by the elicitor, selected by the knowledge provider, identified during domain analysis, or be arrived at through a combination of these. For example, the elicitor may provide a set of case types from which the knowledge provider is asked to select an example. Four case study techniques are discussed here.

Forward scenario simulation

In this technique the elicitor (e.g. Burton and Shadbolt, forthcoming, p. 5) or the knowledge provider (e.g. Grover, 1983, p. 437) supplies an example situation or case and the knowledge provider describes, usually step by step, what would be done in the situation or when handling the case (Breuker and Weilinga, 1984a, p. 28).

If, as in the study by Burton and Shadbolt, the case is not a real one which the knowledge provider has processed, the technique suffers from the disadvantages of other hypothetical questioning strategies and thus an additional source of invalidity may be introduced. (Breuker and Weilinga, 1984a, p. 28). The examples, however, are usually chosen so as to simulate ones the person has been in or handled and so do not send the knowledge provider as far into the realms of fantasy as some hypothetical questions might.

Grover (1983, p. 437) cites three other difficulties with the technique. First, the knowledge provider may use terms and concepts with which the elicitor is not familiar causing confusion and delay. Second, 'rule fanout' problems may arise with the knowledge provider having more rules and strategies brought to mind than can be followed through in the context of the scenario. There is a danger of losing the reasoning path or getting into rules which are too specific to be useful. Third, the job of the reasoner may be confounded with the reasoning method used.

Burton and Shadbolt (forthcoming, p. 5) warn against using the technique with knowledge providers who find it difficult to verbalise knowledge. a warning that should apply to any unstructured technique. They also note that knowledge providers who are prone to *post-hoc* justification are likely to provide spurious decision rules as they work through a case. This is a problem with any introspective technique (see Diaper's discussion of the psychological issues in Chapter 1). Burton and Shadbolt cite the major advantage of the techniques as being the fact that by judicious selection of the example, either a rare case or a mundane one, both of which are likely to be under represented among the cases knowledge providers discuss in the absence of direction from the elicitor, the technique can tap knowledge otherwise overlooked.

Where unusual, rare, difficult or critical cases are employed, the knowledge elicited can be characterised as both typical and atypical. It is typical in so far as it is what the knowledge provider generally does for cases or in situations like the one being used as an example. It is atypical in so far as the example used as the focus is atypical.

Retrospective case description

This is similar to forward scenario simulation except that the cases are not hypothetical ones but are examples of ones which the knowledge provider has handled, preferably in the recent past. If the knowledge provider choses the cases, there is a danger that an interesting rather than a typical case will be selected.

Interesting cases

For some elicitation exercises it is important to have cases from the full range with which the knowledge provider deals. For other elicitation exercises the case chosen is of a specific type such as rare cases, those that take a particularly long time to resolve, those which give the knowledge provider the most difficulty or are particularly memorable. There is a danger that in seeking examples of interesting cases the knowledge provider will have to delve too far into the past to be able to remember the case in detail. This increases the danger of *post-hoc* rationalisation or projecting on to the old case habits and strategies which have been recently used. To avoid using cases from too far in the past, the elicitor may need to settle for less variety. Except where there is some reason to do otherwise, such as the case in point being particularly memorable, the elicitor will need to give less weight to material elicited from very old cases.

Critical incidents

Memorable cases are the focus of the critical incident technique. As with studies of other interesting cases, it is a specialisation of the retrospective case description. The knowledge provider is asked to recall and subsequently to discuss a specific incident or case which was of critical importance in some context. The criticality of the incident is thought to have strongly impressed details on the person's mind. The incident as a source for verbal reports is not only vivid, but in so far as the person relives the incident when it is brought to mind, it approximates a re-enactment of the incident which, it is thought, makes available kinds of knowledge which would not otherwise be recalled. Flanagan, who first described the technique (e.g. Welbank, 1983, p. 21), describes its use with pilots:

> pilots returning from combat were asked to think of some occasion during combat flying in which you personally experienced feelings of acute disorientation or strong vertigo.' They were then asked to

describe what they 'saw, heard, or felt that brought on that experience'. (Flanagan, 1954, p. 329 cited in Ericsson and Simon, 1985, p.
24)

Warnings of two kinds are in order. The knowledge elicited using this
technique is likely to be idiosyncratic and untypical even for the given
knowledge provider. Critical incidents are, after all, those with particular
import, not the everyday occurrence. The second warning has to do with the
validity of assumptions it makes about human information processing and
the nature of memory which have largely been discredited. The critics are
numerous and should not be ignored.

Elicitors should be aware of the difference betwen this use of the term
critical and that implied by a critical path analysis. In the latter, a critical
event or process is one on which subsequent events or processes depend.
The process may be quite routine and unremarkable in itself, but is crucial to
the success or timely completion of the whole. Such a process can and often
is the focus of discussion, but unless it is of particular significance to the
knowledge provider it is unlikely to supply the vividness of recall that critical
incidents described above do. Unfortunately there is no distinction in
terminology used for these different kinds of criticality.

4.2.3   Goal-related tasks

The term *goal* as used in describing these techniques, is a technical term
defined by Hart when describing the *distinguishing goals* method of questioning as 'states of belief, or decisions' (Hart, 1986, p. 59). This use of the
term traces its parentage back to the Newell and Simon's information
processing model of human problem solving (Newell and Simon, 1972). It
can include, for example, any node of a decision tree or step in a plan. Any
intermediate step along a decision path can be described as a goal. Many
goals in this sense would not be thought of as goals in the popular sense of
what people want to accomplish or achieve in, say, their work.

The technical and popular uses of the term are not incompatible. The
difference is less one of kind than range of granularity and orientation to the
goal. In the popular sense goals are typically coarse grained and desirable. In
the technical KBS sense goals can be coarse, but they can also be very fine
grained. They need not be desirable except in the sense that reaching some
resolution is desirable. Applying the term goal to a node in a classification
structure as Burton *et al.* do in one of their examples (Burton *et al.*, 1988, p.
137) or to an undesirable outcome may cause confusion for elicitors new to
the KBS field. Similarly, knowledge providers or domain staff would be
surprised if these were called goals in feedback sessions.

Elicitors should be aware of both uses of the term, realise that the
technical use of the term is much broader than the popular one, and
therefore when using one or more of the four goal-related techniques the
elicitor will need to be careful not to describe the techniques as 'goal related'
nor describe as 'goal structures' material the knowledge provider would not
think of in these terms.

Dividing the domain
The knowledge provider starts with data such as symptoms or bits of evidence, and groups them until a 'goal', such as a diagnosis or a decision, is reached. The reverse of this process is reclassification (Hart, 1986, p. 59).

Reclassification
The knowledge provider is given a 'goal' such as a diagnosis or a decision and asked what evidence would support the view that the 'goal' was the appropriate one (Hart, 1986, p. 59; Breuker and Weilinga, 1983b, p. 543; and Grover, 1983, p. 437).

Distinguishing goals
The knowledge provider is given a 'goal', such as a particular judgement or diagnosis, and is asked for a set of data, e.g. evidence or symptoms, which would be 'necessary and sufficient to distinguish this goal from the other alternatives' (Hart, 1986, p. 59). As described here it is an exercise in identifying minimal sets of discrimination criteria. A set of symptoms, for example, which this task elicits need not contain all the symptoms one would expect to be present in a person suffering from a certain medical condition. It should not generate a full description of the condition, but should elicit just those symptoms which are necessary to distinguish this condition from others and are sufficient to allow the diagnosis to be made. The knowledge provider may not find it easy to leave out symptoms which are typical of the condition but are also typical of alternative conditions and therefore are not effective discriminators. The elicitor can provide some training in the technique in an effort to get the material the technique is intended to elicit and will usually need to check the material for apparently inappropriate criteria and use these as the focus of a subsequent discussion. The latter can be a very revealing strategy. High temperature, for example, may be symptomatic of several conditions and therefore seem inappropriate as a discriminator. On checking, however, it may turn out, for example that the duration of a high temperature, or the pattern of its level (steady or fluctuating) may be the real discriminating factor. This would be missed if the elicitor simply deletes apparently inappropriate material.

Goal decomposition
This involves decomposing 'goals', such as accomplishing a task or solving a problem, into subgoals such as subtasks or subproblems (e.g. Breuker and Weilinga, 1983b, p. 53). The technique will be familiar as the traditional problem reduction approach (Grover, 1983, p. 437) typical of the engineering paradigm where large tasks are broken down into small ones until subtasks are small enough to be tenable and is discussed in some detail by Wilson in Chapter 5. Strictly speaking a (de)composition hierarchy is one in which a higher level item is related to a lower level item by the relation which might be expressed by the label 'has-a-part-called', and a lower level item is related to the higher level item by the relation which might be labelled 'is-a-part-of'. The term is used loosely and hierarchies with other organising

principles, such as logical or temporal dependency, or a mixture of organising principles are sometimes generated as a result of goal decomposition.

As with most techniques, it is the usefulness of the material elicited, not linguistic purity which is important. These other hierarchies may be just what the elicitor wants. If so, the elicitor should be gratefully they arose in spite of the way the technique was labelled. If not, and the knowledge provider begins to generate an inappropriate hierarchy, it may help to get the provider to say something like 'If all these (subgoals) are accomplished I can say the (goal) is accomplished' or 'These (sub-items) are parts of (item).' The alternative is to accept what the provider produces and subsequently extract or infer through analysis, if possible, what is actually required. The latter may be necessary to prevent the knowledge provider feeling over-constrained during elicitation, in spite of its being inefficient.

4.2.4 List-related tasks
Asking the knowledge provider to generate lists is often a precursor to matrix generation whjich is discussed in Section 4.8. Techniques for ensuring that the lists are extensive, representative, and exhaustive are not well discussed in the literature. If one were to read between the lines, however, it would seem that a systematic approach often using some framework such as a list of products, or the daily routine, is often used. Lists can also be extracted from documents or from the analysis of previous elicitation exercises.

The knowledge provider can be asked to compare lists, i.e. to consider similarities between them. They can be contrasted, i.e. differences considered. They can be checked for completeness. The knowledge provider can be asked to discuss lists from different sources and to amalgamate them. This is likely to cause the knowledge provider to note and consider the aptness of alternative expressions of similar items on a list and also to consider the different content of lists from different sources.

Decision analysis
Decision analysis is described by Hart (1986, p. 61) requires a list of all possible decisions and for each decision a list of the possible consequences. A '*worth*' and a '*probability of occurrence*' is assigned to each consequence and those two values are multiplied together to give the '*expected worth*' of the consequence. The expected worth of a decision is calculated by adding together the expected worths of all its consequences. The decision with the largest expected worth is the one to select. The knowledge provider's verbalisations which accompany an exercise such as this may be valuable, as may comments from the knowledge provider about whether the decision indicated by the analysis is 'correct'.

4.3 Teachback
Although Johnson's teachback (Johnson and Johnson, 1987a) is primarily a feedback and verification technique, it can also be effectively used for gathering new material. The process involves a role reversal in which the

elicitor 'teaches' the knowledge provider some aspect of the knowledge which has been elicited.

Teachback episodes can be introduced during a session otherwise taken up with interviewing. This can disrupt or add sparkle to the interview, depending on how the interview is going and on the sensitivity and skill of the elicitor. The alternative, much used by Johnson and Johnson, is to use teachback in a subsequent session with the knowledge provider. This allows the elicitor time to interpret the material and serves as a reminder to the knowledge provider of what went on in a previous session and this gets the knowledge provider 'back into' the process of elicitation. This is important in the light of the fact that although the elicitor may be living and breathing the KBS development, the knowledge provider's contribution to the KBS project is likely to be a peripheral and intermittent activity with respect to their everyday work.

The value of teachback as a material gathering technique arises from its putting knowledge providers on the receiving end of the knowledge. In this way it is similar to Waldron's reflective probes discussed in Section 4.1.2. The situation is rather like having knowledge providers use a prototype in that it gives them the chance to review their expertise from the outside. It is likely that the teachback will remind them of material they had not previously provided and will allow them to supplement and clarify material previously elicited. No less important is the sense of security teachback gives to knowledge providers. Through it they have the chance to retain some control over their contribution by checking the interpretation of the material they have already provided. It can increase their sense of ownership of the system they are helping to develop, the importance of which is emphasised by Bell and Hardiman in Chapter 2, and their trust in the analysis and interpretation processes as well as maintaining their commitment to the KBS development project.

4.4   Construct elicitation

The term *personal construct* arises from George Kelly's work leading to his Personal Construct Theory (PCT) (e.g. Kelly, 1955; Kelly, 1964). Recognition of the potential of PCT outside the field in which it was developed, clinical psychology, has led to its use in business applications (e.g. Stewart and Stewart, 1981) and increasingly in the context of KBS as an elicitation technique and as the basis of a number of developments in automated knowledge acquisition (e.g. Boose, 1985; Lopez de Mantaras *et al.*, 1986; Shaw and Gaines, 1987b; Graham and Jones, 1988). The history and details of the Kelly's theory is well documented in the psychological literature (e.g. Warren, 1964; Bannister, 1970, 1973, 1977; Fransella and Bannister, 1977; Shaw, 1980, 1981), in the literature of social research (e.g. Norris, 1982), in the literature of education (e.g. Pope and Keen, 1981). Related discussions often appear in indexes as 'Kelly Grid' or 'Repertory Grid' or 'Personal Construct Technology' or 'Construct Psychology' or similar permutations. The discussion here is an attempt to put *constructs* in the context of KEL and to clarify some terminology which must be understood if constructs are to be used appropriately for non-automatic elicitation.

To put construct elicitation in context, it is worth noting that although it is primarily associated with the use of the *repertory grid* technique, also pioneered by George Kelly, the data collected using this technique can be used in other analyses such as multidimensional scaling analysis, a detailed discussion of which is beyond the scope of this chapter but is ably discussed by Coxon (1982) and is the subject of a publication by Cordingley and Hammond (forthcoming). It is also worth noting that the notion of constructs bears striking similarity to, but is not identical with, the notion of *contrasts* discussed by ehtnographers such as Spradley. Spradley's Contrast Principle, 'the meaning of a symbol can be discovered by finding out how it is different from other symbols', highlights that 'Whenever we use language we call attention to what things *are*; but we also call attention to what they *are not*. To say 'I'm holding a book, identifies an object in my hand. It also implies that I am not holding a tree, a magazine, a wallet, a house or anything else that we could communicate about. . . . Whenever we talk we convey meaning by these implicit contrasts' (Spradley, 1979, pp. 157–8).

4.4.1 Kelly's personal constructs

The history of PCT accounts for some confusion about terminology. Briefly, Kelly developed a technique for exploring the way people make sense of the world which unfortunately, as it was not really a test, he called the Repertory Test. He later revised the technique and called it the Repertory Grid technique (Radley, 1973, p. 29). The Theory of Personal Constructs consisting of a fundamental postulate and eleven associated corollaries came later. This theory is documented along with the formal aspects of constructs and other relevant terms by Fransella and Bannister (1977, Appendix VI), and will not be restated here. One of the pillars of the work is his notion, the personal construct.

A construct is a mental 'tool' which allows a person to discriminate between elements of his/her world. For example, the employee of a firm may think of external business contacts in terms of the construct 'suppliers–potential customers'. The construct is not applicable to all the people the person knows, but is useful in anticipating the kind of business relations the person will have with people outside the firm with whom she/he has or does business. The person's world will be understood in terms of many such constructs which together make up the person's system of personal constructs. Crucial to the theory and to the grid technique, as used by Kelly and his followers, is that people make sense of the world by anticipating events on the basis of their *personal construct system*. Unless prevented, they creatively understand life as it occurs, actively construing and reconstruing the world in the light of their experiences. An experience which does not fit the anticipated pattern will cause the person to 'think again' about the constructs which led him/her to the violated anticipation. These 'surprising' experiences lead to a 'loosening' of the construct system. Experiences which conform to expectation support the existing system of constructs and 'tighten' the system. Thus new experiences are accommodated in a developing system of personal constructs (e.g. Kelly, 1964, p. 82).

Each construct is a bipolar discrimination which the person funds useful in understanding the world. Each thing, 'element' (e.g. a computer program), for which a construct is relevant can be characterised best by one pole (e.g. easy to use) of the construct or the other (e.g. hard to use). If the person cannot decide which pole best characterises an 'element' or does not find it useful to use the construct to distinguish the 'element' from other 'elements', the construct is not relevant for that 'element' and the 'element' is said to be 'outside the *range of convenience*' of the construct. The usefulness of a construct is essentially a personal thing as are the verbal labels the person attaches to each of the poles, although people with a shared culture are likely to have many common constructs. When the individual tries to share the construct with others, or an elicitor tries to identify constructs which are meaningful to a number of people, the matter of verbal labels becomes problematic and may need to be negotiated.

4.4.2 Bipolarity and scales — constructs and concepts

The bipolarity of the construct is important in the use of personal construct techniques, but it is not well understood. It is not just one concept and its negation. A person may find it easy to give one pole a name (e.g. sociable). That pole, because it was the first named, is referred to as the '*emergent*' pole and the other one then is referred to as the '*implicit*' or the 'contrast' pole. If someone finds it difficult to label the implicit pole they may take the easy way out and use the negation of the emergent pole's label (e.g. not-sociable) as the label for the implicit pole. From the labels 'sociable–not sociable' it is not clear to others whether the construct is, for example, 'sociable–shy' or 'sociable–unfriendly' or 'sociable–teetotal' or 'sociable–drunk' or 'sociable–professional' or 'sociable–a loner'. Provided the person whose construct is being labelled has a clear and relatively stable understanding of what she/he means by not-sociable, the variety of possible meanings will not cause him/her any problem in using the construct to distinguish between elements. It is a bipolar construct for that person in spite of the linguistic ambiguity of the label attached to the implicit pole.

There would, however, be problems in other people being asked to use that construct without some clarification of the sense in which sociability is being viewed. There would also be problems if the person did not attach a relatively stable meaning to tne 'not-sociable' pole. If it is a catchall for everything that cannot be characterised as sociable, there is effectively only one pole, the emergent pole. If one is not confined by the requirements of mathematical terminology, one can visualise a unipolar structure as a small 'region' containing all the elements characterised by the pole surrounded by a large 'region' containing all other elements. The important thing is that the pole region is surrounded by the non-pole region. There are many 'directions' one can take when leaving the region of the emergent pole. A bipolar structure can be visualised as two non-overlapping small 'regions', one containing all the elements associated with one pole the other containing all the elements associated with the other pole, both surrounded by a large 'region' that contains all the elements outside the range of convenience of the bipolar construct. The 'direction' one goes between the poles is determined, although it does not actually matter what 'direction' it is if one is only considering a single construct. A scale can be visualised as a long thin 'region' (if the scale is continuous) or a collection of small non-overlapping 'regions' which are next to each other and arranged in a straight line (if the 'scale' is discrete), containing all the elements for which the scale is relevant in a particular meaningful and relatively stable arrangement. A single scale can also be visualised as being surrounded by a 'region' containing all the elements for which the scale is not relevant.

Humphries' comment that the bipolarity assumption 'maintains that each pole of each construct can be defined as "what the other pole is not" (mutual exclusion), and that cumulatively the two poles exhaust the possibilities of construing along the construct dimension (Humphries, 1973, p. 9) is misleading as it may lead his readers into thinking that the implicit pole of a construct is simply the negation of the emergent pole, although that may not have been what he intended when he wrote the comment. It also seems, by speaking of 'construing along the construct dimension' he suggests, erroneously, that constructs have the nature of continuous scales, although that also may be unintended impression.

The bipolarity of constructs distinguishes them from concepts of conventional logic. As Radley explains:

> Where the latter [*a concept of conventional logic*] might assert that the person chooses between saying 'A is B' or 'A is not B', Kelly proposes that in choosing to say 'A is B' we are also asserting that 'A is not C'. (Radley, 1973,, p. 31).

In terms of the computer program example whis would mean that in conventional logic we can choose between saying 'the computer program A is easy to use' or 'the computer program A is not easy to use'. We can only assert that the computer program A is or is not among the set of things that are easy to use. The concept is unipolar, If, however, we use the bipolar construct 'easy to use–hard to use' and we say 'the computer program A is easy to use' we are also asserting that 'the computer program A is not hard to use'. In this sense the construct is more powerful than the concept.

There is another way in which personal constructs differ from concepts. They do not constitute a continuum along which elements can be placed, although successive use of a construct can order elements as though they were being placed on a scale. This may have implications for the way constructs are elicited and the kind of analysis which is appropriate for material based on the use of constructs. If this is a two-point rating scale, i.e. the person is asked to assign a 1 to the element if it is best characterised by, say, the emergent pole and a 2 if it is best characterised by the implicit pole then the 'scale' is not fundamentally different from the construct unless the rates are later used in calculations which generate scales having values between 1 and 2. Many published accounts of studies using the grid technique fail to address this issue and without comment have the person assign a rating, a number from, say, 1 to 5 or 1 to 7, to each element for each construct or ask the person to rank the elements along the construct as though it were a scale. Grids of rates or ranks are useful, for example, for multidimensional scaling analyses which generate conceptual maps (e.g. Coxon, 1982), or cluster analysis of the kind built into the software developed variously by Shaw and Gaines and Boose (e.g. Boose, 1985; Shaw, 1980, 1981; Shaw and Gaines, 1987a). Both Humphries and Shaw address the issue (Humphries, 1973; Shaw, 1980, Appendix A) but fail to resolve it.

4.4.3 Eliciting constructs

Kelly suggested six ways of eliciting constructs and others have since been developed (Fransella and Bannister, 1977, pp. 14–19). Two of the most frequently used are the method of triads and the method of dyads. To take a concrete example, suppose the elicitor wants to understand how the knowledge provider views computer systems. The elicitor might first find out what systems the person is familiar with and use each of these as an element. Often the elements are written on small cards and handed to the person when she/he is asked to consider the element.

In the method of triads, the person is asked to consider three elements, and to say which two are alike in some way and different from the other. She/he is then asked how the two would be characterised (the emergent pole) and how the other would be described (the implicit pole). Thus, for example, if the three computer programs were WORDSTAR, LOTUS 1-2-3, and SPSS-X the first two might be seen as similar because they can be run on a micro whereas SPSS-X is run on a mainframe. The same three programs might generate other constructs as well. LOTUS and SPSS-X are primarily for use with numbers whereas WORDSTAR is primarily for use with text. WORDSTAR and SPSS-X may be similar because the person knows them well whereas LOTUS has only been seen as a demonstration. When the elicitor is satisfied that all the useful constructs have been elicited from this triad another three computer programs can be considered.

The elements to make up the triad can be chosen haphazardly at the time by the elicitor or by the knowledge provider, or in advance by a random selection process, or according to a non-random pattern, for example one which ensures that all elements are involved in the same number of triads. The elicitor will have to consider which best suits the elicitation process. The decision which will depend upon two things: the relationship that has been established between the elicitor and the knowledge provider, and the analysis which is to be performed on the material. The relationship might be such that it is appropriate for the elicitor to adopt a directive style, instructing which triads are considered and in which order. This makes non-haphazard selection possible. It may be such that it is best to let the knowledge provider select the triads. This makes haphazard selection more likely, although there may be a pattern which emerges from the selection which is in itself of interest to the elicitor. If the planned analysis is based on the assumption of random selection of triads, that selection technique must be adopted. What is more likely, is that the value of the exercise will be based on its utilising all the elements and using any one roughly the same number of times as any other. Then no-random but systematic selection should be adopted.

In the method of dyads, appropriate when the elements are complex and the person finds considering three at a time difficult, the person is asked to consider two elements and say whether they are the same or different and what makes them the same or different (Easterby-Smith, 1981, p. 13 citing Keen and Bell, 1980). This generates the emergent pole. The problem of determining the implicit pole remains. The person may be asked what is the opposite of the implicit pole, but the difficulty is that this often generates the logical opposite, i.e. the negation of the emergent pole rather than the 'real opposite' (Easterby-Smith, 1981, p. 12), i.e. the way the person would really characterise elements in the range of convenience which are not distinguished from elements at the emergent pole.

A large number of triads or dyads will be available. To be sure all elements feature in the elicitation of at least one construct, the elicitor may only elicit one construct from each combination of elements. It will also be important to avoid having some elements dominate the grid by using them markedly more often than other elements. It may surprise someone using the technique for the first time how easily a person begins to get in a 'construct rut'. To help prevent this, it is useful not to have the same construct in successive dyads or triads. The number of genuinely different constructs that can be elicited will depend on the person but it is likely to be between 7 and 25. It would be unusual, but it may be that all the elicitor wants is the constructs themselves. If that is the case the session can end at this point. More typically the elicitor has some further analysis in mind which require that the constructs be used before the session ends.

Eliciting constructs is time consuming and if not handled well can become tedious or unnerving when the knowledge provider gets in a 'constant rut', i.e. when a small set of constructs seem to take over and be all that came to mind. To avoid spending the time, to target the exercise on features of interest, or in search of generalisability, elicitors often supply constructs which are expected to be fruitful or have been used in previous work. This strategy is based on the assumption that the labels attached to poles define the meaning of the construct in such a way that this meaning is the same for all people who are given the construct to use. The assumption of common meaning certainly violates the personal aspect of Kelly's theory and threatens to invalidate the technique. The practice of having the knowledge provider 'grade' elements on each construct also threatens an assumption of the theory, the bipolarity of constructs. The main argument in favour of disregarding the assumptions of the theory is that techniques are robust and that even when used in unorthodox ways the technique interesting and valid (in some sense) results. Elicitors can gather material using methods which are unsound in the terms of a particular theory. The theory, after all, may be wrong or unhelpful for the present pupose. But elicitors should know that the assumptions of the theory are being violated, and the theory should not subsequently be used to determine analysis or justify interpretation. So most of what is reported in KBS literature under the banner of PCT or Repertory Grid technique, should not be so called.

4.4.4   Using constructs

Strictly speaking, as the construct is a discrimination and not a scale, the most appropriate use is to have the knowledge provider indicate which pole of each construct elements are associated with. If the method of triads is used then this will already be known for each element in the triad from which the construct was generated. It will only make sense to place elements within the range of convenience (introduced in Section 4.4.1) of the construct at one pole or the other. However, as the elements are usually 'of a type' and have a functional coherence, e.g. symptoms of diseases, most are likely to be in the range of convenience of most constructs elicited from them. Some elicitors get elements on constructs as each construct comes to light. Thus, in the example above, once the construct 'runs on a micro–runs on a main-frame' was available the elicitor could have the knowledge provider to say which of the other computer programs 'run on a micro' and which 'run on a mainframe'. Typically this will be recorded in some kind of matrix either at the time or after the session is finished. The advantage of using each construct as it emerges is that the knowledge provider remembers what distinction it represents, but some elicitors feel this interrupts the flow of construct elicitation and prefer to elicit all the constructs first and only then have the knowledge provider place elements at one pole or the other of each construct.

There are a number of grids in use (e.g. Fransella and Bannister, 1977, pp. 23–59; Easterby-Smith, 1981, pp. 10–17) and the elicitor will want to become familiar with these and may consider designing one for their own particular needs. There is no one correct format for grids nor only one way to use them. It would be advisable for the elicitor to make a point of reading at least one account of the technique which gives an overview of the possibili-ties, perhaps going back to one of the earlier publications in the field to get a fuller understanding of the technique than might otherwise be available, and then use it appropriately but imaginatively.

It may be what the knowledge provider says while constructs are being elicited and used is the only material from these sessions which the elicitor eventually uses. Construct elicitation is then solely a focus for discussion. In other cases the elicitor uses the constructs and data about how elements are placed on the constructs. Analysis can be confined to careful '*eyeballing*' of the grid, i.e. looking at it carefully for patterns of similarity and difference. A great many insights have been extracted from analyses no more sophisti-cated than this. Such an exercise is recommended as a preliminary step even if other analyses are to be undertaken, because it is a way of coming to 'know' the material well. An elicitor who 'knows' the material well will be less likely to be misled by analytical or clerical errors.

There are a number of software packages in the Personal Construct

Psychology tradition now available which automate elicitation and/or analysis. These include FOCUS, PLANET (including PEGASUS and ARGUS), SOCIOGRIDS, CORE, MINUS (e.g. Shaw and Gaines, 1987). There are also a number of matrix analysis packages which are used with grids but are not so closely tied to this tradition. These include INGRID (Slater, 1987), REVEAL (e.g. Graham and Jones, 1988, pp. 297–300) and a large number of multidimensional scaling packages (e.g. Coxon, 1982).

4.4.5 *Analysis and interpretation*

Kelly suggested certain methods analysis and gave advice about how to interpret results, but there are difficulties with his suggestions and with the current common practice of pooling data from a number of individuals. These are discussed by Radley (1973) and briefly by Coxon (1982, p. 14) among others. One of the main difficulties with the technique is that of interpretation. Constructs are essentially personal and they are not fixed. As a person continually reconstrues the world, some constructs remain largely unchanged but others do not. Personal development is only possible through adjustments in one's system of personal constructs. It is not surprising, therefore that there are difficulties about what a grid means, what it 'measures', what can be inferred from the differences between grids.

Grid analysis methods are very similar to techniques which have non-grid input and will be dealt with, along with non-grid examples, in the Sections 4.5, 4.6 and 4.7.

4.5 Sorting tasks

A technique utilising elements of a domain to understand how the knowledge provider conceptualises this world is 'card' sorting. The things to be sorted, the elements, are either elicited from the knowledge provider, or taken from an analysis of the domain and are each written on a small card. In some cases pictures or diagrams may be more appropriate than words.

There are a variety of ways to proceed from here. If the elicitor requires a binary tree structure the knowledge provider is asked to divide the elements into two piles in a way which is meaningful to the person, and asked to label each pile. She/he is then asked to divide each of these into two and label these, and so on until the person is unable to meaningfully subdivide a pile or until there is only one element left.

An alternative is to give the person two cards and ask whether they are the same or different. If they are the same they are put together in a pile. If they are different they constitute two piles. A new element is provided and the person can either put in one of the existing piles or make a new pile. This continues, one element at a time until all the elements have been assigned to a pile. If the knowledge provider is not allowed to change their decision about which pile an element belongs to, the order in which the elements are offered may affect the outcome. It may be useful to ask for labels for piles as they are created if the order of these concepts is thought to be important. If the labels are not written down as they emerge it is likely that the person will revise them in the course of considering additional elements. An alternative is to give the person all the element cards at once and require them to be sorted into as many piles as seems meaningful and then to name each pile. Both these methods produce a set of mutually exclusive categories which exhaust the population of available elements. There is unlikely to be any structure imposed on these categories, i.e. relations between them are unlikely to emerge unless the elicitor takes some additional steps to elicit such relationships. If there are a large number of piles the person can be asked to group similar piles together and give the new group a name. This can be done several times until they revert to a single pile. If there are few large piles the person can be asked to subdivide them in some meaningful way and name the new piles. In Chapter 7, Clare provides an example of the use of card sorting and comments that while it is possible to use a computer terminal, rather than piles of cards, he says that 'Although some AI toolkits provide means of mapping out such relationships, they do not provide the resolution of a conference room table covered in cards'.

The elicitor can use the piles as the focus for discussion, asking, for example, if there are any piles which seem to be missing and discussing those or looking at the pile which often emerges as the 'other' or 'miscellaneous'. These difficult to classify elements may be of particular interest or significance.

4.6 Laddering

Laddering, described more than twenty years ago by Hinkle (1965) in the context of personal construct studies, was made more widely known by Fransella and Bannister (1977) and has a history of use as part of the battery of repertory grid tools in many domains including business applications (e.g. Stewart and Stewart, 1981). The technique has recently gained prominence as a KBS elicitation technique (e.g. Burton *et al.*, 1988; Graham and Jones, 1988) valuable for generating various hierarchies of concepts. Briefly, to get superordinate concepts the knowledge provider is asked of constructs WHY ...?; to get subordinate concepts the knowledge provider is asked HOW ...?; and to get concepts at the same level the knowledge provider is asked for ALTERNATIVE EXAMPLES OF .... The following examples of the technique in use add flesh to this description.

Example 1

Like personal construct psychologists who have employed the technique, Hinkle used the technique to generate a hierarchy of constructs. He started with a construct on which the subject had expressed a preference for one of the two poles. His standard instructions were:

> Now on this construct you preferred this side to that side. What I want to understand now is why you would prefer to be here [*at one pole*] rather than there [*at the other pole*]... What are the advantages of this side in contrast to the disadvantages of that side as you see it? (Fransella and Bannister, 1977, p. 16; my elaborations in italics).

One construct which was elicited when a number of camera lenses were used as elements to elicit constructs was 'shows more than can be seen by the naked eye – shows what can be seen by the naked eye'. The former was preferred, and when asked why the construct 'one might see something new–no chance of seeing something new' emerged. After checking which was preferred the subject was asked why the preferred pole, 'seeing something new', was important and the subject responded 'you might stumble across a mystery. . .'. Asked why this pole was preferred the subject responded that this 'put you in your place' rather than letting you 'think you were master of everything'. Again the emergent, i.e. the first mentioned, pole was preferred. When asked why the respondent said 'Because only God has the answer to everything and you need to be reminded of that' (Fransella and Bannister, 1977, p. 17).

The session had reached one of the subject's core constructs: i.e. ones for which the subject can answer no more why questions but reiterates the same answer to succeeding why questions; ones which are fundamental to the person's interpretation of the world and which are difficult and traumatic to change. Stewart and Stewart (1981, pp. 24–25) warn users of the technique to be careful of getting too close to these core constructs, because the process may reveal self-deceptions or internal contradictions upon which a person has built a stable and positive self-image. Threatening these pillars of self-esteem without the knowledge, skills and resources to provide alternative supports can be devastating to the knowledge provider. As Stewart and Stewart also point out, it is unlikely that most users of the techniques have a need to explore these core constructs. Unnecessary explorations of these areas are generally a waste of both the knowledge provider's and the elicitor's time. For both reasons it would be well for the knowledge elicitor to be alert for signs, gestures and other signs of discomfort, that indicate the laddering is getting too close to the core constructs. Until one is experienced in using the technique it may be well to follow Stewart and Stewart's rule of thumb not to ladder up more than one level; to use the techniques only in 'safe' areas of inquiry; and only with people who trust you. This may sound slightly extreme because, in contrast to clinical uses of personal construct techniques, knowledge elicitation is designed to tap what the provider knows about the domain, rather than to encourage self-examination *per se*. However, the knowledge provider's self-image may be intimately bound up with the knowledge being elicited. The elicitor may still inadvertently stumble on to dangerous ground, should be sensitive enough to realise when this has happened, and sensible enough to back off.

Example 2
Burton and Shadbolt (forthcoming, p. 17) provide the following description and example of laddering, reproduced here with their permission. The underlining and comments in italics have been added for emphasis and clarity.

Laddered grid method
Step 1:   Start expert off with a seed item.
Step 2:   Move around the domain using the following prompts:
            1. To move down the domain knowledge:
               How can you tell it's <ITEM>?
               Can you give examples of <ITEM>?
            2. To move ACROSS the domain knowledge:
               What <u>alternative</u> examples of <CLASS> are there to
               <ITEM>?
            3. To move UP the domain knowledge:
               What have <SAME LEVEL ITEMS> got in common?
               What are <SAMPLE LEVEL ITEMS> examples of?
               What is the key difference between <ITEM1> and <ITEM
               2>?
            Move around domain at will.

Example laddered grid session
The following interchange could have come from a session in which the
knowledge provider is a Computer Unit Adviser discussing computer
problems.

Q: What examples of a <u>'no response' problem</u> [*The seed item*] are
       there?
A: It's a <u>software problem</u>, unless a <u>small set of keys is affected</u>?
       [*'no response' problems can be divided into two kinds, one of
       which is followed up in the next question.*]

Q: Can you give me an example of <u>what you do</u> if there's <u>a small set of
       keys affected</u>?
       [*Elicitation of actions not additional. A hierarchy with both
problems and actions will be elicited*]
A: Yes. You <u>check the key contacts</u>.

Q: Can you give me examples of actions for <u>software problems</u>?
       [*Now the other kind of 'no response' problem is followed up*]
A: Yes. You <u>intervene</u> or <u>don't intervene</u>.
       [*Two alternative courses of action are given*]
       You don't intervene if <u>there's a user error</u> where they
       [*The users of the system*]
       misinterpret a slow program as this fault.
       [*This might be taken to indicate that there is a third kind of 'no
       response' problem, i.e. on which is a problem with the user's
       understanding of the system and not a problem with either the
       software or when a small set of keys is affected. Alternatively it
       might be taken to be an indication of another kind of 'software'
       problem, i.e. the program has been implemented in such a way
       that the response time is too slow.*]

Q: Can you give me an example of when you <u>intervene</u>?
       [*The second action is pursued*]

A: When there's an <u>editor problem</u>.
      [*The characterisation of the other kind of software problem*]
      Then you use <u>control keys</u> [*The action to deal with it*].

Q: Can you give me examples of <u>using control keys</u>? [*Laddering down*]

A: Press <u>control)c</u>, <u>control-q</u> and <u>control-z</u>.
      [*An expansion of the concept into 3 parts*]

Q: What is the difference between control-c and control-q?
      [*A way of laddering up, here it may lead to a new hierarchy being constructed, one to do with functionality, or it may be an example of the additional knowledge that laddering can elicit.*]

A: Control-q <u>gets you out of control-s</u>
      [*The elicitor can extract the concept 'purpose' or 'function' from this response. A new control key is mentioned here, unless the transcriber of the protocol has made a mistake. The elicitor wil have to keep this in mind and follow it up at an appropriate time.*]
      And control-c <u>gets you out of the program</u>.
      [*Another example of a 'purpose' or 'function'.*]
      Control-q should be used before control-c.
      [*This gives a correct action sequence. There is not enough context to know how this will be used, if at all, in the hierarchy.*]

Q: What is the difference between <u>control-c</u> and <u>control-z</u>?

A: Control-c <u>gets you out of the program</u>
      [*A repeat of material offered in the previous answer. This redundancy serves as confirmation of material previously offered. It is more powerful if there is even more said between the first and second statement of the same material.*]
      and should be used before control-z.
      Control-z <u>quits the system</u>.
      [*This third 'purpose' or 'function' is offered for free*]

The sample session shows the variety of knowledge that can be elicited using this technique and the difficulty in generating a 'clean', homogeneous hierarchy. In most cases trying for a 'clean' hierarchy would diminish the overall value of a laddering session as it would prevent the emergence of valuable material. As with most techniques, the material elicited from a knowledge provider through laddering should be reviewed as raw material that will have to be interpreted rather than knowledge that can be put unthinkingly into a structure such as hierarchy.

Laddering is characterised by Burton *et al.* as a *goal decomposition* technique (1988, p. 137), but this characterisation is likely to be misleading for newcomers to the knowledge-based systems field. Both goals and decomposition hierarchies have been discussed in Section 4.2 above where goal related verbalisation tasks are introduced, but a few additional remarks may be helpful here. As Burton *et al.* recognise themselves, laddering need not be used to generate a hierarchy of goals in the non-technical sense of the word. It can be used to generate many kinds of hierarchy. Expressing this idea in another way. Burton *et al.*'s illustrative classification of animals is a goal hierarchy because it is their goal to create it and/or their intent to use it in some problem solving process. Thus, although it would not be understood as a goal in the non-technical sense, it can be thought of, in the technical sense, as a goal hierarchy. In fact, any hierarchy can be considered a goal hierarchy which makes the word 'goal' in such characterisations superfluous.

Goal decomposition is also misleading because laddering need not be used to generate a composition/decomposition hierarchy. The hierarchy in the classification of animals example is a generalisation/specialisation hierarchy where a higher level item is related to a lower level item by the relation which might be labelled 'a-special-example-of-which-is', and a lower level item is related to the higher level item by the relation which might be labelled 'is-a-kind-of'. The elicitor will want to consider laddering whenever a hierarchy is to be created, not just for the decomposition of goals. Therefore, it is probably better not to characterise laddering as a goal decomposition or goal distinguishing technique.

4.7 '20 questions'

'20 Questions', what Wright and Ayton call context-focusing (1987, p. 22), has been used by ethnographers (e.g. Spradley, 1979, pp. 169–170) as a research technique and is now being used by knowledge elicitors (e.g. Schweikert *et al.*, 1987). It is what its parlour game name suggests. The elicitor selects one from a set (e.g. a situation, a diagnosis, a fault, a problem solution, a state, or an 'outcome') of items known to the knowledge provider. The knowledge provider has to try and determine which one the elicitor has in mind by asking questions which can be answered by the elicitor with 'yes' or 'no'. The knowledge provider reveals underlying contrasts, conceptual categories and task performance strategies through the questions asked rather than through the answers provided. This version of the technique involves role reversal: the knowledge provider asks questions to probe the mind of the elicitor and it is the elicitor who responds. As such, it serves the function of changing the pace of elicitation, as well as providing additional insight into how the knowledge provider partitions and searches the domain.

A '20 Questions' session generates material from which the elicitor later expects to be able to derive such things as the knowledge provider's heuristic rules, information requirements, and questions which discriminate well as the knowledge provider searches through a problem space. It must be borne in mind that these heuristics, requirements, and strategies will be imputed to the knowledge provider and are not provided directly. Where possible, it will be useful for the elicitor to feed back to the knowledge provider such knowledge for confirmation of the interpretation and that it is faithful to the process the knowledge provider uses. The technique requires an elicitor who knows the domain well enough to select fruitful targets for the '20 Questions' and will be able to answer the knowledge provider's questions correctly. Alternatively, a co-operative second expert or domain veteran may be used.

Spradley describes an enhanced version of the technique which makes it reminiscent of knowledge elicitation. In Spradley's version, the items such as a set of computer programs (e.g. WORDSTAR, LOTUS 1-2-3, DBA-SEIII, SUPERCALC, WRITENOW, . . .) would each be written on a card and all are visible to the knowledge provider who asks questions such as 'Is it a word processing program?' In this case the elicitor would respond 'I can answer you if you first tell me which of these are wordprocessing programs.' The knowledge provider identifies those she/he regards as word-processing programs and the elicitor then answers 'yes' or 'no' to the original question. This version of the technique means that the elicitor need not know the domain well to use the technique and has a record of how each of the yes/no questions partitions the space according to a unipolar term.

Killin (1987) describes this technique rather differently, as the elicitor putting a set of questions which require short yes/no answers to the knowledge provider. He mistakenly equates this version of the technique with 'goal decomposition' described by Grover (1983, p. 437) and 'distinguishing goals described by Hart (1986, p. 59). It is not clear from Breuker and Weilinga's report (1984a *see* p. 26) whether they do, as Killin states, see '20 Questions' in this way or as described above.

The comments about goal decomposition in Sections 4.2 and 4.6 above hold for this technique, and, as with laddering, it seems better not to characterise it is a goal decomposition technique.

4.8 Matrix generation
These techniques are particularly useful with knowledge providers who are used to tabulating information. They are most often used to generate tables that are both two-*way*, i.e. have rows and columns, and two-*mode*, i.e. have one 'list', such as component parts of products an organisation sells, written as row headings and a different 'list', e.g. the product names, as column headings. However, it is possible to have one-mode two-way tables, i.e. tables with rows and columns but the same 'list' serving as the column headings and as row headings. These can be used elicit and record relationships between items on the list. A 'component' by 'component' table could be used to record and represent, for example, those that usually are found together in products or those that are associated with the failure of others. Higher modes may be useful, as for example a matrix of components by products by customers, but such tables can be difficult to read so complex multi-mode matrices are often presented as a collection of two-way tables.

Reiss suggests the elicitor 'Consider combinatories; write a matrix of possible solutions [by possible faults] and ask the expert to choose favourites and explain why. This is a way of elicit heuristics' (Reiss, 1986, p. 104). It is also a way to bring combinations to mind which might otherwise have escaped notice or consideration. They are useful for highlighting possible combinations which do not exist or about which there is no information.

Explanations about the non-occurrence of certain combinations can provide valuable insights.

There is a convention about the way tables/matrices are presented with which the elicitor should be familiar, but need not adhere to. The convention is that independent variables, or the values of an independent variable, are usually given along the horizontal axis, i.e. as column headings; and dependent variables, or the values of a dependent variable, are usually given along the vertical axis, i.e. as row headings. Thus in a symptom and fault table, the faults which can be regarded as independent because they 'cause' symptoms, would be used as column headings. Symptoms depend on faults and therefore would be used as row headings if the convention is followed.

Whatever material relates to a particular column heading and a particular row heading can be recorded in the cell which is both in that row and in that column. There are a number of alternatives for how to use the cells. A tick can be put in the cells to indicate that it has been considered and/or discussed. In this case the matrix is a record of how completely the matrix has been covered. The presence or absence of whatever the cell represents can be recorded by, say, plus or a minus respectively. Blanks would then indicate that it is not known whether it is present or not. In Chapter 5, Wilson reproduces an example of a matrix (Table 5.1), taken from Welbank (1987c), that has knowledge elicitation techniques as its rows and types of knowledge as its columns. About 60% of the cells of the matrix are blank. The filled cells are coded as being either 'suitable' indicated by a tick, 'not suitable indicated by a cross, or 'difficult' indicated by a question mark.

Alternatively some measure of association can be recorded in the cells of the matrix. The strength of the association can be quantified either by direct judgement on the part of the knowledge provider or be derived, e.g. the calculation or correlation coefficients. It may be appropriate to have a lower cut-off so some cells are left blank and others have the correlation values if the value is above the threshold. The danger with this is that it is not possible to distinguish between cells whose value is not yet known and those which do not reach the threshold value. Colour coding is sometimes useful, e.g. strong associations in one colour, medium strength associations in another colour and weak associations in a third colour. It may be important to make the matrix eye-catching, but going too far in the direction could be interpreted as inappropriate flamboyance. If the knowledge provider is preparing the matrix these decisions will probably not be the elicitor's. When the elicitor does determine the style of matrix then domain conventions will have to be taken into account.

Symptom-to-fault-linking tables can be created by having all (or as many as possible) symptoms and all (or as many as possible) faults listed either by the knowledge provider or as a result of previous domain analysis or elicitation. The knowledge provider is asked which symptoms are associated with which faults. If a matrix is used with symptoms as one set of headings and faults as the other set, then the cell which is in a given row and in a given column can be used to record material concerning the link between the symptom and the fault. A simple tick to indicate the existence of a link and a cross to indicate none with blanks for those where neither the existence nor non-existence of the link has been established may be all that is required. Alternatives include filling the cells with text indicating the nature of the link or a reference to a document which discusses the link; a measure of association such as a relative frequency, correlation or some other measure between the fault and the symptom; or the names of components for which the fault is indicated by the symptom.

The Morphological Analysis technique of Zwicky, and characterised by Lawson (1984) as a *structured search*, consists of four steps.

> Start with a broad and general statement of the problem. List the essential variables of the problem, also stated broadly. Develop as matrix using each of the variables as an axis. Examine each of the cells thus formed for possible new combinations that could lead to an invention or innovation. (Lawson, 1984, pp. 278–9).

In the terminology given above, there will be as many modes as there are variables. Lawson cites a three-mode three-way example. The general problem is to get from one place to another using a powered vehicle. Three essential variables — power source (atomic power, moving belt, moving cable, magnetic fields, steam, electric motor, internal combustion engine, compressed air), type of vehicle (cart, chair, sling, bed), and media in which the vehicle operates (air, water, oil, hard surface, rollers, rails) — are identified. In the terminology introduced above each of these modes becomes an axis of a three-way (cuboid) matrix with $8 \times 4 \times 6$, i.e. 192, cells each representing a different solution to the general problem. As the term *morphological* in the name suggests, it is the form into which the initial knowledge is put which givees the method power. The three short-lists, identifying only 8, 4 and 6 alternative possible 'values' of a variable of the problem respectively, have been able to bring to mind more possible solutions than would have emerged through other means such as free association brainstorming. Problems with this approach include the fact that few cells of the matrix may generate realistic examples; and that in KBS developments, methods to contain combinatorial explosions are usually required rather than methods for generating them.

4.9 Critiquing

Critiquing might also have been discussed in Section 4.2 as another form of focused talk, but it, in common with the techniques in the following sections, seems to involve display of expertise in addition to knowledgeable talk about the domain.

Introducing critiquing as a way of giving advice, Miller characteristics it as:

> discussing the pros and cons of the proposed approach as compared to alternatives which might be reasonable or preferred. As a result, whereas the more traditional system says in effect, 'This is how I

think you should manage your patient,' the critiquing system says, 'This is what I think of your management plan.' (Miller, 1984, p. 1).

Critiquing requires the person or system performing the critique to be aware of alternatives and to appreciate the approach the person took when originally processing the case. It is particularly useful as an elicitation technique in domains where there is no single 'right' way of doing things.

The knowledge provider can be asked to critique the handling of a case processed by someone else, or the critique can be of the way a prototype system handles a case. Critiquing one's own work is rather more difficult, may be less rewarding in terms of knowledge elicited and can be painful for the knowledge provider. Often knowledge providers will be unaware of their own domain misconceptions and omissions in their domain knowledge. Unless some important increase in expertise has occurred since the case was dealt with, it will only be possible to notice careless errors, areas of uncertainty, or identifying some alternative correct possibilities.

During a critiquing session, the knowledge provider can be asked to identify and correct errors, and indicate what was the likely misconception or missing knowledge which led to the error. If there is more than one way to correct an error, the knowledge provider can be asked to give details of as many of these that differ in non-trivial ways. It is sometimes fruitful to ask how case details would have to be changed in order to make the handling of the case correct or acceptable. An error in the early stages of processing a case can make a nonsense of the rest of the processing. In order to get the most out of the critiquing session, it may be necessary after the first error has been noted and disposed of to have the elicitor of the knowledge provider alter the case details so that it makes sense to proceed. The elicitor can say something like 'Now let's assume the customer did have an adequate credit rating. What about the rest of the work that was done on the case. Is there anything else there that seems incorrect?' As it is not always possible to speak of errors, the elicitor may ask the knowledge provider to point out also those aspects of the case which are unexpected, 'sub-optimal' or unacceptable for some reason such as being inefficient, or making the process vulnerable to unexpected change.

Critiquing can also focus on positive aspects. Good features, both expected and unexpected, of the way a case was handled can be noted and discussed. Case details which might have misled the person who did the original work but which did not can also be mentioned.

4.10 Protocols
The terms protocol and protocol analysis usually appear without definition. It is not entirely clear from accounts of the technique what the protocol actually is, who generates it, and at what stage in protocol analysis one can say a protocol exists. The protocol appears to be either: the standard description of the task; the task which is described; the performance of the task; what the person says while performing the task; the artefacts, such as a completed form in a form-filling task, the person makes while performing

the task; an externally made record, such as a video or audio tape, of what is done and said while the person is performing the task; or a transcription or other processed version of the record made while the person was performing the task. For most discussion the ambiguity does not cause problems, but for clarity *protocols* will be understood here to be the external records, usually on audio or video tape, made when a person reports requested features of a task as it occurs, i.e. in *real-time*, or shortly afterwards, i.e. *retrospectively*.

4.10.1   Types of protocols

Ericsson and Simon distinguish between four different ways of generating protocols. There are real time accounts of three kinds: *think aloud* (relating internal thoughts), *talk aloud* (relating internal 'conversations'), and *eidetic reduction* (relating observations about one's behaviour). Both think aloud and talk aloud protocols are intended to give the elicitor access to the thought process of the knowledge provider who is doing some activity. The distinction between the two is blurred in some presentations (Killin, 1987, p. 9). The third technique, eidetic reduction, can be best described as a real-time self-critiquing. A disadvantage with real-time protocols is that producing a concurrent commentary can interfere with the task performance.

The fourth kind distinguished by Ericsson and Simon, *retrospective reporting* protocol (relating remembered aspects of the activity), is generated after the activity has finished. Retrospective reports capture what is retained in short-term store (STS). There are two reasons for using the retrospective technique. Firstly the reporting does not interfere with the activity itself but comes soon enough after the activity to allow as faithful an account as is possible. Secondly, as there is presumed to be a link between memory and the information which is heeded during the activity, it is felt that the person will recall those details which were important to the conduct of the activity, so relying on recall is not regarded as a disadvantage, but an advantage.

All these ways of generating protocols are predicted on there being a link between cognitive processes and verbalisation, i.e. what someone says about their thoughts and activities has a direct relation to those thoughts and activities. Real time and retrospective protocols are sometimes paired. The person is first asked to give a real-time report and then a retrospective report immediately after the activity is completed.

There are also types of protocol which have been used by elicitors. These include protocols based on descriptions of activities, i.e. *behavioural descriptions*, as they occur in real-time, or as the person watches them occur when a video-tape (or less often an audio tape) is played back, *playback* protocols. For playback descriptions the person is asked to say what they are doing or trying to do at each stage. These are similar to eidetic reduction so far as they are about behaviour, but they are unlike eidetic reduction in so far as they are accounts of that behaviour not critiques of it. They still require one to accept that there is a link between what a person says, the report, and what is 'going through' his/her mind, but it does not require that one accept Ericsson and Simon's model of cognition if they are not reports of cognitions *per se*. There are other kinds of playback protocols as well. The person could be asked to report what she/he was thinking at each stage during a video-recorded task performance.

A situation suggested by Diaper has been used to generate examples of the level of detail different kinds of protocols might elicit. In practice, however, elicitors are likely to get a mixture of kinds of material. It is difficult for knowledge providers to stick to one kind of report. It is even difficult for them to understand the difference between them.

Suppose one makes a typographical error while reporting the activity of writing a paper. The following might appear on the different protocols:

Talk aloud: Damn, I've made a typpo. I must be getting tired. I keep switching the e and the n. Mnet looks stupid sitting there like that.

Think aloud: Will it be quicker to get rid of the n move pass the e and type n there; or shall I cut out the n and paste it after the e; or should I just type en over ne.

Eidetic reduction: This use of the package is not as good as it might be. There is less thought involved in retyping whole sections, but when you are tired that just gives more opportunity for typing mistakes, so I should probably be trying to make better use of the cut and paste facility.

Behavioural description: Notice the mistake, reach for the mouse with the right hand, place the cursor to the right of the offending letter and click the mouse button, while holding it down drag the cursor to the left over the letters that have to be replaced, release the mouse button, put the right hand back on the keyboard and type in the correct letters.

Retrospective report: I was typing along and noticed I'd made a mistake several lines before. I'd typed departmnet rather than department. I corrected it by typing the correct letters over the wrong ones and then carried on.

Playback description: Yes, just there I was trying to fix a typo. I was tired and I kept overshooting the two letters I was trying to select with the mouse.

Criticisms of protocols are based on doubts about the validity and reliability of verbal reports, and concern about how verbalisation may interfere with thinking (Diaper, 1987b), Ericsson and Simon (1984) devote much of their book to consideration of these criticisms, and conclude that protocols and other verbal reports do have value. It is not possible to rehearse the arguments for and against verbal reports here. It can only be assumed that a brief description of what they each involve will, none the less be of interest.

Instructions for generating protocols
All sessions using one of these techniques usually begin with the elicitor giving instructions about the technique and having the knowledge provider go through one or two short warm-up exercises. This training sequence is very important as knowledge providers are unlikely to find self-reporting feels natural.

Think aloud
Instructions to the knowledge provider are likely to include:

— say out loud everything you are thinking from the first time you see the question until you give the answer;
— talk aloud constantly;
— don't think about what you are going to say;
— don't explain what you are saying;

Talk aloud
The knowledge provider is asked to say aloud whatever she/he says to him/herself silently, and to keep up a flow of speech.

Eidetic reduction
In this activity the person is asked to mentally stand aside, view what she/he does critically, and report those critical observations as they occur.

Retrospective reports
Instructions to the knowledge provider who had just worked through a test paper would include:

— tell me everything you can remember about what you were thinking from the first time you saw the question until you gave the answer;
— don't work on solving the problem again, just report everything you were thinking;
— tell if there is anything you are uncertain about;
— try to report your memories in the order in which they occurred when working on the problem.

Behavioural descriptions
The knowledge provider would be asked to say what is happening, including what she/he is doing, as she/he works through the task.

Playback
The instructions for these vary depending on what kind of report is required, e.g. what the person was thinking, what was happening, or what the person is trying to do.

4.10.2 *Protocols in use*
A brief description of two studies will give the flavour of the way protocols are used in KBS system developments. The first is an observational study of users performing set shopping tasks using PRESTEL. The second is a study of subjects filling in a B1 form, the form for claiming Supplementary Benefits in the United Kingdom.

Protocols of teleshopping
The study is described as 'semi-naturalistic' with five subjects each being given a set of eight shopping tasks (e.g. buy roses). Each task was presented

in a scenario (e.g. 'Its your favourite aunt's birthday. She is especially fond of cut roses. You have decided to send her some') Seven scenarios involved use of PRESTEL the eighth involved an 'interactive' system. There were three kinds of elicitation activities which took place during the course of the session, which lasted approximately 2 hours: a concurrent verbal protocol with the screen display was recorded on video-tape while the subject was performing the shopping tasks; a retrospective protocol of the person talking to the elicitor through a mute replay of their own shopping task video was recorded on audio tape; and finally a debriefing interview about the tasks and shopping in general was carried out (Long and Buckley, 1984, p. 367; and Buckley and Long, 1985a, b).

The researchers used the protocols to identify errors and difficulties with the shopping tasks and subsequently to analyse the 'mismatches' (i.e. where the subjects' general knowledge of the shopping task interfered with the system knowledge about what the ideal shopper would need to know in order to complete PRESTEL shopping transaction successfully).

One example of such a mismatch arose with several subjects in this study when, after filling in a response frame to order the goods they are instructed on the screen 'Press1 to send, 2 not to send'. Subjects commented that of course they wanted the goods sent, as what was the good of ordering them via PRESTEL if they had to go to the shop to collect them. 'Send' in the PRESTEL context means send the order for processing to the computer, not send the goods to the customer which is the only delivery option usually available on PRESTEL. Such an error is potentially catastrophic, as escaping from the response frame without 'sending' means that the goods are not ordered. The users would no doubt be irate when their favourite aunt fails to receive her birthday gift. Such information would not have been available from observations of the task without the verbal commentary as the subjects usually responded correctly, but for the wrong reasons.

Protocols of B1 form filling
This work was undertaken as part of the Alvey DHSS Demonstrator Project. It was one of the studies undertaken during the design of the FORMS HELPER, system designed to demonstrate that advanced technology could be used to help members of the public fill in UK welfare benefit forms. In this study, concurrent protocols were recorded on audio tape, in the subjects' home while the subject filled in a paper version of the B1 form (Frohlich, 1986). It is the form used to claim Supplementary Benefit, the UK means-tested welfare benefit for people whose income does not meet their financial requirements as defined by statutory regulations. The form is quite complex as it requires detailed information about members of the person's household and aspects of the current financial situation of all who will be covered by the benefit if it is paid. The version of the form used for the study had not yet been brought into general use, so none of the subjects had used that exact form before.

Four unemployed subjects were asked to imagine they were having to reclaim; four other subjects were asked to imagine they had lost their jobs the previous week and were making a claim. Adopting these roles, all eight were asked to fill in the claim as though it were to be submitted as a real claim. They were told to work in their usual way and at their usual pace on the task which was not to be a test of their performance but an opportunity to find out how they usually filled in forms. They were to read and think aloud as they filled in the form and ask any questions that occurred to them as they went along, although the questions would not be answered in full during the exercise. The protocol was not to be the record of a dialogue between the subject and the elicitor, so when subjects asked non-rhetorical questions the elicitor reflected them back, for example by asking what they would put on the form if they were alone, rather than providing an answer. The reflection of questions was effective in generating comment on the subject's own reasoning processes. Some, but not all, subjects needed prompting to get them in the habit of speaking while they worked. After the form had been filled in there was a debriefing session, in which the elicitor and the subject went over the form together. This provided an opportunity for detailed discussion of particular difficulties the subject had had.

There were three different representations of form-filling that resulted from these exercises for each subject:

— a completed form (later annotated to reflect the subject's form-filling behaviour indicated by the concurrent talk-aloud protocol);
— a question path table, i.e. a table showing the order in which the person visited each question;
— a behavioural events table, i.e. a table showing what the person did at each step along the question path.

These representations were the material upon which subsequent analyses were based.

The annotation of the completed form is a particularly interesting way to making use of the protocols. As Frohlich describes the technique:

> Initially, a copy of each subject's completed form was annotated with information from their verbal protocol and any observational notes made by the experimenter. All textual material read aloud by the subject was highlighted on their copied form. Next to each fragment of spoken reading, the cassette tape counter number was noted at its beginning or end. These numbers could then be used to draw routing arrows between those areas of the form visited consecutively by [the subject], also taking into account any silent question visits evident from the answers provided on the form. Abstracts of the subject['s] own comments and observations were also written on the relevant part of the form, whenever those comments were felt to aid the interpretation of the subject['s] routing behaviour around that time or their written answers to questions in that part [of the form]. (Frohlich, 1986, p. 48).

A facsimile of two pages of a form which has been completed and annotated while listening to the talk-aloud protocol generated while it was being completed is included in Appendix D.

4.11   Role play

Another way of disposing knowledge in use, albeit artificially, which has well documented disadvantages, is to have the knowledge provider adopt a role and enact a situation in which the expertise is used. At least one other person is needed for this technique, either a colleague, someone else from the domain or a member of the knowledge elicitation team. The scenario to be enacted can be determined by those taking part in the role play, but more often it would be determined by the elicitor. The details are usually sketched out and a written copy given to each of the role players. Depending on the nature of the situation being enacted and the knowledge the elicitor requires, the elicitor may decide to encourage the participants to discuss the role play and work it out in concert or may ask them to prepare individually without knowing what the other has been told. The latter is appropriate when one of the tasks of the knowledge provider's is to discover what the other person's situation is.

It is usual to video-tape role play sessions and fruitful to 'debrief' participants afterwards, i.e. to give them an opportunity to discuss the role play immediately after it takes place. The debriefing is particularly important if the roles are likely to engender any disturbing feelings in the participants including concern about their ability to perform the role well in real life. Even experts may suffer self-doubt, especially when put in front of a camera. The debriefing need not, and should not when conducted by most elicitors, be an exercise in psychoanalysis. It should be a simple and straightforward opportunity for participants to reflect on the role play and to say what they felt went well and what seemed to be a struggle and worked less well. As well as being an important outlet for the participants, even if they do not think of it in that way, it usually provides additional insight into the role play itself. It can take place after the participants have seen the video of the role play or without their having seen it.

4.12   Simulations

Simulations are similar to role plays except that the knowledge provider is put into a situation which, though artificial, is made to seem as real as possible and treated as real as far as the performance is concerned. The simulation may or may not require the involvement of another person. The simulation can be very inexpensive to mount, as when the behaviour of a system is simulated by messages to the system being written on pieces of paper by the knowledge provider and those from the system written on pieces of paper by the elicitor. In some domains considerable amounts of money are invested in preparing environments in which situations such as the take-off and landing of an aeroplane can be simulated. The use as a training environment is well recognised. The use for knowledge elicitation has been less well publicised.

One area where simulations have been widely used is in the area of natural language (e.g. Small and Weldon, 1983). Diaper has extensively developed his 'Wizard of Oz' method (Diaper, 1986a; Diaper and Shelton, 1987) in which he simulates an intelligent, full natural language processing interface for expert systems. Subjects in these experiments believe that they are communicating with a real expert system whereas, in fact, they are actually talking to a trained subject in another room via a keyboard and screen. The analyses of these simulations has involved not only the linguistic properties of the recorded dialogues, but also the knowledge such intelligent interfaces, which may themselves be KBS, would need to possess to carry out their simulated duties.

5.   TECHNIQUES FOR GETTING MATERIAL FROM OTHER SOURCES

5.1   Getting data from existing systems

In the development of a KBS to monitor or control, say, administrative processes, the existing system may be one of the most valuable knowledge sources. But getting material from an existing system, whether the system be automated or manual, makes special demands of the elicitor. Special social awareness is required in negotiating with the 'guardians' of the system for access to material, and to provide help in learning to use the system of the elicitor is to use it directly. If the material is being provided through others, the elicitor must still discover what the system has to offer and be able to specify what is required in terms of the content, the format which will be most useful for subsequent analysis and interpretation, and the timescale within which the material must be provided. The social skills, competence to use the source system, and ability to specify needs can all be learned. They do not themselves constitute techniques for 'getting that data', but it is as well to be reminded that they are necessary to the elicitor's 'skill kit'.

The elicitor will need to consider whether the KBS is to differ so much from the existing system as to make the latter irrelevant. Even if the differences are marked and the old system has little direct relevance to the KBS, an examination of the current system will give the elicitor an understanding of current processing practice, and it can serve to stimulate discussion with domain personnel.

The material gathered may be coded information, text, diagrams, formulae, tables, images, sounds or electrical signals. It can be stored in a computer, on disks, magnetic tapes, or, if appropriate, printed. If it is printed, the hard copy is a document and similar to other documents used by the elicitor. Material from the system which must be processed/analysed by a specialist in the domain before it is useful to the elicitor can be regarded as coming from the human specialist rather than being from the existing computer system.

Material generated by the system of its normal processes is likely to be more dynamic than material in guidelines, regulations, or accounts of normal practice. The period during which it is current is likely to be shorter, the frequency of replacement greater. Guidelines, for example, may remain substantially the same for several years whereas management reports will alter in detail if not in style or format each time they are printed. This has implications for feedback and for interpretation. It is important that the elicitor become aware of predictable changes in system output over time and gather material accordingly, getting representative or rare material as required. Changes in output may be of more interest to the elicitor than the output itself. Changes illustrated by output can be one of the topics of focused discussions with domain personnel (Section 4.2). Feedback based on material from the system will have to be accomplished while the material is reasonably current or be expressed in terms of it being of historical value. Not realising that the material is out of date or that it is representative of a cyclical peculiarity, can affect the credibility of the elicitation and the KBS being developed.

Material which is stored by the current system is a valuable information source. The way it is structured, what it contains , what it does not contain, the frequency with which different parts are used and for what purpose can all be sources of insight.

The program of computerised system or the document detailing steps in a manual process are possible knowledge sources. If they are ill-structured or poorly documented the elicitor may feel even more like a detective than usual, but should not ignore their potential because of this, just be aware of the time it may require to gain the insights.

5.2   Getting material from the physical or the social environment

The KADS methodology is among those that explicitly highlight the need for and value of knowledge of the environment. The elicitor will be interested in the physical environment though not in the same way as an ergonomist, someone who designs the physical features of machines and the settings in which they are used. The elicitor must also come to understand the social environment. Practitioners of task analysis place considerable importance on the material gathered directly from the environment and may have experience of using one or more of the four techniques discussed here: observation, object tracing, 'listening', 'collection' of artefacts.

5.2.1   Observation

Observation is being used here to mean the activity of noting and recording features of naturally occurring settings, and of the events and actions within them. Recording features of specially planned activities such as role plays, simulations, exercises from which protocols are produced and case studies have already been covered. The main characteristic of observational techniques, as discussed in this chapter, is that they are passive, with the observer, whether it be a human or a non-human device such as a video camera, being non-directive.

This is not to say that observation activity has no effect on what goes on. A lively debate continues unresolved about the extent to which people, once they become aware they are being observed, alter their behaviour. There is a body of opinion that there is no significant alteration; another that although people may be self-conscious and adapt their behaviour initially, they soon forget the observer and revert to their usual behaviour patterns; another that although there may be alteration it does not invalidate the material collected; yet another that it is possible to take the alterations into account and interpret material appropriately; and finally one that suggests that the technique is so flawed as to be at best useless and at worst misleading. The debate cannot be resolved here. The knowledge elicitor must be aware of the problems. The elicitor must consider the hazards in the light of a particular exercise and judge whether reaction to the observation itself will cause an important and sufficiently large or extended change in what is being observed as to make the material recorded invalid. Equally important, the elicitor must be prepared to justify the decision, whether it is a decision to use the technique or a decision not to do so.

Observations can be characterised in terms of the participation of the human observer, the focus of the observation, and the structure of the record made and these are discussed below.

Participation

Here the participant/non-participant continuum refers to the part the observer plays *in the activities* being observed as this has particular practical implications for the conduct of the elicitation. It is more restricted a use of the term than that used by Spradley, who also includes involvement *with the people* as participation (Spradley, p. 58). Zelditch follows Spradley. He would characterise observation as participant if the observer had some social involvement with the people involved in the activities being observed (Zelditch, 1962, p. 125), even if the observer takes no part in the activities under observation. Although perhaps useful in understanding the social interaction between the elicitation and the activities of the domain (e.g. will the observation be more or less natural, more or less insightful) the broader use of the term blurs a distinction which is important to the conduct of the elicitation process, i.e. whether the elicitor will be in or not be in what is observed. Thus work on participant-observation will still be of interest to elicitors planning what this chapter terms *non-participant observations*.

Focus

A focused observation is one which concentrates on a small portion of the environment. An observation of the physical environment might, for example, be focused on the nature of the furniture to the exclusion of the lighting, acoustic features, layout or personnel. An observation of the social environment might be focused on advice giving interactions between customers and staff to the exclusion of individual actions, interactions between staff members, and other types of interactions with clients. In contrast, an unfocused observation gathers material from as much of the environment or activity as possible. Many features of the physical environment are recorded, as are actions and interactions of many kinds.

Spradley identifies nine features of social situations — space, object, act, activity, event, time, actor, goal and feeling — any of which can provide a focus for observations or together serve as an aid to exploring '...''general cultural domains", categories of cultural meaning that occur in almost every social situation' (Spradley, 1980, p. 102). Some general domains are given in Appendix A. Spradley's book is particularly commended for further reading.

Structure

Unstructured observation involves no preconceptions of what will be important about the phenomenon in focus. Video recording is an unstructured method of recording. Although there may be preselection of what will be video recorded, there is no pre-analysis of what is noted.

A structured observation, on the other hand, implies the knowledge elicitor has a theoretical or practical preconception of what will be important. The observer is likely to use a proforma (e.g. Stacey, 1969, p. 64) with a place for recording each element of the observation. Observers often find it useful to devise a coding system, symbolic 'language', or diagrammatic shorthand to facilitate manual recording of observations. In the same way as choreographers have schemes for recording movements and musicians have one for recording sound, sociometricians, anthropologies and ethnographers have schemes which might be useful to the knowledge engineer.

5.2.2   Object tracing

Object tracing is a technique in which the location and/or use being made of an object is recorded as it goes through some process; alternatively it can be used to record the 'career' of the object and include the details of its creation, each change that occurs to it, and its storage and destruction; or it can do both.

In the first case an electronic or manual record is made and overwritten every time the object changes location or use. The location record is kept in a predetermined place and does not accompany the object as it moves about the environment. An example of this is a library or equipment store checkout system. This kind of system could allow the knowledge elicitor to create a snapshot of where objects of a certain type are, what they are being used for, and how long they have been in that location or being put to that use.

In the second case, new locations or uses are added to the record which also retains previous entries creating a history of the object. The record can be held in one predetermined place, as is the case in many client record systems or progress chasing documents. Alternatively, the records may move about with the object as in the case of a circulation list for a journal being circulated though an organisation or a checklist which accompanies an object which must go through several processes in the course of being prepared or repaired. These object traces allow the knowledge elicitor to discover who has seen or used the object. If the record is designed appropriately it can also allow the knowledge elicitor to know the sequence of events which occurred to the object and their duration.

5.2.3 'Listening'

Listening and making an audio or written record of the sounds is clearly useful for eliciting knowledge from human conversation as in observations (described above), interviews (described below), and monologues as in TA protocols (described below). It can also be useful in gathering other material from the environment. The nature, extent, sequence and frequency of sounds can be important in development of interfaces, monitoring systems, and systems to help an office cope with messages arriving via the telephone. For example, an audio-tape recorder activated by a telephone ring and turned off when the telephone is answered, can make a record of how long it takes calls to be answered and, if there is a record made of the time and duration of recording, how this changes over the day or over longer periods such as a week. A recording of the sound made by equipment during normal and abnormal conditions may be a useful focus for subsequent knowledge elicitation exercises.

5.2.4 'Collection' of artefacts

Artefacts include documents such as reports, guidelines, memos and letters but are not restricted to these. Rough notes may be useful to show how a person or a group processes their information and how they represent it to each other before it becomes part of a polished product. Day books, laboratory journals, card files, topic or client files, object tracing documents, publicity material, duty rosters, training material, staff notices, invoices, timetables, and samples of products may all be useful.

'Collection' may be a matter of noting the existence, content, position (close to hand or not) and extent and nature of use of the artefact. It may, however, be possible to take some material out of the environment for later examination. How selective the knowledge elicitor decides to be in what is requested and accepted depends among other things on the rapport established with the guardians of the artefacts, stage of the development of the KBS, the nature of the artefact, its value to the people in the environment, its anticipated value for the knowledge base, its rarity, its reproducibility, and its bulk. Sometimes it is hard to get access to artefacts for the length of time necessary to study them properly, particularly if the elicitor needs to remove them. Sometimes it is hard to refuse artefacts even though they are unlikely to be of use.

5.3 Getting material from documents

People are so used to gathering material from documents that the separate techniques of reproduction, selection, segmentation, agggregation, and condensation are rarely discussed. The first four are often used in concert as in manual 'cutting and pasting' of copies of original documents to produce material focused on particular themes or structures. A 'theme document', for example, all the material concerning scheduling of activities that appears in elicitation transcripts, is produced by: selecting portions of various documents (the transcripts) which are 'on the topic' (scheduling); cutting them out, usually annotating each with its original location; and putting them in juxtaposition with each other in a single document or file. The knowledge elicitor must decide the boundaries of each segment, i.e. how much cotext (i.e. the surrounding text) is necessary to make a segment meaningful. The elicitor must also decide what addditional information about the segment, its context, is needed for future analysis. It may be useful, for example, to record information such as the name of the source document and why it was created, the segment's location in the source, and how it was used. Once a theme document has been created, the theme can be studied in relative isolation from other material.

A familiar difficulty is that a segment may be pertinent to more than one theme. Several copies can be reproduced and subsequently pasted into separate theme documents. Another technique, used the world over in the preparation of essays, research reports, and dissertations, is to copy each segment on to a separate 'index card' and label them appropriately with the themes to which they contribute. The cards relevant to a given theme can then be selected and shuffled about when trying to make sense of the theme. If the original material has been reproduced in an electronic form, word processing, hypertext systems and other software on the market, such as FACTFINDER and the Oxford Concordance Package (OCP), and ETH-NOGRAPH described below may be of some help.

Selection and condensation of material happens when notes are made of the material in the document rather than selection and aggregation of exact excerpts from the document as described above. The notes, may be summaries or paraphrasing of certain relevant sections. In either case the material has been transformed. It is then secondary rather than primary material.

Although there are numerous computer-based tools for the analyst, few are designed to facilitate analysis of text and few of these are widely available. Three for this purpose on the market now, FACTFINDER, The ETHNOGRAPH, and the OXFORD CONCORDANCE PACKAGE, are described in this section. None of these claim to be hypertext systems (see Nelson, 1980), i.e. systems which allow information to be accessible in a non-sequential way, although each provides the elicitor with a facility for seeing the text in a sequence which is different from that in the original version.

General knowledge engineering tools are not covered here. The following references may be helpful to those interested in knowing more about software that is on the horizon. KEATS, the Knowledge Engineers Assistant, developed by Alvey Project IKBS/020 by staff from the Open University, British Telecom and MIT/Symbolics is described in a number of papers including the final report of that project (Motta et al., 1986). That along with tools such as KADS Power Tool (KPT) to support the KADS methodology of Breuker and Weilinga et al. developed as part of ESPRIT Project 1098, and tools to support the DETEKTR methodology of Freiling et al. are discussed in Anjewierden (1987). The Knowledge Analysts' Tool, and the Knowledge Base Builder (KBB) are being developed by, and currently used within, the Alvey DHSS Demonstrator Project. These are not automated knowledge acquisition software unlike Boose's Expertise Transfer System (ETS), discussed in Anjewierden (1987).

5.3.1 FACTFINDER

FACTFINDER, is a free-form computer-based filing system for the MacIntosh developed by Rudi Diezmann and marketed as a MACWARE Product by Forethought Incorporated, A segment of the textual material, up to several A4 pages in length, is typed or read into an electronic 'factsheet' which acts rather like a one field database record. Keeping segments short, say several sentences in length rather than several paragraphs long, makes the software more useful for creating theme documents, but has its cost in storage, creation and processing overheads.

Keywords are associated with each factsheet by copying words or short phrases from the text of the factsheet on to a keyword list or by typing words or short phrases directly into the keyword list. If a number of factsheets have something in common, such as being material from an interview with the same person whose age, employment status and gender are important for further analysis, it is possible to have those details automatically included in the keyword list for all the factsheets created until the automatic keywords are changed or the facility turned off.

A collection of factsheets, such as segments from a single document or transcript, which are to be stored and processed together is called a 'stack'. Once a stack exists it is possible to process it in a variety of ways using an index of factsheet names, their creation dates, and any keywords used in the stack. Logical operators can be used to set up searches and sorting requests. In particular, one can search for all the factsheets which have a certain keyword or keywords in their keyword list and print or copy them into a stack of their own, thus creating a theme document or topic stack for later use.

As with all software, there are some drawbacks. It is not possible to search across stacks in Version 1.1 of FACTFINDER, so either all the factsheets must be held in one large stack, which means that accessing the stack is time consuming, or each of several stacks must be searched and relevant factsheets from each added to the theme stack. This is possible but tedious. Another difficulty is that some knowledge analysts find the software counter-intuitive. They are used to storing textual material as a whole and dividing it up for analysis rather than storing it in segments and putting together the collection they wish to analyse. FACTFINDER is most powerful if the material is stored in small segments and aggregated for analysis and some analysts find this a difficult way to work.

5.3.2 The ETHNOGRAPH

The ETHNOGRAPH, developed and marketed by Qualic Research Associated provides facilities for the mechanical, as opposed to the cognitive, management of text for qualitative analysis. The software runs on IBM-PCs, XTs ATs and compatibles, and requires at least 256K of memory. The distribution material suggests that a 20-megabyte disk is likely to be sufficient for most ETHNOGRAPH users. This takes into account the fact that during analysis a number of intermediate files are created and is based on 6 to 10 megabytes being required to store material collected for a project of 20 to 30 intensive interviews each generating transcripts of approximately 60 pages with moderately intensive coding.

A body of text, e.g. the transcript of an interview, is put into a special format using any word-processor which can produce standard ASCII text files. Each line of the text is automatically given a number, and will have the text written on one half the page with room on the other half for coding displays. Once an analyst has identified 'interesting' segments of various lengths within the text they can be 'marked' on the file; the segments can overlap with one another and/or have some segments fully contained, i.e. be nested, within others up to 7 levels deep; and a segment can be given up to 12 code words which can later be used to retrieve relevant segments for analyses. The segments are rather like the factsheets of FACTFINDER. Up to 40 'face sheet' variables to identify the material (such as identification code, title , edition, source, author, date, type of document, and current location) can be associated with each data file which acts rather like a FACTFINDER 'stack'. Catalogues of up to 80 files can be created and processed, for example, by being SEARCHed as a unit, which is a notice-able advantage over the separateness of FACTFINDER stacks. Another advantage of ETHNOGRAPH is that it works the way many analysts do, dividing the whole into parts for analysis, rather than crerating the whole out of parts as FACTFINDER does.

5.3.3   OXFORD CONCORDANCE PACKAGE
The OXFORD CONCORDANCE PACKAGE (OCP) project, Director Susan Hockey, has been jointly supported by the (then) UK's Social Science Research Council and the Computer Board to create new machine-indepen-dent concordance software (i.e. software to list words used in a text with or without the words which appear immediately before or after it). Version 1, for mainframe computers, was written during 1979–80. Version 2, available from early April 1988, has similar facilities but, taking advantage of recent developments, it runs three times as fast as the earlier version. Both utilise ideas from COCOA and the CLOC program developed at the University of Birmingham OCPv2 for mainframes will be available from the Oxford University Computing Service. There are discussions afoot about the program being made available to run on MacIntosh hardware.

The program can be made to produce for all, or a portion, of the text (defined by: from ... to; by reference; by string characteristics; or EXCEPT...): a WORDLIST, i.e. a list of words with no references or contexts; an INDEX, i.e. a list of words together with their references but not context; a CONCORDANCE, i.e. a list of words together with their references and contexts; and STATISTICS including total vocabulary size, number of occurrences of each word, type/token ratio and a frequency profile. The amount and position of the context can be varied to suit one's needs. For example all occurrences of a word such as 'welfare' can be printed with, say, the 15 words which precede it and the 15 words which follow it. A different format, but one which provides as many words of context would be to have each occurrence of the word 'welfare' printed along with the 30 words which follow it. Such decisions depend, of course, on what analysis will subsequently be performed. Print-outs can then be examined to see the different ways the word is being used by different individuals or different groups or in different documents.

OCP is being used by the University of Surrey team of the Alvey DHSS Demonstrator Project in developing an advice system. The words of interviewees from the transcripts of some of the 50 interviews with members of low income families have been processed using OCP to elicit a lexicon suitable for the user-interface of the system being designed to give advice to members of the public. OCP is also being used on the KITE Project by a team of linguists at the University of Surrey, headed by Patricia Galloway. On this project it is used for creating termbanks in several languages to facilitate the production of textual material such as user documentation and safety precautions to accompany products in use internationally.

6   'HORSES FOR COURSES': SELECTING AND USING TECHNIQUES

In training, or in order to ensure consistency within an organisation, it may be important to take a strong view on which techniques are 'right' and what is 'the correct' way to employ them. Anyone familiar with the literature will know that it is rich with papers arguing for a particular technique, giving strict instructions about what 'must' be done, and implicitly or explicitly contributing to a methodological debate. As will have become apparent, however, this chapter is not constrained to determining 'the right' technique and it does not attempt to resolve such debates. The far from original stance adopted here is that it is wise for knowledge elicitors to be familiar with the assumptions and various ways of using each of a number of elicitation techniques.

In the course of developing a KBS, elicitors should use as many techniques from their repertoire as seem appropriate, sometimes using only one technique throughout an elicitation occasion, sometimes using several. The use of more than one technique to get material of the same kind can serve as a consistency check (e.g. Welbank, 1983c, p. 35). Elicitors must feel free to use their imaginations in the application of techniques in order to generate and maintain enthusiasm (e.g. Welbank, 1983c, p. 11). They should be open to the possibility of eliciting knowledge throughout the development, iteratively getting material and changing it into knowledge, having it encoded, having the knowledge, base tested to identify errors, ambiguities or gaps, and then starting the cycle again by getting material which will eventually enhance or refine the knowledge base. The concept of elicitation as a linear, one pass activity is at variance with the way it often happens in the real world (e.g. Burton and Shadbolt, forthcoming).

Adopting an eclectic, flexible, iterative, and pluralist approach to elicitation does not mean anything goes. There are certain requirements that should be applied before an elicitation technique is selected for use. It should suit the purpose in hand; be compatible with both the knowledge source, human or otherwise, and with the elicitor; and make appropriate use of the available resources.

6.1   Serving the purpose in hand

The purpose of a particular elicitation activity is determined in part by the nature of the KBS being built, the elicitor's familiarity with the domain and the knowledge provider, the knowledge provider's familiarity with KBS technology, the current stage of the KBS development, what kind of knowledge is still needed, and the framework upon which the development and/or the elicitation is based.

If the system is to be an expert system, i.e. a KBS which emulates some aspect of human expertise, at some stage the elicitor will want to gather material from a human expert. Techniques which can provide insight into the heuristics, i.e. the rules of thumb, the expert uses, and those which allow the demonstration of the way domain knowledge is conceived and organised by the expert are appropriate. If the expertise involves physical manipulation of tools or interactions between the expert and the social or physical environment, then observational techniques are likely to be more appropriate than verbal reports.

In the early stages of the development the purpose may be to introduce the elicitor to the domain and facilitate familiarity with it. It is then appropriate to use tables of contents and indexes of documents such as textbooks, guidelines, or manuals as knowledge sources to get an overview of the domain, its terms, and how it is organised.

It is increasingly recognised that 'there is a preliminary stage of knowledge acquisition when it is more important to establish rapport than to collect information' (Welbank, 1987c, p. 12). The implication of which is that certain productive techniques with which the expert may feel uncomfortable, such as card sorting or highly structured interviewing, are inappropriate. What Welbank may have realised, but fails to make explicit, is that rapport building is a stage in the knowledge provider's relationship to the 'knowledge acquisition' process and to the elicitor rather than a stage of the development process. Unless all human knowledge providers are brought into the development process in its early stages, the 'stage' when establishing rapport is more important than getting information re-occurs during development (i.e. whenever a new knowledge provider begins to participate in the elicitation process). Thus, even if the elicitor is familar with the domain and the KBS is relatively well developed, it may still be appropriate for the elicitor to, avoid techniques known to be stressful to knowledge providers and use more comfortable 'introduction techniques' such as asking a new human knowledge provider to talk in general terms about the domain, i.e. to give a Grand Tour (LaFrance, 1987) or an introductory tutorial. This allows the elicitor to discover if there are any gross differences in approach between this person's view of the field and that which has emerged so far through other sources. It gives indications of aspects of the domain which are of special interest to the person, provides the person a chance to put their personal picture of the domain forward, and allows the knowledge provider to 'get things off his/her chest'. This last recognises the fact that most people carry around cognitive and emotional 'excess baggage' that must be disposed of before the person is prepared to focus on things that interest someone else, a point discussed in more detail by Bell and Hardiman in Chapter 2.

A secondary purpose of a particular elicitation may be to increase the commitment of ther knowledge provider by providing some insight into KBS technology so as to be better able to understand the value of the contribution being made and the kind of system that is envisaged by the developers. In this context, computer-aided elicitation may be appropriate, critiquing existing prototypes should be considered, and it may be appropriate to show the knowledge provider how their material has been incorporated in the system. Knowledge providers who are competent to do so (e.g. some computer programmers, systems designers or logicians) may want to check the system's representation of their knowledge.

Different techniques, of course, are good for different things. Welbank identifies the examination of a prototype as the best way to find out the context in which rules should fire (1987c, p. 15). Cognitive mapping techniques such as MDS, certain repertory grid analyses, and laddering are not very good for eliciting rules, but are useful for identifying and structuring features, including entities, of the domain.

Not surprisingly, different authors identify different strengths and weaknesses of widely used techniques such as interviewing. Some differences arise from the variety of interview styles available to elicitors, others from what contrasts are being made by the author at the time. Bainbridge (1981) contrasts interviews with observational techniques. She is cited as observing that interviews are good for getting general principles, rules, background material, and for consideration of rare events, whereas observational methods can generate detailed contextual material (Welbank, 1983c, p. 20). Burton and Shadbolt (forthcoming) contrast techniques for eliciting procedural knowledge, *knowing how*, with techniques for eliciting declarative knowledge, *knowing what*, a distinction discussed by Diaper in Chapter 1. Burton and Shadbolt characterise both the 'formal' (structured) interview and protocol analysis as primarily eliciting procedural knowledge while characterising card sorting and the laddered grid as primarily eliciting declarative knowledge. In apparent contrast, if one takes strategies to be procedural knowledge, Welbank notes that interviews are not very good for getting at problem solving strategies (1987c, p. 15), a recognition that experts tend to indulge in *post-hoc* rational reconstruction of how they approach problems which seems to differ markedly from their actual problem solving performance. The difference could be explained if in interviews as well as in the protocols Burton and Shadbolt elicit a report of what is done (i.e. an account of the performance) rather than how the person goes about doing (i.e. the strategy behind the performance). None the less it seems unwise to regard multipurpose techniques such as interviewing as too

Table 3.1 — Types of knowledge with appropriate knowledge acquisition methods

Key: √, good; ×, bad, ?, difficult, but possible.

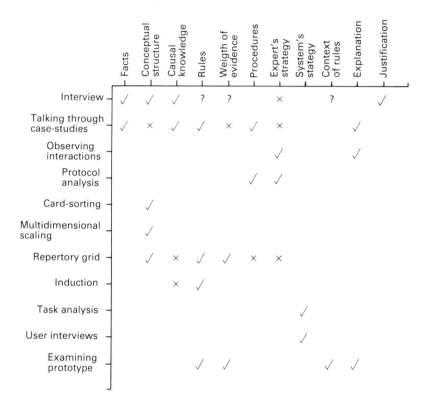

	Facts	Conceptual structure	Causal knowledge	Rules	Weigth of evidence	Procedures	Expert's strategy	System's stategy	Context of rules	Explanation	Justification
Interview	√	√	√	?	?		×		?		√
Talking through case-studies	√	×	√	√	×	√	×			√	
Observing interactions							√			√	
Protocol analysis					√	√					
Card-sorting		√									
Multidimensional scaling		√									
Repertory grid		√	×	√	√	×	×				
Induction			×	√							
Task analysis							√				
User interviews							√				
Examining prototype					√	√				√	√

KEY: √, good;   ×, bad;   ?, difficult, hit possible

closely confined to eliciting a particular type of knowledge. That warning notwithstanding, Welbank's matrix of 'Types of Knowledge' by 'Knowledge Acquisition Methods' (Table 3.1) is a useful summary.

Knowledge about levels of uncertainty is difficult to elicit by asking questions. Some people find it difficult to quanify the strength of a belief, their estimate of how probable an event is, or the utility of a given alternative. If it makes achieving the purpose easier, the elicitor can elicit material which allows quantification to be inferred or use techniques which employ devices such as the 'probability wheel' (introduced in Section 4) or undivided rating scales to allow the person to express these measures without using numbers.

The framework upon which the development is based may be: the analytic methods of a discipline, such as text analysis in linguistics (e.g. Regoczei and Plantinga, 1987) or the qualitative analysis of ethnographers (e.g. Spradley, 1979; Agar, 1986); a development methodology such as

KADS (e.g. Breuker and Weilinga, 1984a); an elicitation framework such as the knowledge acquisition grid taught by LaFrance (1987); an approach to understanding the 'world' for which the KBS is being designed such as the soft systems approach (Checkland, 1981) as used by Taylor and Weaver (1986); a theory providing an approach to understanding aspects of social life such as facet theory (e.g. Canter 1983, 1985), Pask's conversation theory used by Johnson and Johnson (e.g. Johnson and Johnson, 1987a); some other strong model of the domain (e.g. the block interaction model of shopping used by Buckley and Long, 1985b); or the practical limitations imposed by resources or by the way the system is to be implemented (e.g. the shell or language being used).

6.2   Compatibility with source and elicitor

Compatibility with non-human sources is sometimes imposed almost automatically. It is not possible, for example, to employ certain techniques appropriate for use with human knowledge sources, such as the talk-aloud protocol techniques with certain non-human sources, such as a paper document. The document (e.g. a transcript) can be the result of a talk-aloud session, but the session cannot be conducted with the document 'talking-aloud'. It is possible to use the equivalent to the talk-aloud protocol with an electronic system by introducing a facility which produces a journal of all the system transactions. The elicitor must decide whether such a journal would generate material which is likely to be useful and appropriate.

At other times it is the relationship between the source and the anticipated analysis of the material which constrains compatibility. Analysis may require that material gathered be chosen through a process of random selection. Thought must be given to what is to be randomised and whether there is a complete sample frame from which to select the items. One of the major threads of controversy surrounding observational studies relates to how samples of observations were selected. What often happens is that sampling is haphazard, which is unsystematic and often opportunistic, rather than random, which is highly systematic and must be planned in advance. When it is discussed, the selection of the sample of observations is described in terms of one of the several dimensions which may be relevant: time periods, settings, individuals within a setting and a time period, and activities. The other dimensions are often ignored. Conversely the source may put constraints on the range of compatible analyses. It is possible, but often inappropriate to perform quantitative analysis, counting and measuring, of qualitative material. The number of times an expression appears in a text, for example, may have more to do with the verbal style of the author, the formality of the document, or the popularity of the expression at the time the document was produced than with its importance to the issue under discussion. They can be interesting historical or stylistic indicators, but for most KBS purposes conclusions based on simplistic counts and statistics derived from them will be of little value, no matter how 'scientific' they look. Appropriate content analysis of text of the kind made possible by the

OXFORD CONCORDANCE PACKAGE (see Section 5.3.3), for example, requires considerable thought and must be applied to appropriate sources.

The kind of knowledge required can also determine whether certain techniques are compatible with the source. Text analysis to elicit the informal vocabulary of the domain, for example, should not be performed on formal documents.

When the knowledge source is human, there are at least three additional ways the elicitor may need to consider elicitation techniques when deciding whether they are sufficiently compatible to be productive, comfortable and credible. The first has to do with individual differences between knowledge providers. Elicitors will want to employ techniques which are most likely to be productive for a particular knowledge provider and the kind of knowledge needed from a particular session. The second has to do with the differences in the roles played by the elicitor and the knowledge provider during elicitation. Elicitors will want to select techniques with which they and the knowledge providers are comfortable. The third has to do with the credibility and value attributed to the elicitation process and its results. Productivity is of no use if the elicitor does not find the material of any value, and comfort is almost impossible to achieve if the knowledge provider feels the session is a waste of time or the material likely to be misused. Ultimately, both must be convinced of the credibility and the value of elicitation activities.

6.2.1   *Individual differences between knowledge providers*

Burton and Shadbolt (forthcoming) tested whether the knowledge provider's personality (e.g. Eysenck's introvert versus extrovert distinction) and cognitive style (e.g. the field-dependent versus field-independent distinction — see Witkin and Oltman, 1967) affected with elicitation techniques were most suitable for use with a particular knowledge provider. Of the four techniques — a highly structured 'formal' interview, talk-aloud protocol, laddered grid and card sort — studied in their test domain, the only difference personality made was that introverts took longer to complete the interview than extroverts, but that in doing so provided more rules and clauses. Thus the extra time was well spent. Personality made no important difference on any of the other three.

Cognitive style, on the other hand, affected the results with the laddered grid and the talk-aloud protocols. People whose style is field-independent extract features of the problem from the context. They take a systematic approach to problem solving, proceeding step by step and are termed *articulated* thinkers. People whose cognitive style is field-dependent take a holistic, or global, view and make use of the context in problem solving and are termed *global* thinkers (Burton and Shadbolt, 1987, p. 20). Articulated thinkers plod along, if you wish and can accept the term as having no negative connotations, generating many intermediate results. Global thinkers often 'see' the way through a problem as flashes of insight, skipping through the problem-solving process. They generate fewer intermediate results than articulated thinkers and often cannot justify those they do produce. The two styles can be related to Turing's distinction between ingenuity and intuition, two faculties required for mathematical reasoning.

> Mathematical reasoning may be regarded rather schematically as the exercise of a combination of two faculties, which we may call *intuition* and *ingenuity*. (We are leaving out of the account that most important faculty which distinguishes topics of interest from others; in fact, we are regarding the function of the mathematician as simply to determine the truth or falsity of propositions.) The activity of the intuition consists in making spontaneous judgements which are not the result of conscious trains of reasoning. (Hodges, 1983, p. 144).

In Burton and Shadbolt's study, global thinkers, the leapers, had difficulty with the laddered grid and their transcripts of these sessions were harder to convert into rules than those of articulated thinkers, the plodders, with their more systematic style. The talk-aloud protocols of global thinkers provided more rules and clauses than those of articulated thinkers. This was interpreted as indicating that '...perhaps global subjects find it difficult to conceptualise the problem as they do it, hence they make more of a meal of it' (Burton and Shadbolt, 1987, p. 23).

6.2.2   Role differences between providers and elicitors of knowledge

In addition to any individual differences such as personality or cognitive style discussed above there seem to be role differences which affect the compatibility of techniques with the two kinds of participants, knowledge providers and elicitors.

Techniques which are most comfortable to knowledge providers are those that seem performable, relevant, natural, unconstraining and provider-directed. A technique is *performable* if the knowledge provider feels able to provide the required material in the available time. A technique seems *relevant* if the knowledge provider can see how the technique will use knowledge in ways that seem appropriate to the system the knowledge provider envisages being built. It seems *natural* if it allows knowledge to be expressed in familiar ways. It seems *unconstrained* if the knowledge provider feels that neither they, nor the knowledge they are providing, are forced by the structures and formats of the techniques. It seems *provider-directed* if the knowledge providers feel that they have some control over the elicitation process. Thus, for example, the unstructured interview, provided the initiating question is not so vague as to make the task non-*performable*, is often the preferred elicitation technique of experts used to speaking or writing about their work. Observations may be preferred by knowledge providers who rarely verbalise their work, but observations have the drawback of being unnatural to people who are not used to being watched in their work. Video recordings can exacerbate this difficulty.

Techniques which feel comfortable to elicitors are those with which they feel confident of administering effectively, which focus on the knowledge provider rather than the elicitor but over which the elicitor can exercise comfortable, if not necessarily explicit, control. There are certain features of a technique which make it more demanding and potentially stressful for the elicitor. These include having to keep track of many different kinds of material or topics during the elicitation, having to 'think on the fly', having to 'jolly' a lukewarm knowledge provider into co-operation, and having to struggle for control of the session. Thus, because of the amount of material that must be kept in mind and used in subsequent questions, and because the elicitor's desire to 'keep the interview on track' can lead to a struggle for control of the session, unstructured interviews may be more stressful to the elicitor, especially one inexperienced in the technique, than more structured interviews or other better structured techniques. Because of resistance from knowledge providers, techniques like card sorting or role plays may be stressful, at least until the knowledge provider has been 'won over' to appreciating their value, though some never are.

6.2.3 Mapping on to the domain and the KBS

The third way of looking at elicitation techniques classifies them in terms of how well they map on to the KBS and how well they map on to the environment and concerns of domain personnel. This classification can be used to anticipate how highly KBS personnel and domain personnel will value the results of elicitation.

A 2 by 2 matrix such as the one in Fig. 3.1 below can be used to classify

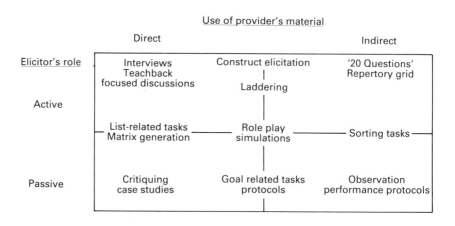

Fig. 3.1 — Categorising techniques.

techniques discussed in this chapter in terms of the involvement of the elicitor and how the knowledge provider's material seems likely to be used. Relatively passive techniques are likely to be least demanding for elicitors, once the knowledge provider has become a willing participant. Techniques which appear to be making direct use of the knowledge provider's material are likely to feel more natural and more relevant and therefore more comfortable for them. Thus the classification can be used to anticipate how the elicitor and the knowledge provider are likely to experience the technique in use. This summary does not, of course, take any of the other numerous dimensions of compatibility into account but can partially guide the selection of techniques or at least alert elicitors to likely difficulties.

The classification is not cut and dried. The extent to which the elicitor takes an active or passive role depends on what variation of the technique is being used, on whether other people are available to take the necessarily active but subordinate roles as in role plays, and on the elicitor's personal style. Most techniques classified as having a direct approach to knowledge also provide material from which other knowledge is derived. Similarly, techniques classified as having an indirect approach to knowledge also provide material which seems to be of direct relevance. So, as with any simplification of complex phenomena, the classification should be viewed as possibly useful, or at least as food for thought, rather than as definitive or, what would be worse, as prescriptive.

6.3   Making appropriate use of resources

Burton and Shadbolt (forthcoming; 1988) also compared the four techniques with respect to the demands on resources and productivity. Laddering and card sorting were taken as exemplars of techniques which elicit declarative knowledge. Structured interviewing and protocol analysis which were taken as exemplars of techniques which elicit procedural knowledge. Of the procedural techniques, protocol analysis took longer and provided less information than the interview. The declarative techniques required similar amounts of time, but the laddering provided significantly more information, at the level of useful clauses, than did card sorting. Burton and Shadbolt are the first to admit that the study they have undertaken with students can only be taken as suggestive of the way other 'experts' might perform using these techniques and that the measures they have used must be carefully scrutinised in order to understand the full implication of the results. The study is none the less a valuable start to the necessary task of empirically investigating the advantages and disadvantages of different elicitation techniques.

7.   CONCLUSION

This chapter has used as its working definition for knowledge elicitation *'those activities undertaken by a person, the knowledge elicitor, to (1) get material from any relevant source, (2) analyse and interpret that material and (3) put it into a form which (a) allows it to be scrutinised by all persons interested in the KBS development and (b) is useful for those who will encode the knowledge in the KBS*: Techniques for step 1, getting material, have been described in some detail with only occasional reference to steps 2 and 3 some aspects of which are covered in greater detail by other chapters in this volume. Only passing mention is made to some of the developing automated knowledge acquisition tools. The extent to which these can partially replace the human elicitor is the extent to which they are outside the scope of this chapter.

Qualities required of elicitors have been given. Advice about how elicitors should conduct and record their activities has been discussed. Though this advice is often predicated upon the expectation that elicitors will be getting knowledge from an expert, most has been seen as applicable to elicitation from non-experts as well. It has been noted that the work of getting material from people is affected by the expectations that the participants, the knowledge provider and the elicitor, bring to the enterprise including: expectations about the KBS; about each other; and about the elicitation session; and it is affected by how they adjust to the interaction while it is in progress (i.e. how great is the rapport between them, how comfortable they feel with the techniques, and their confidence in being able to provide the knowledge being elicited).

Burton and Shadbolt's stance (supported to a lesser or greater extent by Bell and Hardiman in Chapter 2, Johnson in Chapter 4, and Wilson in Chapter 5), that elicitation should be independent of the KBS as well as implementation in order that the knowledge can be used for future enhancements and/or alternative systems is not adopted here for three reasons. Firstly, real world systems are rarely produced in environments which make resources available for more than is required for the system under development. Typically, development teams feel hard pressed to 'bring the system in' in the time allowed with the resources they have at their disposal. In this environment, the recognised 'needs of the KBS' will largely determine what and how material is collected, recorded, interpreted, analysed and used, even if the development team attempts to make elicitation independent of the implementation (in the programming rather than the organisational sense) of the system. Secondly, further analysis of material, though desirable, rarely occurs in practice for several reasons. Turnover in development team personnel is high between KBS development projects even if a team stays together throughout the development of a single system, and the 'not made here' syndrome applies to policies about collection and recording of material as much as about the systems themselves. Each KBS development team has its own views about what material is relevant and useful, they may be intolerant of other styles, and doubtful about the quality of material they have not collected themselves. In some environments it is more difficult to get resources to rework old material — 'If it was so good why wasn't it used first time around?' — then to collect new material. It is often harder, and less efficient to extract what is needed from general purpose material than from material collected with a specific use in mind. Finally, and most importantly, domain realities change. Material collected for the first system can become out of date in subtle ways. Its later use can be seriously misleading to KBS developers especially if the use of previously collected material makes it more difficult for development teams to justify the contact with domain personnel which could bring these changes to light. Thus, though there may be sound reasons for wishing to make elicitation independent of the system, there is a danger that this will become uncritically regarded in the KBS field as the ideal toward which practitioners must strive. The practical difficulties are very real: the fiscal reality of project-by-project funding allows little spare resource for generalised elicitation, a policy which is short-sighted in the eyes of those whose interests span projects but sensible economy to those who are uncertain that additional material will ever be put to use; and the social difficulty of having material collected by other teams accepted as credible and its content valued means much material would still be underused. But the inherent problem, that some domains change too quickly for material to retain its validity across sequentially ordered projects, will remain the most serious difficulty until KBS have a development cycle which is significantly shorter than at present or development and maintenance are integrated with one another with the evolution of the domain. Then knowledge elicitation may become an ongoing, possibly implicit, activity and the problem of independence could disappear.

Attention is drawn to the fact that the terminology used to describe elicitation is far from standard, and some differences and potentially misleading similarities of terms have been pointed out. For example, the prevalent UK and US social science usage of 'focus' and 'structure', used here, is at variance with that of Breuker and Weilinga who, possibly through mistranslation or the fact that European usage differs, seem to have reversed the usual terminology. It naturally follows that it is also at variance with those who base their discussions largely on Breuker and Weilinga's work. Also, neither 'focus' nor 'structure' has been characterised as a dichotomous classification (e.g. focused vs unfocused or structured vs unstructured) as it often is in papers on knowledge acquisition; and they have been seen as separable concepts, i.e. it is possible, for example, for an interview to be both less structured but more focused than another interview. The stance taken in the chapter is not that one usage is correct and another is not, but the meanings of terms should be clearly stated and variations from other work noted so that elicitors will not inadvertently dismiss, ignore, or misuse potentially useful techniques.

Techniques are distinguished from the elicitation sessions, and a number of techniques are described. Some are used when the knowledge source is a person. These include bipartite techniques, ones in which the elicitor and knowledge provider are both involved and there is no other element in the interaction, such as **interviewing** — structured, semi-structured and unstructured. These can be testing for the relationship between the elicitor and the knowledge provider and can be particularly demanding for the elicitor.

Tripartite techniques in which a focus, or a device of material gathering serves as a third element in the interaction, relieving some of the pressure on the elicitor are also described. These include:

Focused discussion — organised around cases
forward scenario simulation
retrospective case description
interesting cases

> critical incidents
> — organised around goals
> dividing the domain
> reclassification
> distinguishing goals
> goal decomposition
> — organised around lists
> a decision analysis strategy

Teachback
Construct elicitation
Sorting tasks
Laddering
'20 Questions'
Matrix generation
Critiquing

Techniques in which the elicitor can be less involved or even absent from the scene in which the knowledge is being provided are described. These include:

Protocols
Role play
Simulations

Techniques for getting material from sources other than humans are described. These include:

Observation
Object tracing
'Listening'
Collection of 'artefacts'

Software which facilitates manipulating text are described

FACTFINDER
The ETHNOGRAPH
OXFORD CONCORDANCE PACKAGE

Finally the selection of techniques is considered. There are three factors that affect the choice of knowledge elicitation techniques: the nature of the source of the knowledge; what form the knowledge takes; and what is allowed to drive the selection of relevant knowledge and the elicitation process itself. But in all cases, effective elicitation means selecting techniques which serve the purpose in hand and are compatible with both the knowledge source and the person eliciting the knowledge. It is important for elicitors to be aware that there is often a tension between a technical orientation of KBS developers and a non-technical orientation of personnel in many domains. The power relation between domain and system development personnel effects the choice of intermediate representation for the knowledge, i.e. how it is displayed outside the system as the knowledge base is being developed, as well as the perceived appropriateness of tools and the credibility of results.

Knowledge elicitors are recommended to cast their net widely: to discover techniques and frameworks for gathering material which can be fruitfully employed for the purpose at hand; to take care to understand the assumptions behind the techniques and the terminology used to discuss them; to use more than one technique in order to get a full and comprehensive understanding of the domain; and to feel free to vary techniques to make them more productive and interesting while not violating the assumptions upon which they are founded.

ACKNOWLEDGEMENT

This work was carried out as part of the Alvey DHSS Demonstrator project, supported by the Science and Engineering Research Council and the Alvey Directorate of the UK Department of Trade and Industry. The project collaborators are ICL, Logica, Imperial College London, and the Universities of Lancaster, Liverpool and Surrey. The views expressed here are those of the author and may not necessarily be shared by other collaborators. The assistance of colleagues on the project especially Marina Jirotka, David Frohlich, and Charlie Portman is gratefully acknowledged as is that of Margaret O'Neill of Loughborough University, Mike Burton and Nigel Shadbolt of Nottingham University, Dushka Johnson of Kingston Polytechnic, Ian Neale of City University Business School, and members of the Alvey Water Industry Expert Systems project at the University of Surrey.

APPENDIX A: SPRADLEY'S GENERAL CULTURAL DOMAINS

Spradley provides an aid for looking at what is going on in social situations. His *general cultural domains* are given as a *cover term* (e.g. Strict Inclusion) and a *semantic relationship* (e.g. X is a kind of Y). The Ys include, but are not limited to, the nine *dimensions of social situation* — space, object, act, activity, event, timer, actor, goal and feeling. The observer may focus on things among the list of Xs for a particular Y. In his study of the grand jury Spradley recounts 'I used the general domain "kinds of actors" as a guide to focusing my attention on domains of this sort. Rather than identifying all the people involved in the grand jury under this domain, I identified several domains. These included (1) kinds of witnesses, (2) kinds of grand jurors, and (3) kinds of officials. The general domain thus led me to three culturally specific domains.' (Spradley, 1980, p. 105).

Below are listed some 'general cultural domains' provided by Spradley as a start on what will be a much longer list of such 'general cultural domains' from which an observer can choose. Elicitors may find them useful both to broaden their conception of possible observations and for deciding on a focus.

1. *Strict inclusion: X is a kind of Y*
      kinds of: acts, time, places, actors, objects, feelings, activities,
            goals, relationships
2. *Spatial: X is a part of Y*
      parts of: activities, places, events, objects
3. *Cause-effect: X is a result of Y*
      results of: activities, acts, events, feelings
4. *Rationale: X is a reason for doing Y*
      reasons for: actions, carrying out activities, staging events, feelings,
            using objects seeking goals, arranging space
5. *Location for action: X is a place for Y*
      Places for: activities, object, seeking goals
      places where: people act, events are held
6. *Function: X is used for Y*
      uses for: objects, events, acts, activities, feelings, places
7. *Means–end: X is a way to do Y*
      ways to: organize space, act, carry out activities, stage events, seek
            goals, become actors, feel
8. *Sequence: X is a step in Y*
      steps in: achieving goals, an act, an event, an activity, becoming an
            actor
9. *Attribution: X is an attribute of Y* (characteristic)
      characteristics of: objects, places, time, actors, activities

(Spradley, 1980, pp. 102–105)

APPENDIX B: LAFRANCE'S KNOWLEDGE ACQUISITION GRID

The Knowledge Acquisition Grid was introduced in Section 4.1.2 and its
question types were discussed in 4.1.3. The other dimension of the grid are
the five forms of knowledge detailed here along with strategies for using the
grid as a framework for knowledge elicitation.

B.1   Forms of knowledge

The forms of knowledge are ways in which experts can represent their know-
how. The five included in the grid — layouts, stories, scripts, metaphors, and
rules of thumb — though not claimed to be exhaustive, provide useful
variety.
      They

> provide a way during knowledge acquisition to catalogue a
> domain's real complexity. ...and encourage broad coverage. In
> seeing knowledge as multi-modal, the knowledge engineer is more
> likely to check whether other modes of expressing the expertise will
> turn up relevant but previously unarticulated know-how. ...each
> Form of Knowledge reflects a different but practical slant on the
> problem domain... One caveat should be mentioned here: even
> though expert knowledge is generally multi-modal, not all Forms of
> Knowledge are evident in all knowledge domains, nor are they used

equivalently by all experts. Nevertheless, knowledge engineers should recognize the potential in each area, and not assume that unfamiliar forms are necessarily unproductive ones. (LaFrance, 1987, pp. 249–50).

The theoretical foundations of this dimension of the grid include 'Minsky's society-of-mind theory [which] proposes that intelligent action emerges from the interactions of many small systems operating within an evolving overall administrative structure (Minsky, 1986).' (LaFrance, 1987, p. 249).

The descriptions below, beginning with the Forms of Knowledge which elicit the more declarative material and going on to those that elicit the more procedural material, closely follow LaFrance's presentation (unless otherwise indicated the quotations are taken from pp. 248–249).

Layouts are verbal descriptions (p. 50) which show how the knowledge provider conceives of tasks, how she/he organizes current information 'in light of prior knowledge and the present context'. Each is a map of some task of interest. It helps make sense of the facts and heuristics used in the task by specifying the goals for which they are to be used. Layouts provide a characterisation of the task in terms of its boundaries, organisation, and basic classifications. The layout helps the elicitor understand how the knowledge provider frames the problem.

Stories are accounts of previous experience, often case studies or talk-aloud protocols, which can be oriented in different ways, for example: to provide explanation or show how a particular outcome followed from events, *explanatory* stories; to show what needed fixing or what was wrong (i.e. a *diagnostic/prescriptive* story).

Scripts (cf. Abelson, 1981) — with their typical roles, standard props, standard sequences of scenes, and results which normally follow certain activities — give the knowledge provider's 'sequential and procedural knowledge of the domain' 'To know an expert's scripts is to have a temporal chart of critical actions, and to be able to understand each action in terms of the prior knowledge required to perform it.'

Metaphors encapsulate the [knowledge provider's] alternative images of ther task, each of which includes unique features, constraints, and options. Metaphors describe one thing by reference to another apparently dissimilar thing so that the first is understood more completely than if the comparison had not been made. Their advantage is being able to present an idea which can later be reconstructed and embellished through probes directed to the [knowledge provider] by the [elicitor].

Rules of thumb 'encapsulate tacit knowledge about which conditions warrant which actions, and about how to gather data on and assess current conditions. [They] are concrete, implementable strategies of minor to moderate scope which can single out and define as issues those specific, limited conditions for which they serve as the most complete strategy.'

B.2 Strategy for use of the knowledge acquisition grid

The grid can be used passively to interpret material from the knowledge provider. It can also be used actively during the elicitation, reminding the elicitor of ways of evoking further material. The grid can be used in a number of ways, one of which is to adopt a cyclical approach moving from general queries to more specific ones, i.e. from grand tour questions through to cross-checking questions, and from declarative forms of knowledge to procedural, i.e. from layouts through to rules-of-thumb. The actual strategy of use will depend on the KBS being developed and the KBS development team's style.

APPENDIX C: PERSONALIZED TASK ELICITATION QUESTIONS

The following is adapted from the task elicitation portion of a course on personalised task representation run by Jim McKenzie for HUSAT. It gives the information that should be elicited about any process.

(1) Basic description
   What: what is done
(2) Temporal ordering
   Before: what processes come before it in time and have a message or a material flow leading to it
   Next: what processes come after it in time and have a message or a material flow leading from it
   Concurrent: what processes happen to occur at the same time but which do not share a common 'before' or 'next' relationship to it
(3) Contingency information
   Or: alternative processes; which one is done depends on predetermined control conditions ('Or' processes do not send messages or materials to one another)
   And: all processes are to be done but in any order ('And' processes may or may not send messages to one another)
(4) Establishing hierarchies
   Why: one is done for the purpose of the other(s); 'Why' relationships establish superordinate/subordinate relationships in hierarchies of purposes; usually the superior sends a control message to the subordinate and receives a data message (a report on progress) back from it.

How: one is done as a means of achieving the other(s); 'How' relation-
          ships establish superordintate/subordinate relationships in
          enabling hierarchies
(5) Production information
   Control: control messages start and stop processes; they express con-
              ditions for actioning processes; identify their source(s) and
              destination(s)
              Concurrent controls: all messages have to be present and all
              have to arrive at the same time for the process to be actioned
              'or' controls: if any of the messages is present then the process
              is actioned
              'and' controls: all messages have to be present but they can
              have arrived in any order for the process to be actioned
   Data: messages which are the informational inputs to processes;
          identify their source(s) and destination(s) and whether they
          come and go directly or via a store (a 'pool')
   Materials: the physical inputs and outputs of processes
   Products: the outputs of the process; they may be messages (data or
              control) or materials
   Tools: what is used by people to help them carry out a process;
          distinguish between types in terms of the process the tool is
          aiding
(6) Scope information
   Boundaries: define in terms of the start (successive before?), the end
              (successive next?), the top level purpose (successive
              why?), and functional primitives (successive how?)
   Who: the agent, object or processor doing the process
   Where: the physical location of the process, message or material flow
   Linked to: non-functional relationships such as similar to
(7) Evaluative information
   How well: attainment compared against some goal
   How liked: how (the full range of) target users like doing it
   How easy: whether (the full range of) target users find it easy to do
(8) Ergonomic information
   Health, safety, comfort: Identify 'hazards'

APPENDIX D: FROHLICH'S DESCRIPTION OF FORM-FILLING ACTIVITIES

The event dictionary comprised of the two tables below was devised by
Frohlich (1986) to code annotations of completed B1 forms in a study
referred to in Section 4.10.2. A facsimile of two pages of an annotated form
follows the tables. It provides an example of an unusual form of protocol
analysis.

Symbol	Event	Definition	Common decriptors (defined in the table below)
S	Scan	A brief look at as page	F,B
V	Vocalisation	A reading aloud	Q,E,I,T
A	Answer	An attempt to provide a satisfactory answer	C,I,c,U
Rep	Repudiation	Written indication that a question is not applicable	
P	Progression	Movement to the next question on the routing path	O,D/o
R	Regression	Movement to the previous question on the routing path	
D	Diversion	Movement to a question more than one step away on the routing path	F.B.

Symbol	Descriptor	Definition	Common events (defined in the table above)
Q	Question	A question on the form	V
E	Explanation	A note of explanation on the form	V
I	Instruction	A routing instruction on the form	V
T	Title	A printed section title	V
O	Oriented	Corectly routed	P,D
D/o	Disoriented	Incorrectly routed	P,D
B	Backward	Towards the beginning on the form	D,S
F	Forward	Towards the end on the form	D,S
C	Consistent	Internally coherent	A
I/c	Inconsistent	Internally incoherent	A
U	Uninterpretable	In a form incapable of interpretation	A

APPENDIX E: FROHLICH'S PRINCIPLES OF READING AND ROUTING OF FORM-FILLING

The results of Frohlich's (1986) protocol analysis suggest 'a pattern for the organisation of form filling . . . characterised in terms of the local application of [the 7] broad principles relating to the location, reading and answering of questions on the form' (Frohlich, 1986, p. 56). The seven principles are:

1. *Principle of linear progression*: work through the questions in the order they appear on the form.
2. *Principle of least reading effort*: only read what seems to be necessary to maintain form-filling progress.
3. *Principle of question routing*: jump directly to a new question if the form tells you to.
4. *Principle of question omission*: miss out questions which don't seem to apply to you.
5. *Principle of question preview*: if in doubt about the meaning of the current question, read the subsequent question.
6. *Principle of question review*: if in doubt about your interpretation of the previous question, review that question and the answer provided.
7. *Principle of topic scan*: if in doubt about the relevance of the current question, scan the local topic context.

(Frohlich, 1986, p. 56)

6 People ~you~ who live with you (93)

a **Do you live alone?**

No ☒

Yes ☐ Now go straight to Part 7 'More about money'.

Please give details about everyone who lives with you. (94)

"where?"

"No"

b Please tell us in this order, partner, children, relatives, lodgers, friends.

Surname and other names	Date of birth	Relationship to you	What do they do? eg work, YTS course, student, school, unemployed, sick)	Do they get Supplementary Benefit?
				No ☐ Yes ☐
				No ☐ Yes ☐
				No ☐ Yes ☐
				No ☐ Yes ☐
				No ☐ Yes ☐
				No ☐ Yes ☐
				No ☐ Yes ☐
				No ☐ Yes ☐

c **Does anyone in this list get Severe Disablement Allowance (SDA)?** SDA replaced the two non-contributory invalidity pensions (NCIP and HNCIP).

(96) "?" ... 107 Stuck

No ☐

Yes ☐ Who gets SDA? [_____]

7 More about money (115)

a **Have you or your partner applied for any benefits or allowances, but not had any money yet?** (117)

No ☐

Yes ☒ Which benefits are they? (120)

[*Unemployment Benefit*]

Who applied for them? (125) "they will"

you ☐   your partner ☐

b **Does anyone owe you or your partner or any dependent children who live with you any money?** For example, maintenance or money from a court order.

No ☒ (132) Now go to the top of the next column.

Yes ☐ How much do they owe?

£ [____]

What do they owe it for?

[_____]

Now go to the top of the next column

c **Do you or your partner get any of these benefits at the moment?** (133) Housing Benefit, Unemployment Benefit, Child Benefit, One-parent Benefit, Family Income Supplement (FIS), maternity benefits, Sickness Benefit, Invalidity Benefit. (136) "They should"

No ☐ Now go on to the next page

Yes ☒ (142)

Which benefit is it?	Who is the benefit paid to?	How much is it each week?
unemploy Benefit	you ☒ your partner ☐	£ 28·50
	you ☐ your partner ☐	£
	you ☐ your partner ☐	£
	you ☐ your partner ☐	£

Go on to the next page

Table 2

d 'More about money' continued (147) " They're asking a lot of questions "

Do you do any kind of work at the moment?

Count work that is

1 paid or unpaid
2 full-time or part-time
3 casual work

Even if you are paid you could still get benefit. (151) " Its obvious they know... "

No ☒ (158)

Yes ☐ How many hours a week do you work?

e **Do you or your partner or any dependent children who live with you have any other money coming in?**

Count things like benefits, allowances, pensions, maintenance, money from a trust fund, money from boarders, or any other money coming in.

No ☒ (161)

Yes ☐ How much is it?

£ _____ every ....

What is it for?

Who is it paid to?

8 Where you live (161)

a **Are you living with your parents, relatives or friends as part of their family?** " They've asked it "

No ☒

Yes ☐ What is the name of the head of the household?

Now go straight to Part 11 'Your Special Needs'

b **Do you own your own home?** _house_ (171)

If it is on a mortgage or a loan, tick Yes

No ☒

Yes ☐ Now go straight to Part 9 'Owning your home'

c **What is the name and address of your landlord, landlady, or council?** (172)

?   " Don't Know "

d **Is your landlord or landlady a relative?**

No ☒ Yes ☐

Now go to the top of the next column

---

g 'Where you live' continued (176) " They've asked this... "

Does the money you pay for where you live cover all your heating costs?

No ☒ Yes ☐ (179)

f **Do you have any joint tenants who share the rent and bills with you?**

No ☒ or Yes ☐ Please tell us below " Same again" "If you... then" (182)

What are their full names?

Which bills do you share with this person?

g **Do you pay board or lodging?** " I pay board" (187)

No ☐ Now go straight to Part 10 'More about where you live'.

Yes ☐ How much board or lodging do you pay?

£ 30 every _week_ (190)

h **Does the money you pay cover any meals?** (191)

No ☒

Yes ☐ How many meals do you get each week?

breakfasts   lunches   evening meals

i **Is there anywhere in the place you live where you can do cooking?** " ? " (193)

No ☐ Yes ☒ (200)

Now go straight to Part 11 'Your Special Needs'

9 Owning your home (201)

This is for people who own their home or have a mortgage or loan. (202) " I don't own it... "

a **Do you own your home jointly with anyone else?**

No ☐ Now go on to the next page

Yes ☐ What are the full names of the other owners?

Do these other owners live in your home?

No ☐ Yes ☐

Go on to the next page

Table 2

Introduction to:
Mediating representations in knowledge elicitation

Nancy Johnson's chapter moves the progress of this book one step on from the previous chapter by Betsy Cordingley (Chapter 3) by describing the 'representation form' and its desirable properties. The chapter starts with the practical observation that after the delivery of an expert system there usually remains no other knowledge representation than that encoded in the system. Such a state makes subsequent modification and maintenance of the expert system difficult or well nigh impossible. Within knowledge elicitation, the notion that 'the production of working code is the real result of work done' is debunked and it is suggested that the premature encoding of knowledge in an expert system-driven representational form is often a hindrance.

The chapter proposes that what is needed is a thorough documentation of the complete design process and within knowledge elicitation Johnson's notion of a mediating representation is offered as one candidate for such documentation. A mediating representation is defined as 'a computer language independent notation used as a conceptual aid in synthesising knowledge ... it "mediates" between verbal data and standardised knowledge representation schemes found in AI software development environments'. The roles of a mediating representation are to 'handle early conceptualization of knowledge in a disciplined way, refine structures and eventually validate the knowledge'.

Mediating representations are contrasted with the more common notion of 'intermediate representations' where the later are described as 'a representation which only exists between flanking representations and is bound to them by clearly defined production rules which map one representation to the next'. Such a view is argued to lack usefulness in the necessary iteration involved in knowledge elicitation, particularly with 'something as philosophically troublesome as "knowledge"'. Nor is a mediating representation merely a 'paper knowledge base' but it is 'the major tool in constructing a machine-independent statement of the knowledge and associated background information ... to provide both a medium of communication between members of the team and a "grammar" of the expert's task'. The properties of mediating representations are discussed in terms of: their explicitness and expressiveness; their economy and power; their communicability; and their ability to guide knowledge analysis.

The form of mediating representation described in the chapter involves the use of Systemic Grammar Networks (SGNs) which in a simple graphical form captures 'the salient features of the domain and expertise' and have the advantage that 'by accepting the discipline of producing a grammar it is possible to be guided in a principled fashion through the knowledge analysis phase'. Applied to interview transcripts and, like Bell and Hardiman in Chapter 2, appealing to the tenets of grounded theory, the transcripts are representable in 'simple abstract terms which lift the analysis one step from the transcripts but with the analysis still "grounded" in the original data'. Two simple SGNs are used to illustrate their basic properties and format and these are discussed in the context of the previously described properties that mediating representations should possess.

4

Mediating representations in knowledge elicitation

Nancy E. Johnson
Department of Computer Science, Brunel University

1. INTRODUCTION

This chapter focuses on the early stage of knowledge elicitation when the knowledge engineer makes those first tentative attempts to understand the expert's problems. Eventually, through sheer hard work and a few insights the knowledge engineer will be confident enough to admit to some collection of ideas, descriptions and procedures which will be termed 'an analysis of the expert's knowledge'. Typically, much of this knowledge is hardly ever reported to other team members and never beyond the project. The knowledge engineer's notes and a few annotated transcripts will be all that is left of the stage of conceptual analysis which preceded the encoding of rules or facts in the KBS. When an expert system shell is the final destination for the expert's knowledge it is not uncommon for there to be no independent statement of the knowledge other than the rule base and some glossaries in the help information of the system. While this state of affairs may be quite acceptable for small scale applications when participants are becoming familiar with the technology it is likely to be quite unacceptable in large scale applications. For where many are gathered together to build an expert system, the team will need access to a statement of the problem and, as the project progresses, to the emergent knowledge not yet expressed in the concepts of the final implementation language. Initially, no one, neither expert nor knowledge engineer will know what subset of the expert's expertise should be selected for implementation. It is the very purpose of knowledge elicitation to make that selection. Premature expression of knowledge in standard knowledge representation languages, although allowing early progress, can become a hindrance to later work. For further analysis of the expert's tasks often suggests radical changes to the structure of the emergent knowledge. Perhaps the tendency of knowledge engineers to rush into high level programming languages or pseudo-code to express domain knowledge is no more than reliving the software development practice of regarding the production of working code as the 'real' result of work done. If this ethos is established in the development of knowledge-based systems, and there is no reason to suppose that developing a KBS system should be much different from developing any other piece of software, then we can all expect similar failures. It is already clear that knowledge engineers can 'get it all wrong' by not fully appreciating the requirements of the user and produce interesting but marginalised systems.

While some would suggest that involving the user more closely is a solution (see Bell and Hardiman, Chapter 2), it is quite reasonable to believe that the problem is the familiar one of software engineering where mistakes made early show up late and are thus more expensive to correct. Thus for software engineering in general (and KBS in particular) flaws in requirements analysis (cf. elicitation stage) may not be apparent until a substantial prototype is in the field. The effect of late detection of early mistakes in conceptualisation is more devastating than discovering mistakes made in the later implementation stages (e.g. having to change an inappropriate classification of domain concepts versus having to add a missing rule during rule base refinement). If the experience of years of system design does not furnish a convincing argument we need only consider the half-life of a software development team to appreciate the problems of maintaining an expert system without documentation of the knowledge separate from the rule base. It is not uncommon for the maintenance team to be unable to give anything other than a historical explanation for the existence of some of the rules (van de Brug *et al.*, 1986). At this point software engineers argue for better requirements analysis and a rigorous specification of the problem and knowledge as the route to more disciplined software design. This chapter argues that the former is unavailable and the latter inappropriate. Taking the inappropriateness of formal specification first, it is easy to forgive the software engineer for misunderstanding the nature of human knowledge and expertise and its resistance to formal specification. Being aware that epistemology is a mature area of philosophical activity has been enough for many of us, including Diaper, Chapter 1, to give up any hope of the silver bullet of a well defined theory of knowledge! In short there is not, nor ever likely to be, a formal specification language expressive enough to capture the nuance of human expertise. It is not so easy to forgive the sleight of hand which suggests that knowledge engineering should solve the bulk of the problems of epistemology and requirements analysis before building knowledge-based systems. Furthermore, while early knowledge elicitation is very like requirements analysis, this is exactly the area which causes major problems for software engineers themselves. It is the least well understood stage in the software development life-cycle area and there are few viable software aids. If we regard KBS development as a particular variety of software development then it could be fruitful to consider documentation of emergent knowledge as a major theme of requirements analysis for the KBS. Perhaps knowledge engineers can contribute to the software engineering field, through disseminating characterisations of the knowledge elicitation process (Cordingley and Diaper this volume are examples). Likewise, informal reports of practices in elicitation (Johnson, 1987a) could be helpful. With luck, the experiences of those who through an absence of any knowledge documentation have been forced to redo the elicitation stage when required to enhance or port a prototype KBS system will not have been in vain.

Whatever the solution to the software design problem, knowledge engineers still need methods which allow knowledge elicitation to proceed in a disciplined way. In this chapter only the problem of the early conceptualisation of the domain will be considered. But there are also the problems of:

- knowledge refinement — giving a more complete description of the knowledge;
- providing a medium of communication between team members, not always dependent on gathering around a screen dump from a knowledge engineeering development environment;
- validating the knowledge with respect to a wider population.

This last stage is hardly addressed in current knowledge engineering practice and is no more than a standard requirement of research that claims made about the status of that which has been discovered should be substantiated. Thus if it is claimed that the procedures and concepts encapsulated in the KBS are 'knowledge' then evidence should be available that either this knowledge is commonplace (a wider population accepts it) or that it is rare and so 'expert'. The former may be had by supporting analysis of literature or cross-checking with other communities of experts, near experts and apprentices. For the latter it may only be possible to produce informal and anecdotal evidence from interaction with the original expert. In no way is it suggested that the expert be subjected to tests of competence. Merely that the claim to knowledge be authenticated by checking against other sources. Validating the knowledge as described here is a quite separate task from 'validating the knowledge base' (checking for completeness and consistency). Validating the knowledge *per se* involves providing some justification for claiming that the description or implementation of the knowledge is *appropriate* and not just internally consistent.

To handle early conceptualisation of knowledge in a disciplined way, refine structures and eventually validate the knowledge, the team will need a flexible preservation medium. The term 'knowledge documentation' can refer to the widest sense of documentation within a KBS project (i.e. not just the user documentation or internal project documentation) and the preservation or representation form warrants some attention. To this end the KBS group at Brunel are experimenting with the idea of a 'Mediating Representation' (Johnson, 1987b).

A mediating representation for knowledge elicitation is a computer language independent notation used as a conceptual aid in synthesising knowledge from talk with experts. It 'mediates' between verbal data and standardised knowledge representation schemes found in AI software development environments. For the group at Brunel the major mediating representation is the systemic grammar network developed by Halliday (1978), used by Winograd (1983) and adapted by Bliss *et al.* (1983). This formalism is a key feature in the process of abstracting and conceptualising expertise in a domain. It provides a means to prepare an explict description of the knowledge in a definitive form for discussion within the KBS development team prior to, and in tandem with, implementation in a knowledge engineering environment. As a research group we are less concerned with tuning applications in a familiar domain and more concerned with developing methods to support fully customised knowledge engineering (new domains or special applications). But it is clear to us that some experience with mediating representations is of immense value. The need arises from simple practical constraints on the division of labour and from a desire to handle the elicitation phase in a disciplined manner. It simply is not possible for the knowledge engineer responsible for implementing the knowledge base to wait for the elicitors to provide a knowledge specification. Furthermore other members of the team responsible for separate parts of the KBS are in need of a statement of the problem as background information. All must start and finish together. Also the knowledge engineering development environment may not be transparent to non-knowledge engineers on the project. Thus software prototypes, of whatever sophistication, are not always the most appropriate channel of communication between members of the team. Here our mediating representation provides a means to document the information gleaned from the expert which can be passed around the group for those early and very influential discussions on the nature of the KBS under development. Subsequently, the implementor can make good use of further 'knowledge drafts' in the same format. In terms of discipline in knowledge elicitation, the very process of building our SGNs forces attention on the fit of structure to the available primary elicitation data, a necessary part of the knowledge validation process. Keeping a largely pencil and paper version of the knowledge distinct from a the current software implementation of the knowledge base has several advantages. First, it allows the team to think *conceptually* without having to translate concepts prematurely into the knowledge representation language of the software prototype. Secondly, the team can make a selection of implementable knowledge without destroying the original representation. Thirdly, the changes which arise through more elicitation can be easily documented, in the next version on paper or screen, without having to adjust the prototype. This is a distinct advantage for the implementor as well as providing a focus of attention for the expert and elicitor. While for the Brunel group it is essential to have a representation and methods to discipline the knowledge elicitation process it is suggested that any team could find use in a mediating representation. The practical reason is that if there is a chance that the first prototype is to be further developed, even if it is a simple rule-based system, then an independent statement of the knowledge will be helpful. Of less immediate practical importance is the advice that tools which encourage *concept analysis* are helpful regardless of the apparent simplicity of the domain.

The next two sections of this chapter examine the nature of knowledge elicitation and the requirements on the mediating or otherwise supporting representations. Two examples of SGNs are described. The first is a toy example to show how an SGN might aid knowledge analysis and the second is a real example. Although this sequence is conceptually sound, glancing through Section 4 before reading Sections 2 and 3 is recommended.

2. KNOWLEDGE ELICITATION AND ANALYSIS: THE NATURE OF KNOWLEDGE ELICITATION

Elicitation involves creating an environment where a domain expert, users and interested parties (as discussed by Diaper in Chapter 1) can generate some kind of description of their activities which the knowledge engineer comments upon, analyses and moulds into a body of 'knowledge'. As Bell and Hardiman (Chapter 2) also suggest, knowledge elicitation is not the discovery of heaps of mature, internalised cognitive structures: nor is it the mapping of incompletely expressed concepts into the seductive precision of a formal system. It is closer to a learning or research activity where a knowledge engineer comes to understand something of the concerns of the others (principally the expert). With varying degrees of appropriateness, the knowledge engineer actively creates the knowledge from a sea of qualitative data produced during their meetings. The two stages of elicitation, raw elicitation (interview, problem solving, etc.) and knowledge analysis (getting it down on paper) are distinct but are used in tandem and knowledge engineers need skills in both. Skill in the use of mediating representation is an essential part of the knowledge analysis stage. Furthermore, as has already been mentioned, there is always the problem of the full custom knowledge engineer working in a new domain and aware that a first generation architecture, typically an expert system shell, may not be adequate. In this situation the knowledge engineer needs a facility for capturing what *may* be relevant and preserving it until a selection of implementable knowledge can be made. Using standard knowledge representation languages (production systems, frame-based languages, associative semantic networks, lisp-like structures, etc.) may already prejudge and thereby eliminate aspects of the expertise or knowledge which, with hindsight, ought to have been implemented.

3. MEDIATING REPRESENTATIONS

This section will describe the desirable properties of a mediating representation, starting with an indication of what it is *not*. First, a mediating representation is not a 'paper knowledge base'. The paper knowledge base is a more restricted form of representation of some of the data from elicitation. It can contain a pretend-it's-English form of potential rules or a prose statement of emergent knowledge. It can even be a computer-based representation scheme, perhaps with loose collections of 'other relevant information'. A paper knowledge base is often used as a focus of activity during elicitation but the aim is to provide a communicable representation of the knowledge base only. A mediating representation is the major tool in constructing a machine-independent statement of the knowledge and associated background information which we call a competence model (Keravnou and Johnson, 1986). The aim is to provide both a medium of communication between members of the team and a 'grammar' of the expert's task.

Secondly, a mediating representation is not a version of the linguists', and latterly knowledge engineers', notion of 'intermediate representation'. An intermediate representation is a representation which only exists between flanking representations and is bound to them by clearly defined projection rules which map one representation to the next. It is obvious to anyone engaged in knowledge elicitation that the ability to translate or map something as philosophically troublesome as 'knowledge' or 'expertise' from one representation form to another is not a task worth undertaking in this lifetime! So intermediate representation is indeed an unfortunate choice of words which carries the sense of iterative knowledge elicitation and translation between representations which most would prefer to avoid. The term mediating representation is preferred to convey the sense of synthesis and coming to understand through the representation which is constitutive of knowledge analysis.

So far in this chapter, no radical solutions have been offered beyond the sympathetic usage of pencil and paper with the desired ability to preserve diagrams and jottings by knowledge engineers. But the creation of a knowledge 'priesthood' with all the true secrets of knowledge elicitation enshrined in cult practices is probably no more desirable than succumbing to the jolly whimsy that automated knowledge acquisition or machine learning will remove the conceptual bottleneck of knowledge analysis. In order to render knowledge elicitation practice more accessible to expert system developers it will be necessary to make available descriptions of tools and methods used by experienced knowledge engineers. A minimum requirement is to publicise the use of those mediating representations which the experience valued. In addition to this minimum, and for the sake of disciplined research, the Brunel group prefer representations which do more than act as a resting place for potential rules and facts. We demand that the representation form and methods will also give rise to an appropriately *structured* description of the knowledge. We might say we need a *grammar* of the expertise or expert's task. Talking in terms of a grammatical metaphor for knowledge elicitation we could imagine how if the expert is a native doer (cf. native speaker) of an exotic task (cf. language) then the knowledge elicitor's job is to create an explicit description which not only characterises the nature of the task (cf. provide terms to categorise the sentences) but also generate descriptions of task sequences or some other meaningful notion in the domain (cf. generate the sentences of the language). This grammar, expressed in the formalism of the mediating representation, can then be tested against the qualitative data collected from the original expert and subsequently validated against a wider population. Thus we ask our mediating representation to do much more than a representation form in a knowledge editing system (e.g. KADS in Breuker and Weilinga, 1984b). A mediating representation must play a part in the very earliest stages of creating the knowledge and evaluation of the knowledge separate from evaluation of the software. At the moment it is clear that no available knowledge engineering environment supports all stages of knowledge elicitation from selection of relevant material from the amorphous mass of expert behaviour through to testing an explicitly represented body of knowledge.

If we pursue the grammatical analogy just a little further some very simple requirements on a mediating representation emerge. Any mediating representation formalism could be assessed in terms of four criteria:

- Is the formalism itself sufficiently expressive?
- Is the resulting description economical?
- Does the formalism aid communication between all members of the development team?
- Does the formalism actually guide knowledge analysis in a significant way?

Each of these will be addressed in turn.

3.1 Explicitness and expressiveness

The major purpose of a representation scheme in knowledge elicitation is to enable the knowledge engineer to build an explicit description of the expert's knowledge or expertise. Any representation scheme has characteristic formal terms, often just nodes and links, which are used to express the content and structure of the knowledge. Those characteristic terms will vary in expressiveness; how well they reflect or make transparent the structure of the knowledge. The knowledge engineer's skill will of course make a difference but primarily, it is the *appropriateness* of the terms for a given domain which will determine how well the representation scheme fits the data of domain knowledge. It is quite reasonable to select the representation scheme on the basis of explicitness and first seek schemes which have well defined terms and for which there is a well understood structuring feature. The most abstract scheme is that of set theory. Here the well defined relationship of set membership with set algebra, elegant and simple as they are, do not adapt well, if at all, to the detail of human expertise. Set membership, union, intersection and complement are simply not expressive enough to reflect the colour of human knowledge. It may be that the notion of 'fuzzy' sets and 'fuzzy algebra' are more appropriate for human expertise but the convenience of well understood structures and methods for handling them is not readily available. Likewise the use of decimal fractions to represent a measure of *human* uncertainty still has a following in knowledge engineering. This despite the advice coming from Eshelman *et al.* (1987) about expert's resistance and the temptation to turn knowledge elicitation into rarefied number crunching. Neither of these representation forms are sufficiently expressive for human expertise, nor is the latter even well enough understood to be called explicit. Perhaps the most common form of knowledge representation language in the KBS field is the use of the IF–THEN rule. Here the computer led representation form is used as a knowledge elicitation 'tool'. Commonly the expert is asked to put his knowledge into rule form for rapid entry into a shell. Building a first generation expert system is typically not much more than a rule writing exercise. It has been known for a long time that the IF–THEN format is simply too bland to explicitly represent all the shades of knowledge which can be implemented and in fact can obscure distinctions. This is the familiar argument from Clancey (1983) on 'compiled knowledge'. Thus the IF–THEN format is not a good candidate for a mediating representation through lack of both expressiveness and explicitness.

With increasingly sophisticated workstations it is now possible to produce a diagrammatic representation of domain concepts which might be loosely termed a 'conceptual graph' or 'knowledge map'. These are networks with nodes and arrow links. Their success as mediating represen- tations is to be judged on an enquiry into how well the terms of the representation capture the spirit of the knowledge and whether the final structure is some way 'signals' incompleteness of the captured knowledge. While it is always possible to force the knowledge into a given formalism or tweak the terms to capture the world, the danger is that purpose-built terms (labels for concepts in the domain) can be made infinitely expressive but at the expense of becoming simply idiosyncratic and therefore lacking in explicitness. However, if we stick to well understood terms the knowledge simply will not fit. Conceptual hierarchies, taxonomies and conceptual graphs of whatever persuasion are prone to the twin failures of being either too elastic or too restricting depending on how the labels or names of concepts are generated. Thus, in the name of more disciplined knowledge elicitation one should expect to have not just a representation form but also guidelines on how the terms of the representation are mapped on to, selected, or generated from the primary elicitation data. A later paragraph (guidance in knowledge analysis) outlines one solution in terms of a process derived from sociological research method plus a commitment to checking the 'output' of the SGNs (the paradigms of section 4). If the process of constructing the structured knowledge is not also made explicit then it is likely that there will be no way of testing for adequacy and fit of structure to primary knowledge data and the representation form will fail to signal incompleteness.

Much of this process of using a representation scheme to construct a structured description of the knowledge can be done with pencil and paper. In fact the early stages *will* be done on paper, perhaps just sketching out possible relationships in order to train the expert into using an automated KA tool. Much more dangerous is the case with which terms may be displayed and elaborated upon until after the nth screen edit a collection of words and arrows transubstantiates into a schema or knowledge structure. (Figure 7 in Rappaport (1987) and Figure 5 in Gruber and Cohen (1987) are but two examples of a proliferating species.)

3.2 Economy and power

The notions of economy and power with respect to descriptions and theories is borrowed from linguistics. These notions suggest that a grammar should be economical in the sense that it assigns structure to *all* and *only* the sentences of a language. Thus mediating representations must capture all the relevant facts, opinions and relationships in the domain and exclude nonsense and contradiction. 'Relevant' here means with respect to the expert's conception. Representation schemes which generate conceptual absurdities or errors of fact are said to be too powerful for the data. Thus an induction algorithm, which even on a restricted set of examples still generates 'unsympathetic' rules, is not providing a good grammar (underlying structure) of the knowledge. While the induction algorithm can produce a finite set of rules, which, when chained together, match the output of human decision makers, it is not uncommon for analysts to be very disappointed in the lack of insight into the problem given by the induction analysis. There is as yet no evidence that representation schemes on paper or on a computer screen have been tested for economy and power. This demands a genuine commitment to empirical work which is almost unknown in knowledge engineering.

3.3 Communicability
The major distinguishing feature of a mediating representation scheme and a knowledge representation language is the purpose to which each is put. A knowledge representation language is a machine oriented scheme where the demands of implementation are entirely appropriate. The purpose of a mediating representation is to provide a grammar-like description of the knowledge for communication between humans in order that appropriate choices of architecture, knowledge representation language and HCI features may be made. It is suggested here that a graphical format is necessary, although never sufficient. Hence it comes as no surprise to hear that experts find critiquing individual rules or other forms of pseudo-code to be an uncongenial experience. Decision trees seem to fare better, but only when pruned! It is now even possible to display knowledge bases in the form of semantic networks on screen with integrity preserved under change. Unfortunately the facility to draw and redraw complex diagrams on screen does not guarantee that well structured accounts of knowledge will emerge. A picture of knowledge, no matter how detailed, will not automatically become a grammar. Nor will it necessarily make knowledge transparent to anyone else on the KBS team. Thus indiscriminate use of sophisticated graphics editors will not make knowledge elicitation, as a conceptual task, very much easier. This is not to say that the use of knowledge editors is to be discouraged. It is merely to say that in knowledge engineering we are not yet harnessing the power of available technology. We lack *methods* not the hardware or software.

3.4 Guidance in knowledge analysis
In the previous discussion of explicitness and expressiveness it was suggested that a sophisticated graphics editor, although desirable, can lead the unwary into producing visually and conceptually confused 'pictures of knowledge'. For the notion of a mediating representation advanced in this chapter we too

require the 'pictures' to be visual displays. But they are to be displays of *grammar-like* structures which reveal important features of the qualitative data arising from elicitation, not just human orientated displays of machine readable code or complex images of uninterpreted and unanalysed names for ideas. For the sake of good practice in knowledge elicitation we require the facility to be able to test the structure against the data for fit and descriptive adequacy. The toy example of the next section shows how this may be done in practice. In principle, we require the mediating representation to do two things:

- Support the process of deriving data driven concepts.
- Generate a description of the knowledge which can be tested against the original data for completeness and soundness (and subsequently against external sources).

In the first requirement, the Brunel group have adopted an approach based on grounded theory (Glaser and Strauss, 1967) and discussed by Bell and Hardiman (Chapter 2). Transcripts of interviews are read closely with much indexing, collating and memo writing to generate simple abstract terms which lift the analysis one step from the transcripts but with the analysis still 'grounded' in the original data. This is one way of tackling the gritty problem known to social scientists as 'forming data driven concepts' or 'qualitative data analysis'. For those using grounded theory the problem is perceived to be one of analysis at a conceptual or semantic level. In knowledge engineering the problem has often been approached through protocol analysis or 'transcript analysis' systems (e.g. KEATS) which only offer protection to the analysis of verbal protocols *after* the selection of 'important' or 'relevant' features of the domain knowledge have been made. These approaches would best be regarded as tools to clean up after a conceptual analysis. It can be argued that before entering any of the current KBS development environments there is always a conceptual analysis stage which is as yet unsupported and for which a mediating representation is essential. Moreover it seems that most knowledge engineers make fundamental choices about the character of the expertise well before entering the KBS environment, usually driven not by the data, but by what can be expressed, and later implemented in that particular environment. The application of denotational semantics to knowledge engineering dubbed ontological analysis (Alexander *et al.*, 1987) is one well publicised example where the formal notation, rather than the characteristics of the data, drives the conceptual analysis. In a less eccentric manner the KADS methodology (Cordingley, Chapter 3 and Wilson Chapter 5) exhorts us to use a 'model' to analyse the knowledge. The notion of models and levels of knowledge in the KADS system rests firmly upon a *computer* architecture which may or may not resemble a model of expertise. Looking to cognitive psychology to help is tempting but as yet not very helpful. A mature approach to KBS development based on the techniques associated with Personal Construct Theory (ETS in Boose, 1987; and PLANET in Gaines and Shaw, 1986) use cognitively real representations (in constructs) but falls far short of being able to represent a structure of an expert's tasks — a primary requirement in the development of second generation expert systems. For more on the topic of task structures and second generation systems see Clancy, 1984; Chandra-sekaran, 1986; and Keravnou and Johnson, 1986.

One solution, favoured by the Brunel Group, is to use the approach of grounded theory to generate names of distinctions in the domain and expertise and to encapsulate those in a Systemic Grammar Network (SGN). The SGN can be traversed to generate 'descriptions' of events or circumstances which ought to represent genuine points of interest in the domain. For example, an SGN which characterises strategies of chip designers could generate descriptions of possible histories of design decisions. These possible histories are suggested by and checked against the original interview transcripts and subsequently shown to other chip designers to 'test' for completeness and soundness. These networks display, in a concise graphical form, nodes whose names reflect the salient features of the domain and expertise. The few and simple links have the advantage of making the displays easy to absorb. The pseudo-code generated by traversing the SGN or picking out combinations of terminal items should describe *all* and *only* possible events of 'objects' in the expert's task. Thus the SGNs with supporting glossaries are custom built to provide a grammar of the task. By accepting the discipline of producing a grammar it is possible to be guided in a principled fashion through the knowledge analysis phase. By repeatedly asking the questions:

> Does our expert approve of the choice of terms used in the SGN?
> Does the total set of combinations (the paradigms illustrated in Fig. 4.3) adequately represent the possibilities the expert described during elicitation?
> Do the sequences of pseudo-code generated by passing through the network generate sensible characterisations of real events or objects with respect to the domain?
> Do the 'failures' say something about the SGN or about holes in the elicitation data?

a series of SGNs will evolve which capture much more of the flavour of the expertise and domain than is normally believed necessary. The short argument is that if explicitness is desirable, then a mediating representation is an essential tool and it should both guide the process and provide a fertile structural format.

4.   SGNs — AN EXAMPLE MEDIATING REPRESENTATION

A systemic grammar network is a well defined system, based on the idea of choice, with no standard rules of application. Essentially the notation provides an empty structure into which a chosen domain of knowledge may be fitted. The 'content free' property of networks is their most useful feature in knowledge analysis. Like other networks, a systemic network is a graph composed of nodes joined by links. All nodes are names invented by the analyst but suggested by the data. The most commonly used links are of two types, a mutually exclusive choice, denoted by a straight bracket and a co-occurring choice, denoted by a curly bracket as in Fig. 4.2. (There is also a recursion symbol and a conditional link.)

For the purpose of illustrating the heuristic use of SGNs imagine a simple classification problem of characterising the range of periodicals and newspapers found on news-stands outside a London Underground station. Our initial data is a collection of publications from one news-stand. The aim is to draw an SGN which will represent the distinguishing features (and attributes) of all the publications in such a way that we may individually characterise each example. By looking at a random collection of publications (for example, the newspapers *The Times*, the *Sun*, and periodicals *Country Life* and *Time Out*) we could form data-driven distinctions such as

Fig. 4.1.

and name the distinctions STATUS and FORMAT concatenating the distinctions thus

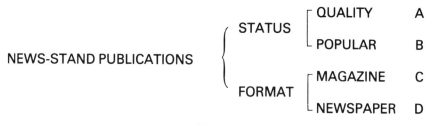

Fig. 4.2.

which can be read from left to right as

NEWS-STAND-PUBLICATIONS have two (co-occurring) features, a STATUS which is either QUALITY or POPULAR and a FORMAT which is either MAGAZINE or NEWSPAPER.

Notice the embryonic network was not constructed from left to right. In fact in this trivial case names for the extreme nodes (left and right) were first chosen and then a name for the middle distinction. This is common practice and at the heart of the heuristic role of SGN writing in knowledge analysis. For while names for the extreme terms may be obvious, the hardest and so most profitable mediation is done through sorting out the middle terms. The 'paradigm' of this network is the set of combinations

A(and)C   quality magazine

AD   quality newspaper

BC   popular magazine

BD   popular newspaper

Fig. 4.3.

which in the sense of Section 3 must 'mean' something in terms of the data. In this paradigm we have a potential characterisation of any individual publication. The most important question is 'Does the paradigm represent *all* and *only* the possibilities?' and for that we need to check with the newstand.

AC is realised as *Country Life*; AD as *The Times*; BC as *Woman's Own* and BD as the *Sun*. So far so good! But what about *BYTE, Buttons* or the *Jewish Chronicle*? Other data-driven distinctions are now suggested. Special Interest Group (SIG) is one example. This may be appended as in Fig. 5.4 where SIG is a distinction of the same rank as STATUS and

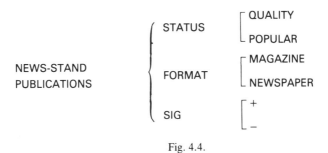

Fig. 4.4.

FORMAT or as in Fig. 4.5 where SIG is a distinction closer to status.

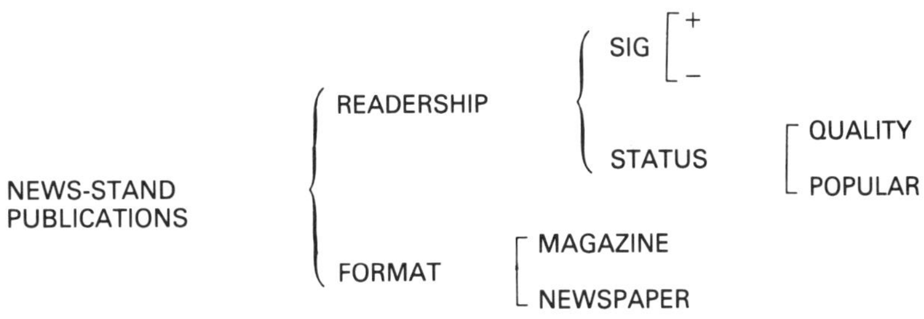

NEWS-STAND PUBLICATIONS
READERSHIP
SIG [+ / −]
STATUS [QUALITY / POPULAR]
FORMAT [MAGAZINE / NEWSPAPER]

Fig. 4.5.

A choice is made between Figs 4.4 or 4.5 on the basis of which structure best reflects the natural divisions of the domain as well as which structure is most economical. At this point the analyst would need to ask for the natural divisions of buying periodicals (seek more data). Thus *BYTE* is a quality, SIG magazine: the *Sun* is a popular, not SIG newspaper and *Buttons* still does not fit! Clearly we need to add more distinctions, COMIC or SHELF LIFE (daily, weekly, monthly, occasional) and eventually by continually testing paths and generating paradigms we could arrive at a one page SGN which was adequate for characterising the limited domain. Building an SGN which fits on to a single page is a desirable feature for readability. The number of distinctions added and the degree of 'delicacy' required will be guided by the purpose of the network and the depth of detail to be expressed. Thus, an SGN characterising peiodicals for printers might contain distinctions pertaining to page size and printing inks used whereas an SGN characterising periodicals for retail outlets might not.

Without checking out paradigms with the data, the focus or purpose of the network can shift and the structure degenerate into a standard AND/OR graph or decision tree. Any given publication may be characterised by a path through the network but it will be hard to see the range of possibilities (the paradigms) in that form of degenerate network.

In Figs 4.4 and 4.5 the names of the publications do not appear in the network. The network *characterises* the domain, it does not generate a representation of the domain. Of course this could be done in another SGN. Also other SGNs could be built to represent buying strategies or the vendor's layout policies. All such SGNs would have one thing in common, that the content is in the choice of nodes and not in the pre-chosen links. For communicability a glossary of the node names must be provided. Fortui-tously this is a welcome discipline in its own right. Bliss *et al.* (1983) provide a more complete account of the application of SGNs. Figure 4.6 is an example of an SGN produced during knowledge elicitation with an architect and an Occupational Therapist (OT) involved in designing for the disabled (Funes, 1987). This SGN is one of a series produced whilst trying to capture the knowledge required to assess the needs of disabled clients and recom-mend changes of abode, adaptations to the existing home or specific aids.

The purpose of Fig. 4.6 was to represent all the important considerations which must be taken into account from the point of view of the experts (architect and OT). In the time available it was not possible to do more than state each of the six left-hand distinctions as being of equal importance. There was insufficient evidence to make clear preferences between the six distinctions although no doubt our architect and OT had preferences which should be expressed. We can think of the absence of a differentiated structure of distinctions as a 'hole' in the SGN arising from lack of data. More elicitation could tease out a more differentiated structure. However, the fine detail of cost or medical condition was known but deliberately not represented at this level. That might be a hole in the network but not due to an absence of data. The analyst would argue that she chose the appropriate level of detail to make a point about the generic structure of the problem.

Looking back to the concerns of Section 3, while Figs 4.4 and 4.5 are not bona fide SGNs in so far as they are fictional, designed only to illustrate the nature of SGNs. Figure 4.6 is a real data-driven SGN and so can be assessed by the standards suggested for mediating representations, namely, fitting the data, being economical yet powerful and being a communication

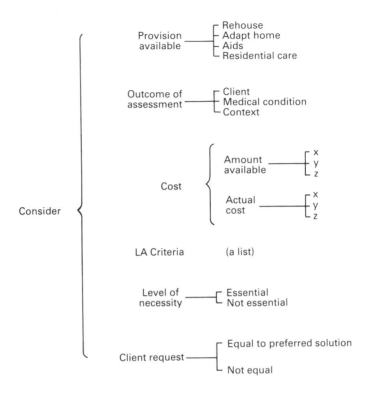

Glossary Term: LA Criteria: Local Authority Criteria

Fig. 4.6.

medium. From the expert's point of view the terms of the network are grounded in the data and are expressive enough to reflect salient features. Even a cursory glance at the paradigms of the network shows that they make reasonable sense. However, it is quite possible that elegance of structure has been sacrificed in favour of ease of reading. As a result of this it is likely that real flesh and blood client's histories do not exist for every single paradigm. Said more abstractly, this SGN may not be as economical as possible and is probably too powerful for the data. But it does (and did) function as a medium of communication. After all it is less arduous to 'interrogate' the SGN than to interrogate the original transcripts. Finally, the very existence of this and its sister SGNs is at least suggestive evidence of the ability of SGNs to guide knowledge analysis.

5 POSTSCRIPT

In this chapter much has been made of the notion of knowledge elicitation as a conceptual process requiring analytic skills by skilled (and human) knowledge engineers. The aim was not to undermine the use of automated knowledge acquisition techniques. The aim was to argue for a more disciplined approach to knowledge elicitation for practical efficiency and in the name of good research. At some point in the knowledge elicitation stage of a KBS project conceptual analysis needs to be done. Given that even now some of the conceptual analysis is done either before entering the knowledge engineering environment or is done outside of it in an *ad hoc* manner, it is reasonable to suppose that knowledge engineers are not getting the best from their elicited data through a lack of *methods* to support elicitation. The mediating representation was advanced as a fruitful idea to guide knowledge analysis. It was argued that a mediating representation should have some of the relationships to elicited knowledge that a grammar of a language has to language. The appropriate fit of structure to data was considered a primary characteristic. To achieve this the formalism used must at least be expressive, allow explicit representation of structure and provide an economical as well as apt structural description of the elicited knowledge in a communicable form. While any representation schema can fulfil some of these requirements. It was suggested through the examples in Section 4 that an SGN via the notion of a paradigm could get closer to fulfilling all the requirements. Furthermore that the discipline of testing the SGN against the data of elicited knowledge was of itself an essential part of knowledge elicitation.

Introduction to:
Task models for knowledge elicitation

In this chapter Wilson provides quite a different, alternative approach to how knowledge elicitation can be structured to that of Johnson in Chapter 4. In the absence of an adequate psychology, as discussed by Diaper in Chapter 1, Wilson proposes that what is needed is the development of a taxonomy of task types. The use of task analysis and its essential, psychological validity are discussed before a number of previously proposed taxonomies for structuring knowledge elicitation are criticised.

The notion of Generic Task Models is introduced as a basis for a consistent and useful task taxonomy that would serve the purpose of: identifying the types of knowledge that need to be acquired; selecting appropriate knowledge elicitation techniques from the set, for example, reviewed by Cordingley in Chapter 3; and directing the process of know-ledge analysis. However, Wilson concludes that only the first of these purposes is served by the currently available generic task models and he sees the other applications, along with issues such as the explanation facilities that should be provided by KBS, as 'still very much research issues'.

The KADS knowledge elicitation methodology is introduced as the 'most complete set of generic task models proposed both in breadth and in detail' and is used to illustrate how such task models may serve the knowledge engineer within the context of design tasks such as: routine design; re-design; innovative design; and creative design.

5

Task models for knowledge elicitation

Michael Wilson
Science and Engineering Research Council
Rutherford Appleton Laboratory

1. INTRODUCTION

In Chapter 3, Cordingley has designed the battery of techniques available to the knowledge engineer when faced with an expert. But the discipline of knowledge engineering has very little to say about what to look for during the analysis of elicited knowledge and which elicitation techniques to choose to make the analysis simplest. If the knowledge engineer is faced with Johnson's example problem in Chapter 4 of developing a KBS for choosing periodicals from a news-stand, which elicitation technique should be chosen? If interviewing is chosen as the elicitation technique which detailed questions should be asked after the initial questions to establish rapport with the experts — experts have a great deal of knowledge which could be elicited but is irrelevant to the task being investigated? If a sorting technique is chosen, which of the terms available from background reading and initial interviews should be selected and which discarded — it would usually take too long to use all the available terms? What should guide the knowledge engineer in making these judgements?.

In this chapter it is argued that to make these judgements efficiently knowledge engineers must hold clear views of the product of knowledge elicitation and the structure of the real world task before the elicitation begins. It is claimed that it is inefficient to elicit knowledge and then consider how to analyse it. It is necessary to consider the knowledge analysis, and therefore the likely structure of the knowledge, before embarking on any knowledge elicitation.

The product of knowledge elicitation will be a representation of knowledge relevant to the task and the processes that operate on the knowledge (e.g. inference strategies) which can be used as a basis for the design and implementation of a KBS. Various tasks in the world have already been analysed and KBS produced to perform them. Therefore a level of representation for the knowledge required for those tasks has already been established, and the inference strategies required to operate on that knowledge

ultimate aim of task based apps
be to produce —

have been described. If knowledge engineering were a better developed discipline it might to be possible to provide a manual which presented a taxonomy of task types and associated with each the most appropriate knowledge representation, the most likely inference strategy, and the techniques best suited to establishing them for any instance of the task encountered by knowledge engineers. Such a manual would direct knowledge engineers as to what they should ask in interviews, what to look for in interview transcripts, and which classes of terms to select for a sorting task. It would thereby guide knowledge engineers in making the judgements demanded by the news-stand example of a classification task, but also those required for other types of task. Unfortunately, knowledge engineering is not sufficiently developed for such a manual to exist.

As the discipline of knowledge engineering develops the components of such a manual will become available. Similarly, as a particular knowledge engineer's experience grows their personal version of such a manual will also develop. This chapter describes attempts to develop the parts of such a manual which describe models of tasks in the world and how they can be used to motivate the decisions made by the knowledge engineer during knowledge elicitation. Several research efforts are reviewed in order that individual knowledge engineers can develop their own manuals as their experience increases, without making the mistake which others have made before them.

In a recent article Hoffman (1987) criticises many papers whose titles indicate that they concern knowledge acquisition but actually contain discussion of abstract inference strategies and representations rather than models to extract knowledge from experts. This chapter is consistent with the body of literature he criticises. This is because a knowledge of abstract inference strategies and representations is necessary in order to make the decisions about which technique to use for knowledge elicitation, and more importantly, what to look for in the results.

2.   TASKS, KNOWLEDGE TYPES AND ELICITATION TECHNIQUES

Before reviewing developments in task models, and task taxonomies as they may aid knowledge engineers, it is necessary to show why a knowledge of tasks is the correct basis on which to make the judgements demanded in the opening paragraph of this chapter.

In order to do this it is necessary to sketch a simple history of knowledge engineering. It is generally acknowledged that people can perform tasks which conventionally developed software could not support or mimic in the early 1970s. The process of knowledge engineering was developed in order to map these tasks on to new types of software structure — which are now called knowledge-based systems. It was acknowledged that because these tasks were performed by humans, some knowledge of human psychology was required to understand their structure. Models of various areas of human psychology existed including semantic net, frame and production rule models of aspects of the memory system (see Conway and Wilson, 1988 for a review). Computer representations based on these models could be used to present some of the knowledge required by humans to perform the tasks. This aspect of knowledge engineering developed support tools such as shells and tool-kits. These had to include processes to act on the representations, so again some aspects of psychological modelling were incorporated, in the form of goal chaining mechanisms. These tools were further developed in a software engineering environment to optimise the code produced and improve the interface for programmers and users. The process of eliciting knowledge to be placed in these tools was then addressed in more detail. The details of interviewing methods for knowledge elicitation were then further developed from a knowledge of the social psychology of the interaction of two or more individuals. It is accepted from psychological theory that people can describe some but not all of the knowledge that they recruit to perform a task. Therefore interviewing techniques could not exclusively be used to elicit knowledge. The performance and psychological distance measures described in Chapter 3 by Cordingley were then added to the knowledge engineer's repertoire of techniques in order to elicit non-verbalisable knowledge. The method of knowledge engineering resulting from these developments is aimed at producing commerical KBS so the process has to be bounded by the constraints of development contacts and the product/client relationships.

In this brief history, the knowledge engineering method has been influenced by a knowledge of the psychology of human memory and information processing during task performance, software engineering, the psychology of self-description and recollection, and project management theory. The representations used in knowledge engineering have evolved though the influences of each of these disciplines. An initial structure has been proposed for a knowledge engineers' handbook of the type described above by relating the knowledge types used in these representations to the appropriate knowledge elicitation techniques. (e.g. Gammack and Young, 1985; Bainbridge, 1986; Slater, 1987; Welbank, 1987a, b, c). Because the knowledge types have been developed by the unrelated disciplines which have influenced knowledge engineering, the resulting classifications are hard to understand as coherent wholes and the arguments for the use of the different knowledge types are incompatible and contradictory. An example after Welbank (1987c) is shown in Table 5.1 which lists a series of techniques, and the knowledge types for which they have been shown by researchers to be suitable or inappropriate.

In the knowledge elicitation literature the types of knowledge presented in Table 5.1 are often described as the units of description which should be extracted from elicited knowledge during knowledge analysis. However, it would be very difficult to go through a transcript and decide if a sequence should be better categorised as a 'rule' or a 'procedure'. A procedure is a method for achieving a goal given some starting conditions, which psychological theory may describe as proceduralised knowledge. In a particular psychological theory of human memory and action this procedural knowledge may be represented as one, or a chainable sequence of, production

Table 5.1 — Types of knowledge with appropriate acquisition methods (after Welbank, 1987c). Key: Y = suitable; N = not suitable; ? = difficult, should be used with care. (Copyright 1987 SD-Scicon plc, reprinted by permission.)

	Facts	Conceptual structure	Causal knowledge	Rules	Weigth of evidence	Procedures	Expert's strategy	System's stategy	Context of rules	Explanation	Justification
Interview	Y	Y	Y	?	?		N		?		Y
Talking through case-studies	Y	N	Y	Y	N	Y	N		Y		
Observing interactions							Y		Y		
Protocol analysis					Y	Y					
Card-sorting		Y									
Multidimensional scaling		Y									
Repertory grid	Y	N	Y	Y	N	N					
Induction		N	Y								
Task analysis								Y			
User interviews								Y			'
Examining prototype				Y	Y				Y	Y	

Key:
Y yes
N no
? difficult, needs care

rules. In expert systems shells such rules are often used as part of the implementation language in contrast to 'facts' (these are usually shells based on the early MYCIN medical expert system). Facts are a way of representing the declarative relationship in an implementation between a small number of items. In psychological theory the set of facts relevant to a problem may be described as the 'conceptual structure' of the problem domain. Therefore, like rules and procedures, facts and conceptual structure are not discretely orthogonal in a taxonomy of knowledge types. When looking at transcripts the knowledge engineer may take in informal distinction between rules which appear as conditional actions and procedures which appear as sequences of such actions. A similar practical distinction may be made between facts and the conceptual structure of a domain. However, in both cases the distinction between the types of knowledge is that one of each pair of terms arose from psychology and the other from an implementation language.

The knowledge types 'context of rules', 'weight of evidence' and 'explanation' arise from the implementation representations used in shells for limited problem types. The context of rules and weight of evidence are used in some probabilistic reasoning systems to derive conclusions. The use of an explanation type of knowledge requires the assumption that some knowledge is used to reason with and other knowledge is used to explain that reasoning to users. The knowledge engineer must determine the scope of the task in order to decide which knowledge will be used to reason about the task, and, if a distinction is appropriate, which will be used to explain it. There is no underlying distinction between these knowledge types in tasks as they are performed or described by experts.

The inclusion of 'expert's strategy' and 'system's strategy' types of knowledge requires the assumption that for any task type these will be an appropriate inference strategy. An implementation language may have a single strategy built into it or it may be possible to specify the one appropriate for a problem. The knowledge engineer must know what range of inference strategies are likely to be encountered and how they vary across problem or task types in order to identify them.

Most of these terms have their roots in some aspect of psychology. Many of the knowledge types have since been constrained or modified to fit the implementation vehicles available. Others such as 'expert's strategy' and 'system's strategy' have been introduced to permit methods and tools to address tasks for which they were not originally designed. The resulting list of knowledge types is not clearly delineated, with the consequence that the knowledge engineer's task of selecting elicitation techniques on the basis of knowledge types expected and analysing knowledge into the categories is confused. If the knowledge engineer is restricted to the types of knowledge derived from the implementation language, then the analysis process and the resulting knowledge will be contaminated by trade-offs made between what the expert actually states and what the implementation language can represent. Conversely, if the knowledge engineer is limited to categories derived from psychological theory then the analysis will be restricted to high level descriptions which will not provide the detail necessary to efficiently develop simple, understandable KBS which can be shown to be correct and can be modified as knowledge changes. KBS which do have such properties will be slow and expensive to develop and will have a short lifespan if they are acceptable at all. As Diaper discusses in Chapter 1, although psychological theory may develop to the level where it can provide the detailed distinctions required in knowledge engineering it is currently inadequate at providing more than high level descriptions.

While psychological theory is developing to the state where it can provide the distinctions required by knowledge engineering an interim solution must be developed which will allow knowledge to be elicited and analysed for a wide range of tasks. One interim solution using a grammar-based mediating representation in the analysis of vebalisable knowledge is presented by Johnson in Chapter 4 of this volume. A second interim solution which should be amenable to a wider range of psychological theory is to rationally contruct a taxonomy of the task types to be addressed, analyse these tasks to determine the processes (e.g. inference strategies) and representations (e.g. knowledge types) relevant to them, and then relate this rational set of processes and representations to elicitation analysis and implementation methods. For this approach to result in a single consistent model of processes and representations which are psychologically valid, the technique used to analyse the tasks must itself be psychologically valid.

3. TASK ANALYSIS

Task analysis techniques divide tasks into components which are usually of pre-specified types. It is this pre-specification of types of components and the relationships those types can hold which differentiates descriptions resulting from the use of task analysis techniques from informal descriptions of tasks in natural language. The pre-specified component types often take the form of sub-tasks where the actions taken and the classes of objects they affect are characterised. The sub-tasks, action and object classes are usually derived from previous analysis, using the available theoretical base. Methods of task analysis have a long history of use in the social/behavioural sciences for breaking tasks into behaviorally (e.g. Miller, 1962), or cognitively (e.g. Rasmassen, 1986; Barnard, 1987) salient units.

A handbook of the type described in the introduction of this chapter would constitute a task analysis method for knowledge elicitation. The pre-specified components would include control processes and knowledge types. The analysis technique would include methods for identifying which control processes and knowledge types were relevant to a task, and which methods should be used to elicit the knowledge for those types. The representation used in such an analysis would not be designed for communication between the knowledge engineer and experts. The task analysis would allow the segmentation of the problem space into units with specified expected knowledge and process types. The analysis technique would describe how the knowledge engineer should choose appropriate elicitation techniques for these units which would include their own mediating representations as discussed by Johnson in Chapter 4 of this volume. The task analysis would then guide the knowledge engineer to look for the expected knowledge in the analysis of the elicited information. To develop such an analysis technique requires the development of a suitable taxonomy of tasks to locate the relevant knowledge and process types.

A variety of knowledge acquisition regimes have been presented in the literature (e.g. Frieling et al., 1985) although most are still informal and unproven. In a generalised regime of knowledge elicitation, such a task analysis technique would take place early in the method to direct later domain knowledge gathering:

(1) Initial problem assessment to determine if KBS offers a cost effective solution?
(2) Initial study of documents and first interviews.
(3) Task analysis.
(4) Full interviews/ performance protocols/indirect measures/simulation.
(5) Develop the intermediate representation.

(6) Re-formulate conceptual structure of the intermediate representation for a particular tool.

In order to allow the tasks which contain different component types to be identified during task analysis it is necessary to generate a structured taxonomy of them. Clancy (1985) observes that 'attempts to make knowledge engineering a systematic discipline often begin with a listing of problem types' which are prone to category errors. Clancy illustrates this with a list of 'problems' or task types which includes: 'design', 'constraint satisfaction' and 'model-based reasoning'. These can also be classed as a type of task, an inference method and a kind of knowledge. Clancey neatly exemplifies the different nature of these terms by combining them into a hypothetical description of VLSI chip design using constraint satisfaction to reason about models of circuit components. To avoid this kind of confusion it is necessary to develop a systematic description of task types at the same level of description, and then to specify the classes of knowledge types. In knowledge elicitation and KBS research such types are often called 'generic tasks'.

4.   GENERIC TASKS FOR KNOWLEDGE ELICITATION

The first problem is one of describing the 'appropriate' level of task. For example, in the task of finding the number of a chemist in a yellow pages directory, one analysis might say that the task is 'to find the number' and that it has an input which is an ill-defined description of the role of the agent whose number is being searched for, and the output is the number itself; consequently, the search is a unitary operation: that is, a single task. A second description might say that the task can be further sub-divided into taking the description and performing an action of comparing it with the headings in a directory until one of them is an acceptable match, then looking down the list of entries under this heading to find one which matches secondary criteria (such as geographical proximity to the searcher) and the result of this match is the output. A third description may subdivide the search task even further and describe the processes which take place during the match in great detail. Such an analysis would describe the perception of the characters on the page and the formulation of words from them, then the matching of these words with memory. This level of description is more detailed but also has a superficial appearance of being more psychologically salient since it incorporates stores such as memory and operations such as human perception. How can knowledge engineers determine in this structure of possible descriptions of a task which is the one that is the most appropriate for the building of KBS's? The answer must be influenced not only by a desire to capture the psychological reality of the description, but also by the computational and functional constraints imposed by the purpose of the desired KBS itself.

A confusion which arises at this point is in determining which task is being described. Experts perform tasks in their natural environments. The

KBS when built will also interact with its user to perform a task thus creating a new environment. The expert may be a cardiac specialist working in a hospital cardiac unit. In contrast the user may be a nurse in the outpatients department who must decide quickly whether to refer patients to the cardiac unit (e.g. Wyatt and Emerson, 1988). Two very different tasks are being performed here, and the task the KBS is performing is only a part of the second task. What is required is an analysis which will map the task performed by the expert (e.g. the cardiac specialist) into the task performed by the KBS (e.g. the non-specialist's tool). It is accepted that there are various different roles such tools can play with respect to the user: adviser, imperative guru, criticising co-worker or teacher. Each of these different roles will require different knowledge to support them, and consequently different knowledge to be acquired by the knowledge engineer. For example, a system in the role of an imperative guru does not require a deep model of the problem to use as the basis for persuasive explanation whereas a critiquing system does. It would be preferable if the task analysis technique would account for the final role of the system in its environment. However, before the task the system is to perform is analysed, the expert's task should be investigated, although it may be different from that performed by the delivered system (Diaper discusses this further in Chapter 1 of this volume).

Returning to the issue of selecting the appropriate 'grain' of analysis, task analyses in other areas of research have performed analyses at levels of description which appear to possess too little detail, intuitively the right level of detail and too much detail. The results of these different levels of analysis of example tasks have then been instantiated in the available technology and the consequences of using the technology on them have been compared with a view of what the desired output should be. This form of sensitivity analysis has shown in previous cases what the appropriate practical level of description is for the available technology (e.g. Card et al., 1983). An attempt can be made to apply the same method of the techology of KBS's. What is required is the level of description of a task which is appropriate for both the technology available to implement it and for the human expert who has to describe it to the knowledge engineer. Thus this technique requires the analyses of tasks previously performed to derive a taxonomy of generic tasks at the appropriate level for knowledge elicitation.

One source of previously analysed tasks that can be used are previously developed KBS. To illustrate the grain of tasks such as an analysis will provide (after Clancy, 1985), the structure of the task of configuring the components of VAX computers performed by R1 (McDermott, 1982) with its order processing front end XSEL could be described as:

SPECIFY + DESIGN { + ASSEMBLE }

while that for the task which the diagnostic medical expert system MYCIN (Shortliffe and Buchanan, 1975) performs could be characterised as:

MONITOR (patient state) + DIAGNOSE (disease category)
+ IDENTIFY (bacteria) + MODIFY (body system or organism)

Before attempting to establish a taxonomy of generic tasks at this level of description, it is necessary to specify what it is useful to state about each task. Since the generic task description is intended to be psychologically valid this will be constrained by the sensitivity of currently applicable psychological theory. A recent review of task analysis techniques relevant to user interface design (Wilson *et al.*, 1988) assesses techniques under four headings:

Knowledge. The breadth of knowledge classes addressed by the technique and the depth of description (i.e. grain) offered of these classes.

Task dynamics. The goals of the task performer, the short-term changes that take place during task performance (in both processing and actions on external objects) and the long-term changes that take place across successive performances of a task (e.g. learning).

Cognitive limitations on processing. The extent to which a functional cognitive model is embodied in the technique and any constraints on cognition which are incorporated in the technique (e.g. capacity, rate).

Use of the technique. How well the technique is unambiguously specified and how much additional skill and knowledge is required to use it.

Applying these criteria to task analyses for knowledge elicitation, the desirable technique would need to include a taxonomy of generic task types, a set of models for each generic task and guidance as to how to elicit the knowledge relevant to each task. Models of generic tasks should address these criteria in the following ways.

To describe the knowledge required to perform the task will require an indexing of the generic task model into the taxonomy of task models and some rules as to their combination. Otherwise, it will take the form of the type of knowledge output by the task (the type of solution), the classes of objects expected, and the classes of attributes that those objects should have. The knowledge available from different knowledge sources (e.g. guidelines, manuals, databases) should be indicated separately.

The task dynamics would include the goals of the task and, to map the model on to the system representation, a description of the inference strategy that is expected for the task in order to account for the short-term changes. The inference strategy will of course interact with and constrain the knowledge of the objects in the task. The long-term changes in the task performance should be decribed as requirements for explanation of the task and requirements for maintaining a model of the task as information changes.

The technique should be stated so that it is easy to use to analyse tasks without the knowledge engineer having to bring a large amount of psychological or other specialist knowledge to it.

Consequently, the generic task model should contain:

- The type of problem the generic task addresses.
- The inference mechanism/strategy expected.
- The form of knowledge used in the solution.

- The classes of objects expected.
- The classes of attributes expected.
- The type of explanation mechanism which is required.
- Requirements and methods for maintaining task knowledge.

The generic task models do not contain user goals since they are to be used in eliciting knowledge of the expert's or source task and not in designing the interface to the task which the user of a KBS developed to perform it will himself perform. Although it may be desirable for generic task models to contain real-time changes in task performance this description does not suggest that they should since these will vary at a lower level of description than the knowledge included in the generic task model from which they are derived. Elicitation techniques using performance measures as data can be used to translate such real-time changes into temporally constrained knowledge (e.g. Wilson *et al.*, 1985).

The task analysis technique will therefore consist of a taxonomy of generic task models each of which contain the information in the above form and a technique for using them to analyse tasks and produce instantiated task models (task descriptions) for particular tasks. Such a technique does not yet exist. We do not yet have a standard set of generic task models which can be fitted to all the tasks which the knowledge engineer is likely to encounter. The goal of several research groups is to develop these, but at present the partial analyses which they have put forward are the best available. These analyses vary as to the task types addressed and the content of the generic task models proposed. The types of task to which KBS's have been applied for the longest are classification and diagnostic tasks, so this group of tasks has been most thoroughly described, whereas the analysis of design tasks is less well developed. As more task types are identified, the structure of the set of generic tasks changes.

The sets of generic tasks proposed by different groups of researchers will be described here to illustrate the methods used for developing task taxonomies and generic task models, as well as the direction of development that current research in this area is taking. Knowledge engineers can expand the set of generic task models themselves with their own experience of developing systems for new tasks. Those presented here are to be used as examples on which to base such development, they do not constitute the only or the best models possible. However, they do provide warnings of knowledge engineers so that flaws previously encountered need not be introduced into their own structures.

The progression illustrated by these examples starts by looking at KBS which have already been developed and attempts to categorise these objects into systematic lists. Then, the tasks which are performed by these various systems are extracted from the whole system and described. This list of tasks is then structured with respect to a theory of systems, and what tasks can be performed on them. Further analyses of tasks performed outside the KBS domain are then introduced to add to this categorisation. Finally, an attempt is made to map the taxonomy that exists on to a cognitive rather than system orientated view of tasks.

Design tasks will be described in more detail than classification and diagnostic tasks since the knowledge engineer who has to tackle design tasks will find less support from current tools and less information on them in the literature, much of which is less accessible than information on other task types.

5.   GENERIC CATEGORIES OF KNOWLEDGE ENGINEERING APPLICATIONS

The first major attempt to structure a set of task models for KBS development was that of Hayes-Roth *et al.* (1983) when they presented a list of generic categories of knowledge engineering applications (see Table 5.2).

Table 5.2 — Generic categories of knowledge engineering applications (after Hayes-Roth *et al.*, 1983)

Category	Problem addressed
Interpretation	Inferring situations from sensor data
Prediction	Inferring likely consequences from a given situation
Diagnosis	Inferring system malfunctions from observables
Design	Configuring objects under constraints
Planning	Designing actions
Monitoring	Comparing observations to plan vulnerabilities
Debugging	Prescribing remedies for malfunctions
Repair	Executing a plan to administer a prescribed remedy
Instruction	Diagnosis, debugging and repairing student behaviour
Control	Interpreting, predicting, repairing, and monitoring system behaviour

These were put forward as distinct types of knowledge engineering applications rather than as generic task models to aid knowledge elicitation. However, the objective of the list was to aid the extraction, articulation and computerisation of experts' knowledge so they serve as a starting point to show the direction in which research is progressing. In explaining this and later classifications the word *system* is used in the sense of any operating process, machine, organisation or device and should not be read in the narrower sense of a computer system of KBS. To contrast with this the term KBS is often used over-restrictively here.

In their analysis, interpretation KBS infer descriptions of system states from observable data about the state. They are used to explain observed data by assigning symbols to them which describe a system state that accounts for the data in systems such as those used for surveillance or speech understanding. Prediction KBS infer the likely consequences of described states in systems such as those used for weather forecasting. Diagnosis KBS infer system malfunctions from described data for such purposes as medical diagnosis or electronic fault finding. Design KBS develop configurations of objects that satisfy the constraints of design problems such as circuit layout or building design. Planning KBS design actions which take place over time. Monitoring KBS compare observations of system behaviour to features that are important to the successful outcome of plans and normally correspond to potential flaws in plans. Debugging KBS prescribe remedies for failures while repair systems develop and excute plans to administer remedies to diagnosed problems. Instruction KBS diagnose student behaviour and attempt to debug it. Control KBS adaptively govern the overall behaviour of a system.

The Hayes-Roth *et al.*, classification of KBS and task types is one of the earliest and thus it is one of the most discussed and criticised. It has been criticised (e.g. Reichgelt and Van Harmalen, 1986) because some of the classes used are more general types of other classes. The criticism is clearly appropriate for several cases: debugging KBS may monitor a system, diagnosis a malfunction, then plan a remedy, and may execute the plan; repair KBS always both plan and execute the plan; instruction KBS monitor, diagnose, plan a remedy and execute the plan; control KBS contain most of the above primitive acts. It is therefore clear that this is not a list of either primitive KBS types or of primitive tasks which should be combined together to produce the task performed by KBSs or experts. It is in fact a list of KBS types that have been developed and classified by the way the developers or users see their roles.

A set of primitive tasks have been produced from this list by Reichgelt and Van Harmalen. They argue that the difference between *diagnosis* and *interpretation* tasks is that while both infer a state description from data, the state description in a diagnosis KBS must be a malfunction while interpretation KBS have no constraint on the type of state they infer. Consequently they view diagnosis KBS as a sub-class of interpretation KBS. Similarly, they argue that planning KBS are a sub-class of design KBS, where the design is a temporally executable plan, and that debugging KBS are a sub-class of planning KBS where the plan is always directed at correcting a malfunction. This argument results in four primitive types of task: interpretation (or classification), monitoring, prediction (or simulation), design.

As with Hayes-Roth *et al.*, Reichgelt and Van Harmalen were looking for a set of tasks which can be used as the building blocks for KBS control structures rather than tasks which could be identified during a knowledge elicitation rather than psychological saliency, it offers a further step on route to a psychologically salient set of task models.

Reichgelt and Van Harmalen draw a distinction between tasks which recursively *monitor* a system's outputs over time and compare them with a plan, and tasks which take a system's outputs (possibly over time) and *classify* them on to a high level description. The distinctions between several tasks are confounded here. The first task translates input data into internal form. A second task classifies sets of internal data (which may be directly re-coded external data or inferred information) against a set of higher level descriptions. There is a third task which outputs higher level descriptions to the user, and a fourth which outputs higher level descriptions into internal form (stored inferences). There is also a distinction as to whether the high level description is a temporal plan, or an atemporal object description. The first three tasks performed once each in succession using atemporal object descriptions make up the *classification* task. The *monitoring* task consists of a cycle of taking input data, classifying it against a temporal plan and storing inferences, with the task of outputting inferences only being introduced when a particular classification (usually an error) is reached. This confounding has serious consequences for Reichgelt and Van Harmalen's purpose of developing machine representations, but may not be a problem for knowledge elicitation since this description appears too detailed to be cognitively salient. However, it is a confounding which has consequences for later arguments in this chapter.

The *simulation* task starts with a system and a requirement for change, and the dependent changes must be inferred. It is usually impossible to enumerate all the possible solutions to such problems in advance. The structure of the task involves a bottom-up control regime whereby changes in the state of the system are interpreted as changes in the behaviour of sub-systems. This information can then be used to predict the changes in the behaviour of the overall system. Consequently, the entities which will exist in this task will include a system, its component sub-systems, features of these which will change, and the mechanisms by which the sub-systems interact.

Since the planning and design tasks of Hayes-Roth *et al.* appeared to differ only in as far as the product was temporally constrained or not, the fourth task Reichgelt and Van Harmalen propose is a general *design* task which involves the construction of a complex entity to meet certain constraints. These constraints will specify both the target or end state and the present state. The present state may be a set of simple component entities which will be specified with constraints as to their combination that will have to be met when constructing the complex entity. In this analysis, the entity under construction may be a spatial system such as a building, or a temporal configuration of actions such as a plan. The major difference between this and the previous tasks is that they were analytical whereas design is synthetic and the solution cannot be found in a predetermined set of possible solutions. There may be conditions under which the solution space is enumerable, although usually it is too large. Reichgelt and Van Harmalen do not further analyse the sub-types of design task or describe the cases where the solution space may be enumerable.

A second criticism of Hayes-Roth *et al.* has been provided by Clancey (1985). He notes the same progressive subsumption in the list as did Reichgelt and Van Harmalen, but he attempts to overcome it by addressing the concept of a *system* in greater detail and trying to avoid the confusions that arise from viewing the types of system as *objects.*, because it is unclear whether programs or procedures are objects or processes. This distinction should not be dismissed as only being relevant to machine representational issues as it does bear on the way the tasks involved in knowledge elicitation are views and analysed.

Hayes-Roth *et al.* describe knowledge as consisting of descriptions, relations and procedures in some domain of interest, although they accept that in practice knowledge does not appear in some precipitated form that neatly fits such abstract categories. Although they differentiate between knowledge and skill, they do not describe a method for analysing a particular problem into generic units during knowledge elicitation. Although Reichgelt and Van Harmalen do not describe the content of their generic tasks in the detail requested above, Clancey takes both the generic task description and the taxonomy itself much further.

6. SYSTEM-BASED GENERIC OPERATIONS

Clancey (1985) argues that a system can be characterised simply in terms of inputs and outputs. He assumes that tasks will either interpret what exists in a system or construct a new system. This results in the tasks of *interpretation* which is similar Reichgelt and Van Harmalen's *classification* (or interpretation) and *construction* which is similar to their *design*. At this level he does not appear to account for their other two tasks. However, Clancey describes both *monitoring* and *simulation* (or prediction) as sub-types of *interpretation* since he provides a hierarchy of task types under each of his two major headings rather than limiting himself to a single dimensional list. His complete hierarchies are shown in Table 5.3.

Table 5.3 — Generic operations (after Clancey, 1985)

Interpret			working system
|	identify		take input and map it on to system knowledge
|	|	monitor	detect discrepancy
|	|	diagnose	explain monitored discrepancy
|	predict		describe outputs for given inputs
|	control		describe inputs to produce given outputs
Construct			Non-working system
|	specify		construct a system description
|	design		conceptual construction
|	|	configure	organise objects as a structure
|	|	plan	organise objects within a process
|	assemble		physical construction of a system
|	|	modify	change the structure of an existing system

The *interpret* tasks all operate on an existing system. Consequently, that existing system can give outputs which can be taken in and *identified* by comparing them with a knowledge base of design and either simply categorise the current state in the system by *monitoring*, or explain that state in terms of discrepancies between the actual system and a standard system. The existing system can be given inputs and the *predict* task used to determine what the outputs of that system would be. Alternatively, a known system may be required to produce known ouputs, in which case the control task can be used to generate the inputs that would be required.

All tasks which operate on a system may be classified by the binary choice of analysis (interpretation) or synthesis (construction) at the top level. The analysis tasks can be broken down into the three categories of recognition (identification), prediction and control on the basis of whether the single unknown is the input, output or system itself.

There is a conflict between the *monitoring* and *classifying* tasks proposed by Reichgelt and Van Harmalen and the *monitoring* and *diagnosing* tasks suggested by Clancey which is worth further examination. A confounding was shown above in the distinction between Reichgelt and van Harmalen's two tasks. This was due to the way in which they accounted for time in both the performance of the task and the type of descriptions being used for the classification. The monitoring may occur at one time or recursively, and the data structure could be temporal or not. Clancey's tasks both take place on a 'running' system and detect a deviation from a standard. He does not distinguish between whether the description is temporal or not, but between whether the task involves the 'detection' of discrepancies or 'explains' the monitored behaviour in terms of discrepancies. That is, the output from *monitoring* is a less rich description than that from *diagnosis*. As with Reichgelt and Van Harmalen's distinction, both tasks include the same initial input of data, and the distinction between them arises with the process which produces a different output from each task. For Clancey, the *simulation* task is subsummed as a special task of *prediction* where a computational model which is complete at a known level of detail is used to predict the outputs resulting from known inputs. This is not the same as Reichgelt and Van Harmalen's *simulation* where a system itself is modified in a simulation and then its outputs can be tested for known inputs and its inputs tested for known outputs. These two tests correspond to Clancey's *simulation* and *control* tasks, although the modification prior to the testing is a *construction* task.

Whereas Reichgelt and Van Harmalen only described one task which covered all forms of design, modification, construction or planning, Clancey provides a richer analysis of these tasks. The first task of the *construct* type is *specify* which refers to the operation of constraining a system specification in respect of both other defined systems and the real world. *Assemble* is a general task referring to the physical construction of a system. This task would require robot assembly in a computer system performing the task. The one sub-task *modify* is included to cover the transformation of a system to effect a redesign by 're-assembly' given a required design modification.

Design is characterised as a general conceptual operation describing the spatial and temporal interactions of components including a characterisation of both structure and process. Having united them under the same task of *design* Clancey then draws a distinction between the two tasks of *configuration* and *planning* which had existed in Hayes-Roth *et al.*'s analysis. Reichgelt and Van Harmalen's arguments for the computational equivalence of the two tasks are not being denied here. Clancey's use of a hierarchical structure of tasks permits both the computational generality and the colloquial distinction to be expressed which their list would not. However, Clancey does not use the temporal nature of plans as the basis for his distinction. The *configure* task pieces together components into a whole so that the functional totality will show desired properties. A typical example of this would be VLSI design where physical components are pieced together so that the behaviour of the parts interact to produce the desired system behaviour. In contrast the *planning* task does not operate on well-structured systems but on a general system (e.g. the world) which surrounds and transforms an entity (e.g. a person).

Chandrasekaran and his co-workers (Brown and Chandrasekaran, 1986; Bylander and Chandrasekaran, 1987, pp. 236, 237) have produced a potential generic task model for the *configure* task which they suggest can not only act as a component of a KBS but also be used to guide knowledge elicitation:

Problem type: object synthesis by plan selection and refinement.

Problem: Design an object satisfying specifications. An object can be an abstract device, e.g. a plan or program.

Representation: The object is represented in a component hierarchy in which the children of a node represent components of the parent. For each node, there are plans that can be used to set parameters of the component and to specify additional constraints to be satisfied. There is additional knowledge for selecting the most appropriate plan and to recover from failed constraints.

Important concepts: The object and its components.

Inference strategy: To design an object, *plan selection and refinement* selects an appropriate plan, which, in turn requires the design of sub-objects in a specified order. When failure occurs, failure handling knowledge is applied to make appropriate changes.

Examples: Routine design of devices and the synthesis of everyday plans can be performed using the generic task, e.g. MOLGEN (Friedland, 1979), R1 (McDermott, 1982).

This generic task model does not provide information on the explanation mechanism required for the task, nor any guidance in maintaining the system. Also, the description of the representation is very implementation orientated, and would be of little use in guiding questions during knowledge elicitation, but it illustrates a step closer to the desired generic task description than those offered by earlier analyses.

However, these general descriptions still do not offer a specification of the structure of knowledge required which is detailed enough to motivate knowledge elicitation.

7. GENERIC TASK MODELS IN KADS

The most complete set of generic task models proposed both in breadth and in detail are presented in the KADS knowledge elicitation methodology. This is currently under development (see Breuker and Weilinga, 1987; Hayward, 1987) and a complete task taxonomy and library of task models will be available in the *KADS Handbook* with supporting software tools (see Anjewierden, 1987). Table 5.4 shows an initial taxonomy of problem types from this methodology which is a development of that presented by Clancey. These tasks are intended to be accepted by knowledge engineers as the appropriate categories. However, is is assumed here that knowledge engineers will modify any taxonomy of tasks on the basis of their own experience and therefore the reasons why the distinctions have been made will be described to provide a basis for personalisation.

The top level categories of *analysis* and *synthesis* are similar to Clancey's *interpret* and *construct* tasks. In Clancey's analysis there was some confusion about whether systems should exist or merely that designs for systems be known. Similarly, it was not clear that *modify* was a valid form of assembly since a system had to exist for the *modification* to take place, whereas it could not for *assembly*. To overcome these doubts the third category of *modification* has been introduced to illustrate that a continuum and not a discrete cut-off exists between *analysis* tasks, where a solution has to be identified, and *synthesis* tasks, where a solution has to be constructed.

The analysis tasks here are an expansion of Clancey's *interpretation* tasks. The use of a hierarchy has permitted the further differentiation of these on the basis of principles already mentioned.

The *synthesis* tasks, however, are somewhat different to Clancey's. The top level classification is made on the type of input and output that the task has. Design tasks take functional requirements as their input and produce descriptions of an artefact as output. The distinction from Hayes-Roth *et al.* between *design* operating on artefacts and *planning* on temporal events has been revived here despite the criticisms made of it earlier. Otherwise these two tasks are the same. The *modelling* task takes the same inputs as design, but in addition it requires a set of 'data' of which the solution must be an abstraction. In many cases descriptions of component elements must be abstracted from the data. The output of the task is a description of an artefact as for design. The *transformation* task takes as input a description of an artefact and a known transformation to apply to it. The output is a description of a new artefact after the trasnformation has been applied. This is a task which could be classified as either design or modification, illustrating the continuum that exists between them.

The set of generic task models proposed for design tasks in KADS is richer than any of the previous sets. The generic task model for general

Table 5.4 — Taxonomy of problem types (after Breuker *et al.*, 1987)

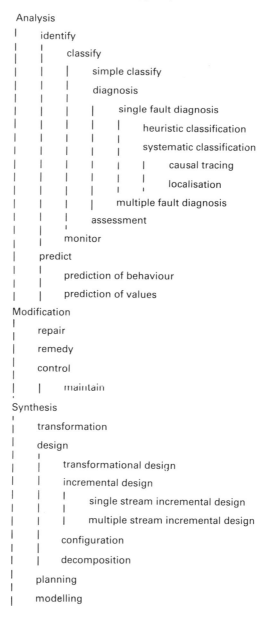

```
Analysis
|    identify
|    |    classify
|    |    |    simple classify
|    |    |    diagnosis
|    |    |    |    single fault diagnosis
|    |    |    |    |    heuristic classification
|    |    |    |    |    systematic classification
|    |    |    |    |    |    causal tracing
|    |    |    |    |    |    localisation
|    |    |    |    multiple fault diagnosis
|    |    |    assessment
|    |    monitor
|    predict
|    |    prediction of behaviour
|    |    prediction of values
Modification
|    repair
|    remedy
|    control
|    |    maintain
Synthesis
|    transformation
|    design
|    |    transformational design
|    |    incremental design
|    |    |    single stream incremental design
|    |    |    multiple stream incremental design
|    |    configuration
|    |    decomposition
|    planning
|    modelling
```

design task can be used to illustrate the greater depth of description that KADS achieves over the earlier attempts.

It is assumed that design is a process whereby an entity must be synthesised to conform to a collection of specified requirements or constraints. The requirements are usually ill-specified, therefore the first stage of the design task is to analyse the informal requirements and to produce a formal specification. The second stage of the task will be to synthesise a detailed design from the formal specification. There are therefore five concepts involved at this level of description: two processes — *analysis* and *synthesis* — and three objects — *informal requirements, formal specification* and *detailed design*. The process of analysis can be performed on the informal specification by either its *expansion* or its *transformation*.

This model is further elaborated in KADS to take into account the conceptual model of the final product which specifies the structure of the product entity. This conceptual model is required for design tasks that involve configuration since the global structure of the product object is not specified in these. This conceptual model will have been developed prior to the detailed design from the formal specification. Therefore the single process of *synthesis* must be decomposed since a process is required to *select* or *aggregate* elements of the formal specification into the conceptual model. A second process is required to *transform*, expand or *refine* this conceptual model into the final detailed design. The resulting structure for the design process is shown in Figure 5.1.

Earlier in this chapter it was suggested that a generic task model should contain not only the type of problem the task would address and the inference mechanism, but also the form of knowledge used in the solution. The KADS system has presented a taxonomy of problem types, including sub-types of design. It has included in the description of design various objects and processes. For the first time in this series of task models these are further expanded to describe the type of knowledge expected in each. For example, the object *informal problem statement* is described as (after Breuker *et al.*, 1987).

> *meta-class* **informal problem statement**. This is the input of the design process, an informally formulated specification of the structure to be designed. Examples: input/output specification, specification by analogy, description, component/function specification.
>
> *consists of:* **informal_system_specification** constraints, requirements.

Similarly, the other object types are described as meta-classes of objects, and have types within the metaclass further defined and exemplified. In the same way, the processes are described, although in the terminology of KADS these are called *knowledge sources* following the use of that phrase in blackboard models. For example, the process which builds a formal specification from an informal specification of a problem is described as (after Breuker *et al.*, 1987).

> *knowledge source:* **transformation and expansion** These knowledge sources build a complete formal specification of the system to be built.
>
> *input:* **informal problem statement** This is a description of the problem that does not necessarily include all parameters, function and constraints, but just the major ones.
>
> *Output:* **formal specification** The formal specification is a description of

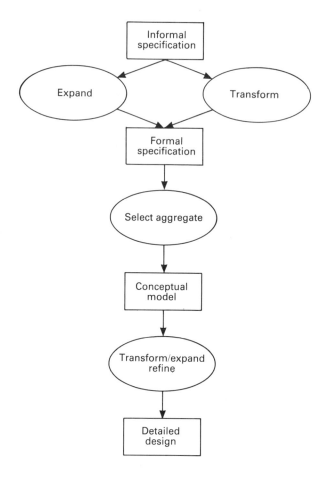

Fig. 5.1 — Global structure of the design process (after Baker Breuker *et al.*, 1987).

the system to be designed which holds all constraints, functions and parameters. This statement is given in the language of the domain.

methods: Currently the methods are not specified by KADS although they are assumed to be domain dependent.

domain knowledge: This probably includes knowledge about the functions required in systems the expert knows about, knowledge about what is achievable, etc.

Currently these illustrate that although the KADS project attempts to develop knowledge type descriptions acknowledging that they are a desired feature of a generic task model, it has not yet been computed for design tasks. Considerable further research is required in analysing design tasks for these to be completed but they illustrate for the first time the depth of description required.

There are several options as to how the sub-types of the design task can be structured. Those shown above are only tentative within the KADS method, but they can be used to illustrate the alternatives and the grounds for assessing them. It is generally agreed that design involves objects that have attributes which can be set to values. It is also agreed that constraints can be applied to determine acceptable values. There are three major distinctions possible.

The first distinction to be drawn is whether all the constraints can be stated initially as requirements or whether some can only be generated in response to a design. The first option provides the general KADS design model. The second requires a loop to exist which allows the analysis (or diagnosis) of a design to produce new constraints which can be fed into the requirements phase. This process could combine the KADS *design* and *analysis* tasks together into a more complex design task.

The second distinction relates to this and determines when the loop should terminate, by setting the standards of acceptable diagnosis in design. The first option is to accept a design which meets the set of constraints provided. The second option is to determine all the designs that meet the provided constraints and then look for constraints which will select among these, until only one optimal design remains. The constraints applied may be very individual and apparently informal (such as the colour preferences of the managing director) but they do act as constraints on the design. When a non-reducible set of designs remains a random selection will be required, although usually constraints will be applied to leave only one design. The first option is usually associated with engineering design (e.g. the generic design model suggested by Chandrasekaran above) and the second with artistic design.

The third distinction relates to how the constraints are applied to the whole design and sub-parts of it. It may appear that design components would have to be altered, but even in engineering design the range of options can be broad (after Chekayeb, *et al.*, 1987):

(1) Routine design — Select a known entity and transform it by modifying attribute values, e.g. bigger bottle. When the entity and the attribute values are known this task becomes the *transformation* type of synthesis task in KADS. The process of determining the transformation and applying it constitute the *transformational design* task.
(2) Re-design — Select an old design for an entity, then modify values of attributes of its components. Modifying one component may affect other relationships to other components and further constraints will be brought to bear. This will require the *decomposition* of an old design followed by *transformational design* in an overall process often called *hierarchical design*.
(3) *Innovative design* — Synthesise a new configuration from old primitive objects. This becomes the *configuration* task in KADS.
(4) Creative design — create new primitives — then apply innovative design to these primitives. New primitives are genuinely new to the domain of

use although they can be created by translating elements that already exist in the relation lattice of another domain.

The fourth distinction is whether all the options in the design space are generated before the constraints are applied or whether the constraints are applied to each step in the generation of the design solution space in order to restrict the solution search. Gero and his colleagues (e.g. Rosenman *et al.*, 1987; Oxman and Gero, 1987) have developed design synthesis systems which generate all possible design solutions that can result from a present state before applying constraints to them. This may be computationally effective when the solution set is small, but psychological evidence (Johnson-Laird, 1987) suggests that it is not a method used in human creative reasoning and therefore should not provide a generic task model for knowledge elicitation.

Within this set of options a large number of design tasks can exist. The correct set of 'generic tasks' for knowledge elicitation can only be derived through further research and analysis. This statement of the options however, should allow the selection of possible interpretations for any design task facing a knowledge engineer.

8.   THE STATE OF RESEARCH INTO GENERIC TASK MODELS

It is necessary for the knowledge engineer to develop a view of the analysis of elicited knowledge before embarking on knowledge elicitation. This view will direct the elicitation toward the knowledge sought, and away from extraneous information. This view can also be used to guide the analysis of knowledge. A view of the knowledge required to perform tasks could be obtained from generic tasks models. The information which these should present about tasks has been outlined. Attempts to develop taxonomies of generic tasks models and to specify the knowledge that they should present have been reviewed at length in this chapter. However, it will be necessary to refer to the *KADS Handbook* to use the full range of the defined models put forward there.

It is clear from this chapter that current models do not meet the criteria laid out for them in the introduction to this chapter. The taxonomy of models has been reasonably developed for analytic tasks, although it is still incomplete for synthesis and modification tasks. Consequently the description of real tasks in terms of generic task models is not supported by an easy to use method. However, the examples given show that it is possible to describe some real tasks in terms of generic tasks. The purpose of using generic task models is to provide the knowledge engineer with sufficient information to know what types of knowledge to acquire, to guide the choice of elicitation techniques which can acquire this knowledge and to direct the knowledge analysis. The present set of models are not sufficiently developed to do this. Although they describe the inference strategy expected and begin to describe the classes of knowledge expected these are not linked to elicitation or knowledge analysis strategies. The other major problems with the present models are that they do not address the issues of explanation in the task that the KBS user will perform or maintenance by the user of the KBS. These two aspects of generic task models are still very much research issues.

Although task models are still under development, knowledge engineers should see the advantages offered by their use during the analysis of acquired information from this review. They should also be in a better position to develop their own models as their experience progresses. It should of course be remembered that the task models described here are to be used by the knowledge engineer in analysis and to structure sessions with domain experts, rather than being presented to the experts during knowledge elicitation.

Introduction to:
Knowledge elicitation: some practical issues

Professor Geoffrey Trimble now moves the book on to the practical side of knowledge elicitation. He starts by suggesting the factors that promote the commercial success of expert systems by drawing an analogy between the established success of Network Analysis Techniques (NAT) such as PERT and CPM and the current state of commercially useful expert systems. He emphasises the organisational context in which development takes place and strongly argues for the importance of the commitment of the client organisation's senior personnel. He also argues that it is essential to avoid the solutions (expert systems) looking for applications approach and suggests that greater commercial success will follow simple, rather than complex, applications.

The chapter reviews the types of knowledge that may be elicited, the techniques that may be employed, and a range of human factors issues associated with knowledge elicitation. The chapter thus draws together much of the work described in more detail in the preceding chapters within a practical context. The chapter finishes with general advice that should be of considerable benefit to those about to commence building an expert system and the key issues are outlined as 11 points in the conclusion section.

6

Knowledge elicitation — some practical issues

Geoffrey Trimble
Department of Civil Engineering, Loughborough University of Technology

1. INTRODUCTION

In recent years a team in the department of Civil Engineering at Loughborough has been studying the practical problems of building expert systems with particular reference to the knowledge acquisition process. This team has built or is building eight systems covering a wide spectrum of domains. The author has also been involved in a survey of 70 'real world' expert systems again with the objective of exploring the knowledge acquisition process. This involvement has revealed that there are two types of situation in which a system may be built.

(1) An identifiable client requires a system and has instructed a contractor or employee to produce it. The client has a reasonably good idea of why he wants the system and how it will be used when complete.

(2) There is no identifiable client. An enthusiast (or group of enthusiasts), initiates a system with the objectives of exploring the subject of expert systems and producing a demonstration system.

It is considered that the problems of knowledge acquisition can only be explored realistically in situations of type (1). In type (2) situations the enthusiasts usually have domain expertise themselves so there is little need to elicit expert knowledge from the domain expert via a non-domain-expert (e.g. a knowledge engineer) to prepare some form of intermediate representation.

This background has prompted the team to seek systems that are working in the real world or at least are being developed with the intention of real use. This analysis has led to the identification of the kind of situation that will promote the development of useful systems and the factors that inhibit their development. In some ways this parallels a study (Arditi, 1973) to explore the factors that make for success in the application of network analysis, i.e. computer-based project scheduling and control. Section 2 of this chapter explores this parallel and offers tentative advice as to the factors that are likely to promote the development of successful real world systems. The other sections are as follows:

- The situation in which the process is undertaken.
- Knowledge elicitation methods.
- Human factors.
- The special problem of uncertainty.
- Some general advice.
- Conclusions.

The systems the team have built are summarised below.

CONPLANT (Wijesundera and Harris, 1985) — selection of materials handling equipment for multi-storey construction sites.
BREDAMP (Allwood *et al.*, 1988) — diagnosis of the cause of dampness in buildings.
CRANES (Cooper, 1987) — selection of tower cranes for multi-storey constructions sites (incorporating a graphics interface).
BID/NO BID — decision support for a design and construct contractor on whether to bid for new contracts.
NETWORK — diagnosis of faults in a national computer network.
MATSEL — material selection for boiler pressure parts.

The first five systems utilise the SAVOIR commercial shell program and run on an IBM PC XT. The last-named uses the IBM shell ESE and runs on an IBM mainframe computer. The unreferenced systems are described in research reports which have not yet been published. CONPLANT is an 'enthusiast's' system which drew largely on the expertise within the author's department and on expertise from Taylor Woodrow plc and Tarmac plc.

All other systems were developed either within a type (1) situation (i.e. with an identifiable client) or as near to this situation as it was possible to engineer.

BREDAMP was specifically commissioned by the Building Research Establishment.
CRANES was developed using expertise from Geo Wimpey & Co; BID/NO BID is based on input from I.D.C. Ltd. These companies were encouraged to act as though they were clients and in particular to reject any part of the system which they considered unrealistic.
NETWORK was developed for a retail chain.
MATSEL was undertaken in association with Foster Wheeler Ltd.

Currently under development are two further systems funded by the British government's Alvey Directorate. These are in association with Stewart Hughes Ltd, Rolls-Royce plc and GEC plc. Both concern the interpretation of sophisticated analyses of vibrations in rotating equipment. One assists in the diagnosis of faults in aero engines; the other in the balancing of the rotors of very large alternators. The author was also a member of two of the Community Clubs (PLANIT and ARIES) established by the Alvey Directorate. These comprise groups of industrial organisations with a common interest in exploring particular applications of expert systems. PLANIT explored the use of expert systems as an interactive aid to project managers; ARIES was formed by the insurance industry and produced one prototype system to assess premiums for fire insurance and another as an aid to investment managers in selecting equities.

2. FACTORS THAT MAKE FOR SUCCESS

In the early 1970s Arditi studied the factors that promote success in the application of Network Analysis Techniques (NAT) such as PERT, CPM, etc., in construction. At the time of the study the techniques were already widely known and quite widely applied (Harris and Trimble, 1974). It was therefore feasible to assemble data about real world applications of NAT and to examine them using statistical techniques. This is in contrast to the present (1988) position regarding the application of expert systems. However, the expert system study suggests that there may be some parallels that are worth examining. These are:

(1) The early study demonstrated that success was strongly correlated with initial and continuing support from senior management. Where there is a clearly identifiable client it can usually be reasonably assumed that management support has been obtained. Successful expert systems have been developed in this type of situation. However, where systems have been developed by enthusiasts there has been no need to define a client role. Such systems are seldom adopted in the real world.
(2) The motivation of those involved, particularly the more senior people, was shown by the study to be a key determinant of success. This motivation was most often generated by the commitment of managers, for example the commitment that is made by spending money on the development of special purpose software. Parallels are more difficult to find in this case but it seems likely that, where a client can be clearly identified, the person in the client role sees himself or herself as having commitment.
(3) The early studies showed that simpler applications of NAT were more likely to succeed than complex ones. For example the integration of cost control with NAT reduced the success rate and even regular updating of networks had a negative influence. Although the evidence is limited it does seem that a very substantial majority of successful expert systems deal with relatively simple domains.
(4) It was also found that success with NAT was greater when the need for the techniques was identified within the organisation (i.e. the contractor in this case) than when their use was imposed upon it by contractual requirements. A loose parallel with this has been seen in the recent very successful work of Stone & Webster inc. of Boston, Mass. This company approaches expert system applications simply as real-world problems that may respond to some form of analytical treatment. They make no prior commitment to the use of expert system technology but look only

at the problem. If the solution is wholly or partially an expert system they are pleased; if it is a solution that cannot in any way be described as an expert system they are equally pleased! Their criterion is solely whether the solution does its job effectively in real-world application.

(5) Although it is too early to assemble good statistical data regarding real-world applications of expert systems, experience with other types of system that people have applied does seem to provide some interesting pointers. The writer concludes that if the objective is to provide systems for the real world the following advice may be helpful.

- Ensure that senior management is involved and has contributed to defining the problem and knows how the eventual system will actually work.
- Keep the system as simple as the domain conditions permit.
- Avoid the danger of techniques looking for applications. Rather, identify the problem and judge success by the efficiency of whatever solution is found.

3. SITUATIONS THAT AFFECT THE ELICITATION PROCESS

It is clear that the nature of the situation within which the knowledge is elicited will have a major influence on the knowledge elicitation methods to be selected. The categories so far identified are:

(1) The knowledge is held in largely intuitive undefined format.
(2) As category (1) but where some closely similar domains have been examined previously.
(3) Cases can be defined that reflect a body of decision-making within the domain.
(4) There is published material about the domain.
(5) The domain expert has sufficient knowledge about expert systems to enable him to define the knowledge (or at least to play a significant role in its definition).

Superimposed on this list of categories are other dimensions such as:

- The 'depth' of knowledge to be represented, i.e. does it represent fundamental knowledge such as that relating to molecular structure or 'heuristic' knowledge which includes a substantial amount of personal opinion.
- The attitude of individual experts to the system.
- The extent to which a consensus among experts can be found.

The foregoing categories are now elaborated.

3.1 Intuitive knowledge

Some knowledge engineers favour a method which requires the development of a prototype system based very often on the prior knowledge of the knowledge engineer. The prototype is demonstrated to the domain expert who suggests modifications and amplification. The changes are made and the revised system demonstrated again. The iterations of this process continue until the domain expert is satisfied that the model is acceptable. If a good initial model is produced this method can be very productive. However, it can have the effect of prejudicing the responses of the expert and thus diverting him from some of the subtle, more intuitive knowledge that might be of crucial importance in the operation of the system. Diaper (Chapter 1) deals extensively with the limitations of the prototyping approach.

An alternative is to start with a blank sheet of paper and ask the domain expert to tell you what he knows. A fairly extensive set of knowledge is then assembled before the initial system is coded. This approach is fundamentally better but its success is critically dependent on the time that the domain expert can devote to the process. An example of what can be achieved when access to domain experts is severely restricted is described by Clare in Chapter 7.

Techniques for eliciting knowledge from domain experts are briefly described in the next section and comprehensively so by Cordingley in Chapter 3.

3.2   Intuitive knowledge with precedents

Where systems have been produced for very similar domains it may be safe to introduce a short-cut in the form of structured interviews based on the content of the previous systems. Again the danger of prejudicing responses must always be borne in mind.

3.3   Defined cases

There are several computer programs that will induce rules from sets of cases. Of these EXPERT-EASE is probably the simplest and best known. At first sight this approach has much to recommend it. However, extensive trials of the early programs have revealed some disconcerting problems. One of these is that the natural sequence of questioning that is inherent in a domain is not respected. For example a pair of questions might be:

- Is the pipe a drain?
- Have you performed a drain-test?

If the sequence of these questions is reversed, as it may be when automatic rule-induction is applied, then the confidence of the user may quickly evaporate. Another problem is that, like regression analysis, rule-induction works on cases irrespective of any causal connections. Bramer (1978) has made similar, more detailed, criticisms of automated rule induction with respect to the popular ID3 algorithm (Quinlan, 1979; 1986).

It is not, of course, imperative to use the rule-induction program. Manual examination of sets of cases will often indicate relationships that can be coded on an *ad hoc* basis and Bramer has suggested using only a 'semi-automated' form of rule induction. The expert will frequently find it easier to recall his knowledge through the recounting of case histories than through other forms of interview.

3.4   Published material
There is a lot of interest in the use of expert systems to guide users in the interpretation of regulations and codes of practice. Clearly, in this situation, there should be no problem of human interaction as the views of the human experts should be fully recorded in the published text. As an aside, and as discussed by Diaper in Chapter 1, attempts to 'computerise' regulations were made before the recent surge of interest in expert systems. These attempts often revealed inconsistency and vagueness which made 'compu- terisation' difficult. Perhaps this should be anticipated since differences between the views of the members of the original committee that drafted the regulations eventually have to be resolved by compromise.

3.5   Coding by the expert
When the domain expert is also a reasonably competent user of computers it may be possible for him to produce his own expert system without the use of a human intermediary. This approach is only possible where the expert exhibits a high degree of self-knowledge and is likely to be unsuccessful where the knowledge is largely intuitive. Diaper (Chapter 1) discusses in detail the problems of people accessing their knowledge, particularly for highly practised tasks, which he suggests may be represented procedurally and which in consequence are difficult to verbalise. The expert may or may not be inclined to use an expert system shell to assist him (and constrain him) in his efforts.

4.   SELECTING ELICITATION METHODS
The previous section identified the following methods of knowledge elicitation:

- Unstructured interviews.
- Structured interviews.
- Case histories.
- Prototype systems evolved iteratively.
- Rule induction.

   To this list should be added:

- Observation.
- Paper models.

All of these techniques, with the exception of the automated aspects of rule induction, are described in detail by Cordingley in Chapter 3.
   The Loughborough team have recently focused attention on the use of paper models after seeing the successful use of this technique by the ARIES Alvey Community Club. The knowledge engineer creates a document

detailing the rules elicited and develops this as knowledge elicitation progresses. The document records the status of each rule — i.e. finalised, tentative, needs review, etc., and hence provides a formal record of the knowledge elicited. A natural format is adopted so that the paper model can in many cases be reviewed by the domain experts. Furthermore this review process can itself stimulate further knowledge acquisition. Bell and Hardiman (Chapter 2) adopt a similar technique and the properties of paper models are discussed more fully by Johnson in Chapter 4.

Initially the team started with the view that it should be possible to isolate situations (or combinations of factors) that would point to the selection of a single method. Experience has not borne out this view and, for example, in one of the applications studied four different methods were used at different stages. Thus the current advice is in line with Cordingley's conclusions (Chapter 3) that what is required is for the knowledge engineer to acquire a feel for the alternative methods and to use them flexibly as the position unfolds. The following comments augment those in the preceding section.

Unstructured interviewing has the great merit of not prejudicing the responses of the domain expert. Thus less obvious points emerge that can be very important. The method, however, is time-consuming and requires patience on the part of the expert.

Structured or focused interviewing achieves results quickly and is appropriate when the knowledge engineer is fairly confident of his understanding of the domain. This understanding may result from prior knowledge or from the results of earlier elicitation methods. Interviews can be broadly focused or narrowly focused. During a broadly focused interview a knowledge engineer might pose questions such as 'describe the parts of a typical boiler system' whereas during a narrowly focused interview 'are there any welding problems associated with carbon steel?' would be more typical

Prototyping has much to recommend it particularly as each interaction can provide cues to prompt the expert in his thoughts about his intuitive knowledge. As with structured interviewing, however, there is a danger that less obvious points may be overlooked.

Rule induction appears to be satisfactory for simple well-defined applications. However, for applications involving only quite modest levels of complexity, it appears that rules prepared by induction are unsatisfactory for direct incorporation in the expert system. Despite these shortcomings, attempts to apply rule induction to limited modules of a total application can encourage the expert to consider factors that are not revealed by other methods. This must improve the validity of the knowledge base even if the induced rules are themselves discarded.

The author has very limited experience of observational methods. However, it must be a beneficial approach in providing at least the initial evidence that the knowledge engineer will require in structuring the problem. Furthermore observation can be used to check that the expert performs his tasks in the way he claims to use during inverview sessions, i.e. during interview sessions he may be telling the knowledge engineer how he thinks the job ought to be done rather than how it is done in practice. The use of observational methods, and task analysis in particular, are extensively discussed by Diaper (Chapter 1) and by Wilson (Chapter 5).

5. HUMAN FACTORS

Knowledge elicitation for expert systems is a human process and several of the human aspects have already been mentioned. The purpose of this section is to itemise the human problems that arise so that readers can be aware of them. This is not to suggest that definitive solutions can yet be offered; the process is likely to remain largely *ad hoc* for some time. Before proceeding it is worth repeating that the goal of knowledge acquisition is the transfer and transformation of expertise from some source (usually human) to a computer program.

5.1 Resistance

Domain experts may fear that, by giving up their knowledge, they will weaken their position within their organisation. Unless some incentive can be engineered such an expert is unlikely to provide the basis for a useful system. Organisational resistance may also arise and has been observed in the Community Clubs established in Britain by the Alvey Directorate. For example one club member may provide an expert but then realise that commercially valuable knowledge could be transmitted via the system to a competitor. It should be noted, on the other hand, that positive motivation may be encountered when an expert is bored with providing personal advice in one subject and would welcome the chance to have this process automated.

5.2 Accessibility and prejudicing responses

Experts may have the necessary knowledge and motivation but may have other duties that prevent them spending an adequate amount of time with the knowledge engineer. The dangers of prejudicing responses by over-structuring interviews and by offering detailed prototypes have already been mentioned. However, the methods that prejudice responses are usually quicker so some compromise is often necessary.

5.3 Cues and examples

Experts are often better at doing things than explaining what they are doing and why. So one method of obtaining knowledge is to watch the expert at work and then ask why he did what he did. The problem, as already mentioned, is that the expert often cannot access the rules and relationships that have become intuitive. A method that also deals with this problem is to generate artificial examples as cues and to ask the expert what he would do in these circumstances. Obtaining the Bayes factors for BREDAMP is one illustration of this method (see below) and Cordingley (Chapter 3) discusses such methods and their limitations in more detail.

5.4 Rapport and roles

Clearly the knowledge acquisition process will proceed more smoothly and effectively when rapport is established between the knowledge engineer and the domain expert. As a corollary to this, it is usually better to separate the tasks of knowledge elicitation from that of encoding the information for the computer. This enables the knowledge engineer to concentrate on the knowledge as perceived by the expert and on establishing a good human relationship with the expert, as emphasised by Bell and Hardiman (Chapter 2) and Cordingley (Chapter 3).

The background of the Loughborough team is in construction and engineering and this has facilitated the development of good rapport with experts during the development of systems in engineering domains. Their experience, however, has alerted them to the danger that knowledge engineers who are well versed in the domain being studied are in danger of distorting the expert's knowledge by introducing their own ideas.

6. THE SPECIAL PROBLEM OF UNCERTAINTY

The BREDAMP system generated some useful insights into the problems of uncertain knowledge. This system was commissioned by the Building Research Establishment, a long-established British government laboratory with extensive expertise relating to building construction and building defects. The purpose of the system is to diagnose the cause of dampness in buildings. The domain expert was exceptionally cogent and well motivated. However, it was necessary to attach probabilities to the goals, e.g. to conclude that there was a 90% likelihood that the cause of the dampness was rising damp. For this the dependencies between variables are calculated using Bayes' theorem for which affirmative and negative factors must be established. While the domain expert could be expected to describe the behaviour of dampness, it was impractical to obtain from him estimates of the Bayes factors. To overcome this problem, the key factors relating to each cause (or goal) were first obtained from the domain expert. These were then compiled into tables in the following form and the domain expert was asked to suggest values to replace the question marks:

Factor	*Suggested values*	
Evidence	A stain	A stain
Height of stain	9 inches	15 inches
Age of building	8 years	9 years
Component wetter inside than out	Yes	Don't know
Positive salts test	Don't know	Yes
Probability of rising damp	?	?

To derive Bayes factors from these data it was sufficient to use an *ad hoc* approach i.e. a combination of simultaneous equations and trial and error. A better approach would have been some form of regression analysis although it can often be difficult to elicit a sufficient number of cases to make this approach possible.

This case illustrates a further point, namely confidence limits. At present BREDAMP offers only a set of probabilities for each of the defined causes of dampness. For example:

Rising damp	90%
Rain penetration	27%
Others	less than 5%

The rising damp figure may in fact mean that the probability is in the range 89–91% or it may mean that it is in the range 80–100%. A user would react differently if he had these ranges available. With a narrow range, users are likely to conclude that they have gone as far as the system will allow and may then decide to take remedial measures to cure the problem on the assumption that the cause is in fact rising damp. If the wider range (80–100) is shown they will probably undertake additional, quite cheap, tests to improve the reliability of the diagnosis. This extension of the information provided by a system has been mentioned in several contexts, but no actual implementation has so far been identified by the author.

7 GENERAL ADVICE

Before attempting to develop any expert system knowledge engineers need to be clear about their own objectives. If they are motivated by the wish to solve real-world problems they need to be alert to the dangers of seeking applications for interesting techniques; they should concentrate instead on solving the problem using the most effective technique available. Whatever the nature of the technical solution ensure that senior management is involved and committed.

It is worth bearing in mind also that simple applications are generally more successful than complex ones. If, instead, the knowledge engineer wishes to advance the technology of expert systems he is less constrained. The debates about fundamental and applied research may act as a guide. However, if one is seeking enlightenment on knowledge acquisition then it should be recognised that no real knowledge acquisition occurs when the person (or team) developing the system starts with substantial knowledge about the domain. It was this consideration that caused the author to look at real-world applications.

Having confronted these issues and when starting in earnest on the knowledge elicitation process the following comments may help. The approach to knowledge elicitation must be flexible and be specific to the domain under consideration. The general approach can be characterised as the following progression:

(i) one or two unstructured sessions
(ii) case histories and broadly focused interviews
(iii) narrowly focused interviews
(iv) prototyping and iteration

The author has found that the demonstration of a prototype system to the experts has provided a valuable stimulus to further knowledge elicitation. However, the point at which the expert first sees this prototype should be selected with care. On the one hand the knowledge engineer may become prematurely over-enthusiastic about the system and as a result demonstrate a piece of code which is trivial, thus losing the confidence of the expert. On the other hand, experts have been encountered who had serious misconceptions about the capabilities of the system being developed, and such misconceptions must be dispelled at an early stage. Each situation is different and the only general advice that can be offered is to be aware of the pitfalls. The author has found that demonstrating the prototype as soon as it is capable of giving a piece of recognisable and plausible advice is one useful approach. Each knowledge engineer is likely to generate his own guidelines as his experience accumulates.

Following some recent work it is also recommended that a paper model should be developed as a means of documenting the knowledge elicitation process and as a focus for discussion with the domain experts. Johnson discusses the advantages of such documentation in detail in Chapter 4.

8. CONCLUSIONS

The following are offered as reminders of the key points in this chapter.

- System development should be client led.
- Simple applications are more likely to succeed than complex ones.
- Knowledge elicitation methods depend much more on the situation than on the domain.
- Flexibility of approach is essential to the knowledge elicitation process. Factors which will determine this approach include:

  - the form in which the knowledge is available;
  - the depth of knowledge (i.e. fundamental or heuristic);
  - the degree of consensus among experts;
  - the attitudes of individual experts to the system.

- It is unlikely that a single method of knowledge acquisition can be adopted for development of an application — rather a number of methods will be required.
- Cues and examples can help an expert to recall intuitively held knowledge.
- Using a computer program to induce rules from cases may provide some enlightenment but is unlikely to provide working rules except perhaps for simple systems.
- Even with a very responsive expert, ascertaining Bayes factors is best done by examples.
- The prototype system should be demonstrated to the experts as soon as it starts to give plausible and recognisable advice. This dispels misconceptions at an early stage and in general provokes further knowledge elicitation and promotes enthusiasm on the part of the expert.

- Using a paper model as an intermediate representation for the knowledge elicited helps the knowledge engineer cope with the mass of information gathered, and with the right experts can itself be used as a knowledge elicitation tool.
- Be aware of the danger of finding applications for techniques. The greatest success in expert systems in construction has been achieved when the work is problem-orientated.

Introduction to:
Knowledge elicitation for financial dealers

The final chapter reports a study where 'the objective was to demonstrate to a commercial organisation how they might benefit from the use of Knowledge-Based techniques'. The study uses knowledge elicitation techniques to identify how dealers on the New York Stock Exchange could be supported in their dealing tasks. The demonstrator developed was a victim of its own success as 'It clearly showed that aspects of specialised expertise could be enhanced' and this led to the project's participating organisations, who are competitors on the Stock Exchange, not wishing 'to share with each other such a valuable resource'. Jeremy Clare's chapter thus contains a cautionary note on the relationship between knowledge engineering organisations and their clients.

As the final chapter, it puts into context much of the preceding work and very powerfully describes how essential it is to understand the environment in which the potential application will be used and the psychology of the personnel involved. It also demonstrates that a considerable amount can be achieved with only very limited access to domain experts and this is in part achieved by the sensible selection and tailoring of a variety of knowledge elicitation techniques. Within its few pages the chapter outlines a range of models, though perhaps unfortunately not how they were derived, that clearly reflects a theoretically driven approach rather than an *ad hoc* or *post hoc* one.

7

Knowledge elicitation for financial dealers

Jeremy Clare
Cambridge Consultants Ltd

1. INTRODUCTION

As part of a demonstration of the application of techniques and methods associated with Knowledge-Based Systems (KBS) in financial dealing rooms it was necessary to undertake a knowledge elicitation exercise. A major constraint was that the six dealers could each only make one day available. The chosen knowledge election method was heavily focused on understanding the tasks carried out and the knowledge needed to undertake those tasks. The method consisted of first observing the work activity. Secondly, a full day interview with full video recording. Finally, further observation of the workplace was carried out. The transcripts from the interviews were analysed to identify the objects in the dealers world, his goals and objectives and the principal tasks carried out. Part of the approach to this knowledge elicitiation exercise was a classification of the expert behaviour. In the case of a dealer we may class his expertise as being performance orientated. This is in contrast to a mathematician, for example, whose expertise is based on knowledge of theoretical relationships, while that of a loan assessor is based on rules and and procedures.

Based on the knowledge elicitation exercise a demonstration system was developed which included facilities to allow rapid assimilation of information and to allow fast input of information. The key aspect of the demonstration being a potential system which would neither get in the users way nor would it prevent him being in control.

The work reported here was part of the development of a demonstration of a financial dealer's workstation. The original premise was that the dealing room was an appropriate area for the demonstration of KBS techniques as the activities are complex in terms of information flow and processing. Further, these activities have a high value for the institutions.

A key step in developing the demonstration system was knowledge elicitation. As Diaper, in Chapter 1, and Cordingley, in Chapter 3, have pointed out, there are a number of initial steps to be undertaken before knowledge elicitation is commenced. The first steps in this project were to identify the objectives of the demonstration system, to understand the environment in which a full system would operate and to identify the benefits that could accrue from such a system. Only after these steps were carried out was the knowledge elicitation exercise undertaken.

This chapter sets out to give an understanding of the knowledge elicitation exercise. However, first the dealing room environment is described to provide a context. Then the objectives and benefits are briefly outlined. The next sections describe the knowledge elicitation approach, followed by a discussion of the chosen demonstration system, and finally there are some proposals for the further development of the knowledge elicitation approach

2. THE DEALING ROOM

The particular type of dealing room that formed the basis for this study is to be found in New York financial institutions which hold large portfolios of equities. In these institutions dealers buy and sell equities to make up these portfolios. The size of the operation in each institution was such that there would be six to twelve dealers working in a room together. Their task being to locate stockbrokers who either had equities for sale, or were willing to purchase, and then to arrange a deal. Although this sounds a relatively simple task, the dealer requires skill in a number of areas.

In dealing the first skill is to find sellers or buyers without letting the market know the equities of interest. In some cases this is relatively easy in that the equity is listed for sale. However, in many cases, because of the institution's position in the market, the size of the deal is larger than any single offering on the market. Thus, as deals were initiated the market would react by changing the value of the offering. Therefore dealers attempt to locate the largest offerings without revealing their intentions.

The second area of skill is understanding the market dynamics in order to make the deal at the most advantageous time. There are many levels at which this skill may operate from the seemingly intuitive to the highly analytical.

The third area of skill is the effective use of the various support tools. These include a variety of quotation services which provide advice on current offerings from stockbrokers, information provided on past dealing, information and news services such as Reuters, in house analytical services and the various telephone systems which provide very fast connections to stockbrokers and other dealers.

The dealer exercises these skills from a dealing desk, which typically has four to six screens displaying various types of information. In addition, he has telephones with direct connect keypads, these give single button dialling. The environment can become extremely frenetic with a dealer undertaking up to 1200 telephone conversations lasting for as little as six seconds during a working day. In addition as relevant information is obtained it is shouted to the other dealers for them to note and use. This activity level means that in highly volatile situations the dealer covers his desk with pieces of paper on which are recorded snippets of information.

Moving in and out of this environment are the portfolio managers who may come to update their orders for the day based on charges in the market. In addition there will be the head dealer trying to impose a degree of overall control in terms of balancing the activity and ensuring that the institutions overall position is not threatened.

This environment may at first seem bizaare, but it must be understood in the context of any marketplace. A marketplace is where individuals have items for deal where they attempt to achieve the optimal deal for themselves. The dealer and the broker act as agents in the financial marketplace. As agents they make their living on a commission basis. Thus it is in their collective interest to ensure the maximum activity to generate the right combination of circumstances in which to make optimal deals. The actual behaviour of any market depends on its tempo, the nature of complexity of items being traded, and the extent of the risks and the margins available. Thus, in the range of international financial and commodity markets behaviours can be observed ranging from the intensely analytical, where mainframe and super computers are used to analyse the opportunities, through to the futures markets characterised by the 'barrow boys' shouting their waves and clamouring to make a deal.

The US equity market is not normally the most frenetic of markets although it has seen some intense periods of activity since the Stock Market crash on Black Monday, 19 October 1987. However, at the time of the study the market was stable and not subject to excessive changes.

3. THE OBJECTIVES AND BENEFITS

The principle objective was to identify how the techniques from KBS could be applied to this environment. The method chosen to achieve that objective was to develop a demonstration system which would show the type of system a dealer might use in the future. The demonstrator was to illustrate the concepts rather than specify function or to outline a final architecture. It was seen as necessary that the demonstration should have a clear set of specific objectives, from which it would be possible to identify a clear set of benefits for the participating institutions. The specific objectives were:

(a) Provide the dealer with assistance in his task while leaving him with overall control and responsibility. It was not the intent to provide an 'expert' system that would replace the dealer himself. This would have been a far too challenging project since the dealer exercises a wide range of human skills including complex reasoning, judgement, analysis and practices considerable common sense.

(b) The solution should not impose extra tasks on the dealer which would detract from his normal activity. It was taken as an axiomatic that there would be no additional screens or input devices to those already present at the dealing desk.

(c) Any implementations would need to be capable of full integration with the existing and planned data and information feeds within the dealing environment.

(d) The demonstration would have to be readily understood by the dealers and their management. Thus careful attention would have to be given to providing an easily understood functionality. In addition there would have to be clear paths to implementation.

(e) The study would have to be conducted with the minimum disruption to dealers and other key staff within the participating institutions.

With this ambitious set of objectives there had been an identification of clear benefits that would have to be large to justify the cost of developing a full system. The judgement was made that if the integrated system was to be developed then it would require several man years of effort for full scale implementation. At the time of the study the principle benefits for typical institutions included the following:

(a) Better control and monitoring of the overall position of the institutions. The individual dealer has to have a considerable degree of autonomy in his activities. However, the head dealer has responsibility to maintain a strategic level of control. An important aspect of this is in the obligations owed and given to other institutions in return for information and preferential treatment. This aspect is highly dependent on the head dealer's judgement but he needed to have a clear understanding of who was negotiating what, with whom, in order to manage this process.

(b) To provide the individual dealer with a better safety net as his individual cognitive capacity, skill and knowledge limits were reached. The nature of the job is such that dealers can normally only undertake it for a few years. A benefit would be provided then with a significant support so as to extend their potential working careers. In addition training new dealers is expensive as at present the only effective training is 'on the job' and mistakes can be expensive for the institution.

(d) To provide support for the new dealer to protect him from some of the more obvious mistakes. There are a few situations which are comparable to a 'fools mate' which he should be warned about before he commits himself.

These benefits were identified in general terms as the demonstration was to show that they could be achieved rather than to fully cost justify their value. The latter was intended to be the basis of subsequent work. At the same time it was decided that no direct dealing benefits would be sought since these are highly dependent on market dynamics and subject to many external factors, for example, loss of confidence in the US economy. It was also seen that there were many current developments in analytical technique which can provide dealing benefits which have yet to show their full promise.

3.1   The knowledge elicitation approach

The approach used was based on the experience gained by the AI team at Arthur D. Little over a number of years. It was also firmly based on a wide base of skills and techniques from various social sciences including anthropology, sociology and psychology. A principal assertion was that the observer should try to rationalise on the basis of his own knowledge the nature and behaviour of a novel social group. The approach is named task environment analysis, since it attempts to place the nature of the individual's behaviour and expertise clearly in the context of the environment within which they occur. Thus the approach is to develop a description of the behaviour and expertise which is rational within its own context.

The major steps in the approach are to identify the object and entities in the individual's world, to then relate these to each other and finally to identify the underlying constructs which provide the higher level structure to the individual's world, for further discussion of the structuring of knowledge see Diaper (1984) and Diaper and Johnson (1989). Once the individual's world is so described then the words of individuals acting together are compared to identify the common points of reference and process.

There are two parts to the activity of identifying the objects and entities in the individual's world. Firstly, the place of work is inspected and all important sources of information are noted. A simple measure of importance for any source of information is in terms of the ease of access to it by the individual. In this study the desk at which the task is carried out and its immediate surrounds are the key workplace of the dealer. For the dealer his screens, keypads and telephones are clearly major sources. In addition there are the many pieces of paper that contain the information resulting from the plan for the day, which includes instructions from the portfolio managers and the outcome of the early morning pre-trading briefing session. Although not all the dealers used paper to record this information, its existence pointed to its importance for some. It also pointed to the importance of the pre-dealing briefing session. This is a meeting where the dealers, portfolio managers and analysts and researchers share knowledge about the day. The meeting may be very informal and held during breakfast. All the individuals concerned are avid readers of newspapers and news services on their way to work and for the first part of the day.

The second part in identifying the objects and entities is done in an interview. The dealers were asked to talk freely about their working day and what information sources they used and why. Based on the observations of the workplace they were asked to explain the meaning of the various items that had been observed. This interview session also addressed the actions performed. Thus additional importance could be assigned to objects and entities together with their relationships through action. As each dealer talked through his day it was also possible to identify the high level structure of his world. Interview and talk-through techniques are extensively described by Cordingley in Chapter 3.

There was a limited availability of each dealer, this meant that each

individual was only available for a single day. In a full system implementation it would be necessary to interview individuals more than once. The
actual number of times will depend on the effectiveness of the analysis that
can be made and the degree to which the individuals are articulate about
their world.

Six dealers were interviewed for the present study, each was the head
dealer of the six participating institutions. Thus the relationships between
individuals had to be interpreted across institutions. In this particular
environment this was not a major problem as all individuals work in the
same marketplace. This means that the range of options to any individual
are broadly similar with only a limited set of ways of achieving a particular
outcome. Institutional factors constrain an individual's behaviour but do not
change it fundamentally. An interesting aspect was that many individuals
from institutions in this marketplace gathered together on social occasions
which included poker games. In fact it was not clear to the analysis team
whether these poker games were social occasions or merely an extension of
the working day where they practised their skills in bluff and risk taking.

In order to improve the analysis of the interviews, full video and audio
recordings were made. Although this technique can have a disturbing effect
on the individual in some cases, as discussed by Cordingley in Chapter 3, the
nature of dealers is such that no problems were experienced. This is an area
where there seems to be a divide between USA and UK practice. In the
USA people accept and use video recording very widely. In the UK many
knowledge elicitors report that it disrupts the individual's behaviour.

A full transcript of the audio track was then produced. This is a tedious
business and it helps to have experienced transcribers. The Arthur D. Little
team used agencies for this work and were able to find one that was very
good in that the typists typed what was said, rather than trying to interpret
coherent sentences. The 'ugh' is a useful pointer to an individual grasping for
a concept or idea that is difficult to express. Using typists is in contrast to Bell
and Hardiman (Chapter 2) who recommend that the knowledge elictor
undertake their own transcript production. The problem for commercial AI
groups is that the knowledge elicitor's time is too valuable to spend large
portions of it in transcript production.

The transcripts are then analysed in conjunction with reviewing the
video recording. To sound a note of warning to anyone setting out to become
a knowledge elicitor, these recordings are always embarrassing as they point
out your own incompetence where you have asked inappropriate questions
and interrupted useful discourses.

The method of analysis used was to write on coloured cards the objects,
entities, actions and meta structure. The next stage is to lay out the cards on
a table according to the relationship between objects and entities, the use of
colour facilitaties the visualisations of patterns. Although some AI tool-kits
provide means for mapping out such relationships, they do not provide the
resolution of a conference room table covered in cards.

4. TYPES OF EXPERT BEHAVIOUR

Based on experience in a number of knowledge elicitation exercises is has been found useful to identify types of expert. If we understand the appoach and motivation of the individual experts we can then use the most appropriate way to elicit their knowledge. We have found it useful to classify the individual expert behaviour into one of four basic types. Although it is expected that individuals may show a mixture of the types of expert behaviour from time to time. The four types may be characterised as:

(a) Practitioner
(b) Academic
(c) Craftsman
(d) Samurai

Practitioner expertise is based on an organised set of principles and methods. These may be acquired on the basis of some theoretical knowledge or developed from experience and practice. It is this type of expertise that is usually called to mind in describing expert systems. However, it must be recognised that such expertise is rare in that the motivations, experience and work environment of most individuals distracts them from acquiring a fully coherent basis for their expertise. The consequence is that three types will be encountered in the majority of cases.

Academic behaviour is often found where an individual has moved to a position where he is expected to guide, direct and teach others with respect to his own expertise. There is considerable pressure for the individual to organise his methods and practice and to put them in a clear theoretical structure. This leads to a tendency to discard the expertise of practice if it cannot be fitted to a theoretical basis, and the solution to any problem must be shown to have been arrived at by a method. The problem is that areas of expertise are discarded or ignored if they do not fit the theory. Thus areas of useful knowledge are discarded. The resulting expertise is only good if the theoretical basis is a sound one. It should be noted that the demonstration of a knowledge representation structure to such an expert may often lead him to adopt it as his theoretical basis. This may further reduce the applicability of his own expertise.

Craftsman behaviour is most often found in routine activities where the individual is concerned with solving a series of similar problems. An example of this type is the claim assessor in an insurance company. This type of expertise is often characterised by rote learning of methods and procedures. For the individual there is often no organising principles or coherent understanding. It is quite likely that this type of expertise may have many contradictions and conflicts at the higher level. These are controlled by the individual who segments his activities into clearly separable parts. This behaviour may be considered as irrational. The goal of the individual in this context is to achieve the 'right' solution. This type of expertise is the most widely distributed in the workplace, and such individuals may be characterised as practical knowledge workers.

Samurai behaviour is characterised by the way in which expertise is performed. For the individual the perfomance is the key aspect, the final outcome is only a consequence of the performance. This type of expertise is clearly demonstrated throughout the performing arts and in sport. The individual learns by sitting at the feet of a master and by doing and practice. Much of the dealer's experience falls into this class. Each day brings a set of circumstances in which he must perform well. The day will come when he can no longer perform and so he will retire. This type of expertise is rare in the general workplace, but it may be observed in many organisations where social skills or other performance activities are required. It is the most difficult type of expertise to externalise and represent since its basis is internal to the individual. However, it does not prevent the building of systems that allow the individuals to extend and enhance their performance.

5.   THE DEMONSTRATION SYSTEM

The analysis from the knowledge elicitation exercise identified the critical information in the delear's world. The relationships that were identified in the patterns of cards showed how the information should be grouped. The exercise also showed how important it was for the individual to have the right information on which to execute his experience. Based on this analysis a demonstration system was put together. The basic features were as follows:

(a) Bringing together the relevant information on to a single screen. By understanding the various tasks the appropriate information from various sources can be sorted and displayed on a single high resolution screen. Thus the operation buy '9000 IBM' requires display of who is offering IBM equity, the recent history of price and volume movements, and any relevant research and news information. This is all displayed on the left-hand side of the screen.

(b) Rules to identify if the deal is simple or complex. A deal is simple if the equity is stable, there are offers available and there is no news stories about it. To just identify this status for any deal means that the dealer can process it at any time when there is a hold in his other activities. It is estimated that, at the time, about 25% of deals fell into that category. This information is displayed on the right of the screen.

(c) If the deal was complex then to point the dealer to the major cause of complexity. Thus if the equity is volatile or performing badly with respect to the industry Dow Jones index, the dealer's attention can be directed to these aspects. However, at this point the system is clearly advisory and the dealer responsible for his own actions.

(d) Identifying certain market related anomalies set to catch the unwary. In the particular marketplace a stockbroker may advertise equities which he does not have for sale. Hoping to find buyers so that he can negotiate with possible sellers. A few simple rules were found that could identify these instances.

(e) Providing an easy means of inputting and updating information gleaned over the telephone. If the system was to contain a full representation of information then the telephone call data had to be captured. An analysis of information flow in telephone calls showed that a very constrained syntax and vocabulary were used. Thus about 50–100 dedicated keys could be identified so that news snippets and deals could be recorded in 4 to 8 key strokes.

(f) Providing a clear and uncluttered display, considerable attention was given to ensuring that the display was well laid out so that separate sources of information were clearly separated. In addition the actual information was displayed in an easily legible form and contained sufficient appropriate information for clear understanding.

The project came to a halt at this point. The demonstrator had shown the value of knowledge-based techniques in the dealing room. However, the justification for development for a full sale system depends on many factors. One aspect is the cost of development and in this respect the demonstration created its own paradox. It clearly showed all aspects of specialised expertise could be enhanced. However, it also showed the value of that expertise, which meant that the participating institutions did not want to share with each other such a valuable resource.

6. FURTHER DEVELOPMENTS OF THE TECHNIQUE

An important area for development is in the description of the task environment. There are a number of structured techniques for task analysis which may be applicable. Some of these are based on a data flow and other software modelling approaches, e.g. Mobbs (1986a) and Yourdan (1979). Others are derived from traditional ergonomic and work study practice. Finally there are those that have been developed by the various human computer interaction centres such as GOMS (Card *et al.*, 1980; Barnard, 1987).

In using structured methods to describe the task environment there are a variety of requirements. In the initial stages the need is for a description which imposes a minimum of structure. As the knowledge elicitation proceeds then the observed structure needs to be described. The principal requirement is to have a tool which in itself imposes a minimum of structure. Of the various methods those based on a data flow model would appear most useful.

A further area of development is in the introduction of additional techniques to the interview for eliciting knowledge. Recent advances in knowledge elicitation (Kidd, 1987; Burton and Shadbolt, 1987), have demonstrated a number of techniques which can improve knowledge transfer. These techniques need to be applied at appropriate stages in the knowledge elicitation process and for the right type of knowledge. Some of the techniques are very simple, such as twenty questions. Other techniques are more complex, such as repertory grid. In twenty questions the expert is allowed to ask questions to identify the solution the elicitor has written out on a card. The power of the technique comes from the order in which questions are asked as well as the type of question. Repertory grid is a technique based on the Personal Construct Theory (Kelly, 1955). It provides a way for a domain to be explored with the minimum of knowledge of the language, syntax or semantics. These techniques are reviewed more thoroughly by Cordingley in Chapter 3.

7. CONCLUSIONS

In the study reported here the objective was to demonstrate to a commercial organisation how they might benefit from the use of knowledge-based techniques. The approach used was directed towards understanding the organisational context in which a system would be implemented. For that reason the analysis approach concentrated as much on the environment in which the expertise would be practised as the expertise itself. An important part of understanding any expert behaviour is being able to identify the personal goals of the expert and the way in which he exercises his expertise. As part of this understanding the four types of expert behaviour have been identified.

The work described here is one of a series of similar projects carried out to demonstrate the value of knowledge-based techniques for a wide range of organisations. The overall approach has been used in all these projects. In most projects the experts have been mostly craftsmen. The nature of these commercially based projects is such that it is only feasible to report those that have in some sense failed. This particular project was halted because the participating institutions did not want to share expertise that had been demonstrated to be valuable to them.

References

Abelson, R. P. (1981) The psychological status of the script concept, *American Psychologist* **36**, 71–729.

Agar, M. H. (1986) *Speaking of ethnography*, London: Sage.

Aleksander, I. (1984) *Designing intelligent systems: an introduction*, London: Kogan Page.

Adrian, E. (1966) Consciousness, in Eccles, J. (ed.) *Brain and conscious experience*. Springer-Verlag.

Alexander, J. H., Freiling, M. J., Shulman, S. J., Rehfuss, S. & Messick, S. L. (1987) Ontological analysis: an ongoing experiment. *International Journ. Man–Machine Studies* **26**, 4, 473–486.

Allwood, R. J., Shaw, M. R., Smith, J. L., Stewart, D. J. & Trimble, E. G. (1988) Building dampness: diagnosing the causes. How the BREDAMP system was developed. *Building Research & Practice No. 1.*

Alty, J. & Coombs, M. (1984) *Expert systems: concepts and examples*, NCC:UK.

Anjewierden, A. (1987) Knowledge acquisition tools, *AICOM* **0**, 1, 29–38.

Apperley, M. & Field, G. (1984) A comparative evaluation of menu-based interactive human–computer dialogue techniques, in Shackel, B. (ed.) *Interact '84 — First IFIP conference on human–computer interaction* **1**, 296–299. Elsevier/North Holland.

Arditi, D. (1973) *An investigation into the behavioural and technical factors affecting success in the use of network analysis in the construction industry of Great Britain*. PhD Thesis. Loughborough.

Babbie, E. R. (1979) *The Practice of Social Research*, 2nd edn, Belmont, California: Wadsworth.

Bainbridge, L. (1979) Verbal reports as evidence of the process operator's knowledge, *International Journ. of Man–Machine Studies* **11**, 431–436.

Bainbridge, L. (1981) Verbal reports as evidence of the process operator's knowledge, in Mahamdani, E. H. & Gaines, B. R. (eds) *Fuzzy reasoning and its applications*, London: Academic Press, pp. 343–368.

Bainbridge, L. (1986) Asking questions and accessing knowledge, *Future Computing Systems* **1**, 143–150.

Banff 87 (1987) *Second knowledge acquisition for knowledge-based systems workshop*, sponsored by AAAI, Banff, Canada, October 1987 (to appear in *International Journ. Man–Machine Studies* 1988).

Bannister, D. (ed.) (1970) *Perspectives in personal construct theory*, London: Academic Press.

Bannister, D. (Chairman) (1973) *Repertory grid methods*, invited papers present at a workshop on Repertory Grids in November 1973 at Bedford College, London, British Physchological Society, Mathematical and Statistical Psychology Section.

Bannister, D. (ed.) (1977) *New perspectives in personal construct theory*, London: Academic Press.

Barber, M. & Kempson, J. (1984) Preparing hospital staff for the changeover to computerised records, in Shackel, B. (ed.) *Interact '84 — First IFIP conference on human–computer interaction.* **1**, 209–213. Amersterdam: Elsevier/North-Holland.

Barnard, P. J. (1987) Cognitive resources and the learning of human–computer dialogues, in J. M. Carroll (ed.) *Interfacing thought: cognitive aspects of human–computer interaction*, Cambridge, Mass.: MIT Press.

Barr, A. & Feigenbaum, E. (1981) *The handbook of artificial intelligence*, **1**, Reading, Mass.: Addison-Wesley.

Basden, A. (1984) On the application of expert systems, in Coombs, M. (ed.) *Developments in expert systems.* 56–76. Academic Press.

Bell, J. (1987a) *The human side of knowledge engineering*, Educational Media International **24**, 2.

Bell, J. (1987b) *Notes to accompany the course: the human side of knowledge engineering*, Winchester: JB Associates.

Bem, D. J. (1972) Self Perception Theory, in Berkokwitz, L. (ed.) *Advances in Experimental Sociol Psychology, 6.* New York: Academic Press.

Bjorn-Andersen, N. (1984) Training for subjection or participation, in Shackel, B. (ed.), *Interact '84 — First IFIP conference on human–computer interaction.* **2**, 349–326. Amsterdam: Elsevier/North Holland.

Bjorn-Andersen, N. (1986) Understanding the nature of the office for the design of third wave office systems, in Harrison, M. & Monk, A. (eds.) *People and computers: designing for usability.* 65–77. Cambridge University Press.

Bliss, J., Monk, M. & Ogborn, J. (1983) *Qualitative data analysis: a guide to the use of systemic networks*, London: Croom Helm.

Boehm, B. (1984) Verifying and validating software requirements and design specifications, *IEEE Software*, 75–88.

Boose, J. (1984) Personal construct theory and the transfer of human expertise, in *Proceedings of the National Conference in Artificial Intelligence, Austin, Texas*.

Boose, J. H. (1985) Personal construct theory and the transfer of human expertise, in O'Shea, T. (ed.) *Advances in artificial intelligence*, Amsterdam: Elsevier/North-Holland.

Boose, J. (1986) Rapid acquisition and combination of knowledge from multiple experts in the same domain, *Future Computing Systems* **1**, 191–216.

Boose, J. H. (1987) Uses of repertory grid-centered knowledge acquisition tools for knowledge-based systems, in Banff 87.

Boose, J. & Bradshaw, J. (1987a) AQUINAS: a knowledge acquisition workbench for building knowledge-based systems, in Addis, T., Boose, J. and Gaines, B. (eds) *Proceedings of the First European Workshop on Knowledge Acquisition for Knowledge Based Systems*.

Boose, J. & Bradshaw, J. (1987b) Expertise transfer and complex problems: using AQUINAS as a knowledge acquisition workbench for knowledge-based systems, *International Journ. Man–Machine Studies*, **26**, 3–28.

Bramer, M. A. (1987) Automatic induction of rules from examples: a critical analysis of the ID3 family of rule induction systems, in Addis, T., Boose, J. and Gaines, B. (eds.) *Proceedings of the First European Workshop on Knowledge Acquisition for Knowledge Based Systems*.

Bramer, M. (1985) Expert systems: the vision and the reality, in Bramer, M. (ed.) *Research and development in expert systems*, 1–13. Cambridge University Press.

Brennen, M., Brown, J. & Canter, D. (eds) (1985) *The research interview: uses and approaches*, London: Academic Press.

Breuker, J. (ed.) (1987) *Model-driven knowledge acquisition interpretation models*, Deliverable task A1, Esprit Project 1098, Department of Social Science Informatics, University of Amsterdam, Herengracht 196, 1016 BS Amsterdam, The Netherlands.

Breuker, J. (ed.) (1987) *Model-driven knowledge acquisition interpretation models*, Report of Esprit Project 1098, Department of Social Informatics, University of Amsterdam, The Netherlands and STL, Stevenage, UK.

Breuker, J. A. & Weilinga, B. J. (1983a) *Analysis techniques for knowledge based systems. Part 1: Methods for knowledge acquisition*, Esprit Project 12, Report 1.1, University of Amsterdam.

Breuker, J. A. & Weilinga, B. J. (1983b) *Analysis techniques for knowledge based systems. Part 2: Methods for knowledge acquisition*, Esprit Project 12, Report 1.2, University of Amsterdam.

Breuker, J. A. & Weilinga, B. J. (1984a) *Techniques for knowledge elicitation and analysis*, Esprit Project 12, Report 1.5, University of Amsterdam.

Breuker, J. A. & Weilinga, B. J. (1984b) Interpretation models for knowledge acquisition, in O'Shea, T. (ed.) *Advances in artificial intelligence*, North-Holland.

Breuker, J. A., Weilinga, B. J. & van Someren, M. W. (1986) *The KADS system functional description*, Esprit Project 1098, Deliverable T1.1, University of Amsterdam.

Breuker, J. A. & Weilinga, B. J. (1987) Use of models in the interpretation of verbal data, in Kidd, A. (ed.) *Knowledge acquisition for expert systems*, New York, NY: Plenum.

Breuker, J. A. & Weilinga, B., van Someren, M., de Hoog, R., Schreiber, G., de Greef, P., Bredeweg, B., Wielemaker, J., Billeaut, J.-P.,

Davoodi, M. & Hayward, S. (1987) *Model-driven knowledge acquisition interpretation models*. Deliverable Task A1, Esprit Project 1098, Commission of the European Community.

Brew, A. (1988) *Research as learning*, Ph.D. Thesis, School of Management, University of Bath, England.

Brooke, J. (1986) Usability engineering in office product development, in Harrison, M. & Monk, A. (eds) *People and computers: designing for usability* 249–260. Cambridge University Press.

Brown, J. (1985) An introduction to the use of facet theory, in Canter, D. (ed.) *Facet theory: approaches to social research*, New York: Springer-Verlag, pp. 17–57.

Brown, D. C. & Chandrasekaran, B. (1986) Knowledge and control for a mechanical design expert system, *Computer* **19**, 92–100.

Brynner, J. & Stribley, K. M. (eds) (1979) *Social research: principles and procedures*, London: Longman in Association with the Open University.

Buchanan, B. G. (1985) *Some approaches to knowledge acquisition*. Dept. of Computer Science, Stanford University.

Buchanan, B. & Feigenbaum, E. (1978) DENDRAL and Meta-DENDRAL: the applications dimension, *Artificial Intelligence* **11**, 5–24.

Buckley, P. K. & Long, J. B. (1985a) Identifying usability variables for teleshopping, *Contemporary ergonomics 1985*, Proceedings of the 1985 Conference of the Ergonomics Society, Taylor and Francis.

Buckley, P. K. & Long, J. B. (1985b) Effects of systems and knowledge variables on a task component of "teleshopping", In Johnson, P. and Cook, S. (eds) *People and Computers: Designing the Interface*, Proceedings of the Conference of the British Computer Society Human Computer Interaction Specialist Group, Cambridge: Cambridge University Press.

Bundy, A. (1985) Intelligent front ends, in Bramer, M. (ed.) *Research and development in expert systems* 193–204. Cambridge University Press.

Burton, M. & Shadbolt, N. (1987) A formal evaluation of knowledge elicitation techniques for expert systems: domain 1, in Pavelin, C. and Wilson, M. *Proceedings of a SERC Workshop on Knowledge Acquisition for Engineering Applications* 20–28. Rutherford Appleton Laboratory, RAL-87-055.

Burton, M. & Shadbolt, N. (1988) 'Characteristics of the experts in knowledge elicitation'. Unpublished paper given at the BCS HCI/Expert Systems Northern Group, 27 January.

Burton, A. M. & Shadbolt, N. R. (forthcoming) Knowledge engineering, *Technical Report 87-2-1* (forthcoming in Wiulliams, N. and Holt, P. *Expert systems for Users*, London: McGraw-Hill.)

Burton, M., Shadbolt, N., Hedgecock, A. & Rugg, G. (1987) A formal evaluation of knowledge elicitation techniques for expert systems: domain 1, in Addis, T., Boose, J. and Gaines, B. (eds) *Proceedings of the First European Workshop on Knowledge Acquisition for Knowledge Based Systems*.

Burton, A. M., Shadbolt, N. R., Hedgecock, A. P. & Rugg, G. (1988) A formal evaluation of knowledge elicitation techniques for expert systems: Domain 1, in Moralee, D. S. (ed.) *Research and Development in Expert Systems IV*, Proceedings of Expert Systems 1987, the Seventh Annual Technical Conference of the British Computer Society Specialist Group on Expert Systems, Cambridge: Cambridge University Press.

Butcher, H. (1968) *Human intelligence: its nature and assessment*, Methuen.

Bylander, T. & Chandrasekaran, B. (1987) Generic tasks for knowledge-based reasoning: the 'right' level of abstraction for knowledge acquisition, *Int. Journ. Man–Machine Studies* **26**, 231–243.

Cameron, J. (1983) *JSP & JSD: the Jackson approach to software development*. IEE Computer Society Press.

Canter, D. (1983) The potential of facet theory for applied social psychology, *Quality and Quantity* **17**, 35–67.

Canter, D. (ed.) (1985) *Facet theory: approaches to social research*, New York: Springer-Verlag.

Card, S. K., Moran, T. & Newell, A. (1980) The keystroke-level model for user performance time with interactive systems, *Communications of the ACM* **23**, 396–410.

Card, S., Moran, T. & Newell, A. (1983) *The psychology of human–computer interaction*, Hillside, N.J.: Lawrence Erlbaum.

Carver, M. (1988) Practical experience of specifying the human–computer interface using JSD in Megaw, E. (ed.) *Contemporary ergonomics 1988*. 177–182. London: Taylor & Francis.

Chandrasekaran, B. (1986) Generic tasks in knowledge based reasoning. *IEEE Expert* **1**, 3 23–32.

Checkland, P. B. (1981) *Systems, thinking, systems practice*, Chichester: Wiley.

Chekayeb, Niedzweeki & Conner (1987) Paper presented at Second International Conference on Engineering Applications of AI.

Church, C. (1988) *Time, budgets and contacts ... knowledge acquisition in the commercial context*. Unpublished paper given at the BCS HCI/Expert Systems Northern Group, 27 January.

Clancey, W. J. (1983) The epistemology of a rule based expert system — a framework for explanation, *Artificial Intelligence* **20**, 215–251.

Clancey, W. J. (1984) Acquiring, representing & evaluating a competence model of diagnostic strategy, *HPP Memo 84.2*, Stanford University.

Clancey, W. J. (1985) Heuristic classification, *Artificial Intelligence* **27**, 209–350.

Clark, D. A. with Crossland, J. (1985) *Action Systems: An Introduction to the Analysis of Complex Behaviour*, London: Methuen.

Clement, D. (1984) Empirical guidelines and a model for writing computer documentation, in Shackel, B. (ed.) *Interact '84 — First IFIP Conference on Human–Computer Interaction* **2**, 108–112. Elsevier/North Holland.

Collins, H. (1987) Domains in which expert systems could succeed, in *Third International Expert Systems Conference*. 201–206. Oxford: Learned Information.

Conway, A. & Wilson, M. D. (1988) Psychological studies of knowledge representation, in Ringland, G. A. and Duce, D. A. (eds) *Approaches to knowledge representation*, Letchworth: Research Studies Press.

Cooley, M. (1987) Human centred systems: an urgent problem for systems designers, *AI & Society* **1**, 37–46.

Cooper, C. N. (1987) *CRANES — a rule-based assistant with graphics for construction planning engineers*, 3rd Int. Conf. on Civil and Structural Engineering Computing, London, September 1987.

Cordingley, E. S. & Hammond, S. (forthcoming) *Practical fundamentals of multidimensional scaling*, Department of Sociology Occasional Paper, Guildford: University of Surrey, Guildford.

Coxon, A. P. M. (1982) *The user's guide to multidimensional scaling*, London: Heinemann Educational Books.

CSO (1976) Ask a silly question, booklet prepared by the Survey Control Unit of the Central Statistical Office, London: HMSO

Davis, W. S. (1983) *Tools and techniques for structured systems, analysis and design*, London: Addison-Wesley.

Dawkins (1987) Applications of expert systems to office automation, in *Third International Expert Systems Conference*. 423–434. Oxford: Learned Information.

Diaper, D. (1982) *Central backward masking and the two task paradigm*. Unpublished Ph.D. thesis, University of Cambridge, UK.

Diaper, D. (1984) An approach to IKBS development based on a review of conceptual structures: information processing in mind and machine by J. F. Sowa, *Behaviour and Information Technology* **3**, 3, 249–255.

Diaper, D. (1986a) Identifying the knowledge requirements of an expert system's natural language processing interface, in Harrison, M. and Monk, A. (eds) *People and computers: designing for usability* 263–280. Cambridge University Press.

Diaper, D. (1986b) Will expert systems be safe? in *Second International Expert Systems Conference*, 561–572. Oxford: Learned Information.

Diaper, D. (1987a) POMESS: a People Orientated Methodology for Expert System Specification, in Addis, T., Boose, J. & Gaines, B. (eds) *Proceedings of the First European Workshop on Knowledge Acquisition for Knowledge Based Systems*.

Diaper, D. (1987b) Designing systems for people: beyond user centred design, in *Software Engineering*, Proceedings of the Share European Association (SEAS) Anniversary Meeting, 283–302.

Diaper, D. (1988a) Task analysis for knowledge descriptions: building a task descriptive hierarchy, in Megaw, E. (ed.) *Contemporary ergonomics 1988*. 118–124. London: Taylor & Francis.

Diaper, D. (1988b) The promise of POMESS (a People Orientated Methodology for Expert System Specification), in Berry, D. and Hart, A. (eds) *Human and organisational issues of expert systems*.

Diaper, D. (1988c) Natural language communication with computers: theory, needs and practice, in *Proceeding of the conference on KBS in Government 1988*. 19–44. Blenheim Online.

Diaper, D. & Shelton, T. (1987) Natural language requirements for expert system naive users, in *Recent developments and applications of natural language understanding*. 113–124. UNICOM Seminars Ltd.

Diaper, D. & Shelton, T. (1988 — in press) Dialogues with the tin man: computing a natural language grammar for expert system naive users, in Peckham, J. (ed.) *Natural language understanding: recent developments and applications of natural language understanding*. London: Kogan Page.

Diaper, D. & Johnson, P. (1989 — in press) Task analysis for knowledge descriptions: theory and application in training, in Long, J. and Whitefield, A. (eds) *Cognitive ergonomics*. Cambridge University Press.

Dillon, A. (1987) Knowledge acquisition and conceptual models: a cognitive analysis of the interface, in Diaper, D. and Winder, R. (eds) *People and Computers III*, Proceedings of the Third Conference of the BCS HCI Specialist Group, Cambridge: Cambridge University Press for the British Computer Society.

Douglas, R., Ettridge, D., Fearnhead, D., Payne, C., Pugh, D. & Sowter, D. (1988) *Helping people work together: a guide to participative working practices*, National Institute of Social Work Papers No. 21, London NISW.

Duda, R., Gaschnig, J. & Hart, P. (1979) Model design in the PROSPECTOR consultant program for mineral exploration, in Michie, D. (ed.) *Expert systems in the microelectronic age*. Edinburgh University Press.

Easterby-Smith, M. (1981) The design, analysis and interpretation of repertory grids, in Shaw, M. L. G. *Recent developments in personal construct technology*, London: Academic Press.

Eden, C., Jones, S. & Sims, D. (1983) *Messing about with problems*, Oxford: Pergamon.

EKAW 87 (1987) *Proceedings of First European Workshop on Knowledge Acquisition for Knowledge Based Systems*, Computer Science Dept., Reading University, Reading, Berkshire, UK, September 1987.

Ericsson, K. A. & Simon, H. A. (1985) *Protocol analysis: verbal report as data*, London: MIT Press.

Eshelman, L. (1987) A KA tool that buries certainty factors, in Boose, J. H. & Gaines, B. R. *Proceedings of Second AAAI sponsored Knowledge Acquisition for Knowledge Based Systems Workshop*, Banff, Canada, October.

Fahnrich, K-P. & Ziegler, J. (1984) Workstations using direct manipulation as interaction mode — aspect of design, application and eveluation, in Shackel, B. (ed.) *Interact '84 — First IFIP Conference on Human--Computer Interaction* 2, 203–208. Elsevier/North Holland.

Farris, C. & Lucas, R. (1986) PROLOG rule acquisition via a natural language interface, in *Second International Expert Systems Conference*. 377–390. Oxford: Learned Information.

Feigenbaum, E. A. & McCorduck, P. (1984) *The fifth generation*, London: Pan Books.

Fielding, N. G. & Fielding, J. L. (1986) *Linking data*, Qualitative Research Methods Series 4, London: Sage.

Fitter, M., Brownbridge, G., Garber, R. & Herzmark, G. (1984), in Shackel, B. (ed.) *Interact '84 — First IFIP Conference on Human--Computer Intertaction*. **2**, 203–208. Elsevier/North Holland.

Flanagan, J. C. (1954) The critical incident technique, *Psychological Bulletin* **51**, 327–358.

Fodor, J. (1981) The mind–body problem, *Scientific American*, Jan., 124–132.

Fowler, C., Macaulay, L. & Siripoksup, S. (1987) An evaluation of the effectiveness of the adaptive interface module (AIM) in matching dialogues to users, in Diaper, D. & Winder, R. (eds) *People and computers III*. 345–360. Cambridge University Press.

Fransella, F. & Bannister, D. (1977) *A manual for repertory grid technique*, London: Academic Press.

Friedland, P. (1979) *Knowledge based experiment design in molecular genetics*, Ph.D. thesis, Computer Science Dept. Stanford University.

Frieling, M., Alexander, J., Messick, S., Rehfuss, S. & Shulman, S. (1985) Starting a knowledge engineering project: a step-by-step approach, *AI Magazine* **6**(3), 150–165.

Frohlich, D. M. (1986) On the organisation of form-filling behaviour, *Information and Design Journal* **5/1**, 43–59.

Frost, R. A. (1986) *Introduction to knowledge base systems*, London: Collins.

Funes, M. (1987) Knowledge Elicitation using teachback Methoodology and SGNs, MSc Thesis (Intelligent Systems) Brunel University, Uxbridge, UB8 2PS UK.

Gammack, J. & Young, R., (1985) Psychological techniques for eliciting expert knowledge, in Bramer, M. (ed.) *Research and development in expert systems*. Cambridge University Press.

Gardner, H. (1985) *The mind's new science: a history of the cognitive revolution*, New York: Basic Books.

Glaser, B. G. & Strauss, A. L. (1967) *The Discovery of Grounded Theory*, Chicago: Aldine.

Gotts, N. M. (1984) *Knowledge acquisition for medical systems — a review*. Artificial Intelligence in Medicine Group, University of Sussex.

Graham, I. & Jones, P. L. (1988) *Expert systems: knowledge uncertainty and decision*, London: Chapman & Hall.

Grishman, R. & Kitteridge, R. (1986) *Analysing language in restricted domains*, New Jersey: Lawrence Erlbaum.

Grover, M. D. (1983) A pragmatic knowledge acquisition methodology, *IJCAI*, **1**, 436–438.

Gruber, T. & Cohen, L. (1987) Acquiring strategic knowledge from experts, in Boose, J. H. and Gaines, B. R., *Proceedings of Second*

AAAI sponsored Knowledge Acquisition for Knowledge Based Systems Workshop, Banff, Canada. October.

Grudin, J. & MacLean, A. (1984) Adapting a psychophysical method to measure performance and preference tradeoffs in human–computer interaction, in Shackel, B. (ed.) *Interact '84 — First IFIP Conference on Human-Computer Interaction.* **2,** 338–342. Elsevier/North Holland.

Halliday, M. A. K. (1978) *Language as a Social Semiotic,* London: Edward Arnold.

Hammond, N., Hinton, G., Barnard, P., MacLean, A., Long, J. & Whitefield, A. (1984) Evaluating the interface of a document processor: a comparison of expert judgement and user observation, in Shackel, B. (ed.) *Interact '84 — First IFIP Conference on Human–Computer Interaction.* **2,** 135–139. Elsevier/North Holland.

Hammond, N. & Allinson, L. (1987) The travel metaphor as design principle and training aid for navigating around complex systems, in Diaper, D. and Winder, R. (eds) *People and Computers III.* 345–360. Cambridge University Press.

Hardiman, R. J. (1987a) *Naturalistic Knowledge Engineering,* School of Management, University of Bath, England.

Hardiman, R. J. (1987b) *A naturalistic methodology for knowledge engineering,* Proceedings of the First European Workshop on Knowledge Acquisition for Knowledge Based Systems, University of Reading, England.

Hardiman, R. J. (1987c) *Packaging distance learning; a meeting place for educational technologies? Educational Media International* **24,** 2.

Harries, T. W. & Trimble, E. G. (1974) *Factors which effect success in network applications.* Fourth Internat. Congress. Paris.

Hart, A. (1985) *Expert systems: an introduction for managers,* London: Kogan Page.

Hart, A. (1986) *Knowledge acquisition for expert systems,* London, Kogan Page.

Hayes-Roth, F., Waterman, D. & Lenat, D. (eds) (1983) *Building expert systems,* Reading, Mass.: Addison-Wesley.

Hayward, S. (1986a) A structured development methodology for expert systems, paper given at KBS 1986, Wembley, July 1986.

Hayward, S. (1986b) 'Models, Structure and Abstraction — Issues for an emerging methodology', paper given at the Esprit Conference, October 1986.

Hayward, S. (1987) How to build knowledge based systems: techniques, tools, and case studies, in *ESPRIT '87: proceedings of the Esprit Conferences,* pp. 665–687. Commission of the European Community: Brussels.

Hayward, S. A., Weilinga, B. J. & Breuker, J. A. (1987) Structured analysis of knowledge, *International Journ. of Man–Machine Studies* **26,** 487–498.

Heppe, D., Edmondson, W. & Spence, R. (1985) Helping both the novice and advanced user in menu-driven information retrieval systems, in

Johnson, P. & Cook, S. (eds) *People and computers: designing the interface*. 92–101. Cambridge University Press.

Heron, J. (1977) *Catharsis in human development*, British Postgraduate Medical Foundation, London.

Heron, J. (1981a) *Experiential research methodology*, in Reason, P. & Rowan, J. (eds) *Humans inquiry: a sourcebook of new paradigm research*, Chichester: John Wiley.

Heron, J. (1981b) *Philosophical basis for a new paradigm,* in Reason, P. & Rowan, J. (eds) *Human inquiry: a sourcebook of new paradigm research*, Chichester: John Wiley.

Heron, J. (1986) *Six category intervention analysis, second edition*. Human Potential Research Project, University of Surrey, Guildford.

Herzberg, F. (1968) *Work and the nature of man*. London: Staples.

Hilgard, E. (1980) Consciousness in contemporary psychology, *Annual Review of Psychology* **31**, 1–26.

Hinton, G. (1981) Implementing semantic networks in parallel hardware, in Hinton, G. & Anderson, J. (eds) *Parallel models of associative memory*. New Jersey: Lawrence Erlbaum.

Hinton, G. & Sejnowski, T. (1983) Optimal perceptual inference, in *Proceedings of the IEEE Computer Society Conference on Computer Vision and Pattern Recognition*. Washington, DC.

Hockey, S. & Marriott, I. (1980) *Oxford concordance program version 1.0 users' manual*, Oxford: Oxford University Computing Service.

Hodges, A. (1983) *Alan Turing the enigma of intelligence*, London: Counterpoint.

Hoffman, R. R. (1987) The problem of extracting the knowledge of experts from the perspective of experimental psychology, *AI Magazine* Summer 53–67.

Humphries, P. (1973) A review of some statistical properties of the repertory grid (and their cognitive implications), in Bannister, D. (Chairman) (1973) *Repertory Grid Methods*, invited papers present at a workshop on Repertory Grids in November 1973 at Bedford College, London, British Psychological Society, Mathematical and Statistical Psychology Section.

Johnson, L. & Johnson, N. E. (1987a) Knowledge elicitation involving teachback interviewing, in Kidd, A. L. (ed.) *Knowledge acquisition for expert systems: a practical handbook*, London: Plenum Press.

Johnson, L. & Johnson, N. E. (1087b) A knowledge elicitation method for expert systems design, *Int. J. Systems Research and Info. Science*, **2,** Gordon & Breach, London.

Johnson, N. E. (1985) Varieties of representation in eliciting and representing knowledge for IKBS, *Int. J. Systems Research and Info. Science* **1**, 2 69–90.

Johnson, N. E. (1987a) Knowledge elicitation in practice, *Insight Study No. 6*, Systems Designers Scientific, Pembroke Broadway, Camberley, Surrey GU15 3XD, UK.

Johnson, N. E. (1987b) Mediating representations in knowledge elicitation, in *Proceedings of the first European Workshop on Knowledge Acquisition for Knowledge-Based Systems*, September 1987, Reading University and the Institute of Electrical Engineers.

Johnson, P. (1985) Towards a task model of messaging: an example of the application of TAKD to user interface design, in Johnson, P. & Cook, S. (eds) *People and computers: designing the interface* 46–62. Cambridge University Press.

Johnson, P., Diaper, D. & Long, J. (1984) Tasks, skills and knowledge: task analysis for knowledge based descriptions, in Shackel, B. (ed.) *Interact '84 — First IFIP Conference on Human–Computer Interaction* 23–27. Elsevier/North Holland.

Johnson, P., Diaper, D. & Long, J. (1985) Task analysis in interactive systems design and evaluation, in Joannsen, G., Mancini, G. and Martensson, L. (eds) *Analysis, design and evaluation on man–machine systems*. Oxford: Pergamon Press.

Johnson, P., Long, J. & Visick, D. (1986) Voice versus keyboard: use of a comparative analysis of learning to identify skill requirements of input devices, in Harrison, M. & Monk, A. (eds) *People and computers: designing for usability* 546–613. Cambridge University Press.

Johnson-Laird, P. (1980) Mental models in cognitive science, *Cognitive Science,* **4,** 71–115.

Johnson-Laird, P. (1983) *Mental models: towards a cognitive science of language, inference and consciousness.* Cambridge University Press.

Johnson-Laird, P. N. (1987) Reasoning, imaging and creating, *Bulletin of the British Psychological Society* **40**, 121–129.

Jones, K. (1987) Expert systems blossom, *Computer Weekly*, Jan., 189.

Jones, S. (1985) The analysis of depth interviews, in Walker, R. (ed.) *Applied Qualitative Research*, Aldershot: Gower.

Kant, I. (1781) *Critique of pure reason* (Translated by Kemp Smith, N. — 1958) New York: Random House.

Kaster, J. & Widdel, H. (1984) Graphical support for dialogue transparency, in Shackel, B. (ed.) *Interact '84 — First IFIP Conference on Human–Computer Interaction* 1, 302–306. Elsevier/North Holland.

Keen, T. R. & Bell, R. C. (1980) One thing leads to another: a new approach to elicitation in the repertory grid techniques, *International Journ. of Man–Machine Studies* **13**, 25–38.

Keen, M. & Williams, G. (1985) Expert system shells come of age, in Bramer, M. (ed.) *Research and development in expert systems* 13–22. Cambridge University Press.

Kelly, G. (1955) *The psychology of personal constructs*. New York: Norton.

Kelly, G. A. (1964) in Warren, N. (ed.) (1964) *Theory and Methodology og George Kelly*, the Report of a Symposium on Construct Theory held at Brunel College, London, Autumn 1964 (mimeo).

Kelly, G. A. (1970) A brief introduction to personal construct theory, in Bannister, D. (ed.) *Perspectives in personal construct theory*, London: Academic Press.

Kelly, G. A. (1977) The psychology of the unknown, in Bannister, D. (ed.)

New perspectives in personal construct theory, London: Academic Press.

Keravnou, E. T. & Johnson, L. (1986) *Competent Expert Systems: a case study in fault diagnostics*, London: Kogan Page.

Kidd, A. (1982) Problems in man–machine dialogue design, in *Proceedings of the 6th International conference on Computer Communication: Pathways to the Information Society*, 531–536.

Kidd, A. L. (ed.) (1987) *Knowledge acquisition for expert systems: a practical handbook*, London: Plenum Press.

Killin, J. (1987) Interview techniques, a knowledge acquisition module for the course 'Pragmatic knowledge engineering' given at the Knowledge-Based Systems Centre, South Bank Polytechnic, London: unpublished.

Kolb, D. (1984) *Experiential learning*, New Jersey: Prentice-Hall.

Labaw, P. J. (1980) *Advanced questionnaire design?*, Mass:

LaBerge, D. (1974) Acquisition of automatic processing in perceptual and associative learning, in Rabitt, P. and Dornic, S. (eds) *Attention and performance V*. New York: Academic Press.

Laberge, D. (1981) Automatic information processing: a review, in Long, J. and Baddeley, A. (eds) *Attention and performance XI*. New Jersey: Lawrence Erlbaum.

LaFrance, M. (1987) The knowledge acquisition grid: a method for training knowledge engineers, *International Journ. of Man–Machine Studies* **26**, 245–255.

Lawson, H. W. (1984) Computer architecture education, in Tiberghien, (cd.) *New Computer Architectures*, London: Academic Press.

Lincoln, Y. S. & Guba, E. G. (1984) *Naturalistic inquiry*, California: Sage.

Long, J. & Buckley, P. (1984) Transaction processing using videotext or: shopping on PRESTEL, in Shakeb, B. (ed.) *Interact '84 — First IFIP Conference on Human Computer Interaction*, Amsterdam: Elsevier Science Publishers BV, Vol. 1, 365–369.

Lopez de Mantaras, R., Agusti, J. & Plaza, E. (1986) Knowledge elicitation and analysis for approximate reasoning systems. *CIIAM 1986*, 91–108.

Mandler, G. (1975) Consciousness: respectable, useful and probably necessary, in Solso, R. (ed.) *Information processing and cognition: the Loyola Symposium*. New Jersey: Lawrence Erlbaum.

Marr, D. (1972) *Vision: A Computational Investigation into the Human Representation and Processing of Visual Information*. San Francisco: Freeman.

Martin, J. & McClure, C. (1985) *Diagramming techniques for analysts and programmers*. Englewood Cliffs: Prentice-Hall.

Marshall, J. (1981) *Making sense as personal process*, in Reason, P. & Rowan, J. (eds) *Human inquiry: a sourcebook of new paradigm research*, Chichester: John Wiley.

McDermott, J. (1982) R1: a rule based configurer for computer systems, *Artificial Intelligence* **19**, 39–88.

McClelland, J. & Rummelhart, D. (1986) *Parallel distributed processing*.

explorations in the microstructure of cognition, Volume 2: Psychological and Biological Models. Massachusetts: MIT.

Miller, G. (1962) *Psychology: the science of mental life.* New York: Harper & Row.

Miller, P. L. (1984) *A critiquing approach to expert computer advice: ATTENDING,* Research Notes in Artificial Intelligence 1, London: Pitman Advanced Publishing Program.

Miller, R. B. (1962) Task description and analysis, in R. M. Gagne (ed.) *Psychological principles in system development.* New York, NY: Holt, Rinehart & Winston.

Minsky, M. (1986) *Society of mind,* New York: Simon & Schuster.

Mobbs, A. J. (1986) *STARTS debrief on CORE,* NCC Publications.

Modesitt, K. (1987) Experts: human and otherwise, in *Third International Expert Systems Conference.* 333–342. Oxford: Learned Information.

Moran, T. (1978) Introduction to the command language grammar. *Report No. SSL-78-3.* Palo Alto: Rank Xerox.

Moran, T. (1981) The command language grammar, a representation for the user interface of interactive computer systems. *International Journ. of Man–Machine Studies* **15,** 3–50.

Moser, C. A. & Kalton, G. (1978) Question wording, in Brynner, J & Stribley, K. M. (eds) *Social research: principles and procedures,* London: Longman in Association with the Open University.

Motta, E., Eisenstadt, M., West, M., Pitman, K. & Everstz, R. (1986) KEATS: the knowledge engineer's assistant, final project report, *Technical Report No. 20,* Human Cognition Research Laboratory, Milton Keynes: The Open University.

Neale, I. M. (1987) Knowledge acquisition for expert systems: a review and case study, MSc dissertation, Loughborough University of Technology.

Neale, I. M. (forthcoming) Knowledge acquisition for expert systems: A review of methodology, *Knowledge Engineering Review,* **3,** 3.

Neisser, U. (1967) *Cognitive Psychology,* Appleton-Century-Crofts.

Nelson, T. (1980) Replacing the printed word: a complete literary system, *Information Processing 80,* IFIP, 1013–1023, Amsterdam: North-Holland.

Newell, A. & Simon, H. A. (1972) *Human problem solving,* Englewood Cliffs, New Jersey: Prentice-Hall.

Nisbett, R. E. and Wilson, T. D. (1977) Telling more than we can know: verbal reports on mental processes. *Psychological Review,* **84,** 231–259.

Norman, D. (1968) Towards a theory of memory and attention, *Psychological Review,* **75,** 533–536. (Reprinted in Coltheart, M. (ed.) *Readings in cognitive psychology* 1972, 222–237 Holt, Rinehart & Winston).

Norman, D. & Draper, S. (1986) *User Centred System Design.* New Jersey: Lawrence Erlbaum.

Norris, Marg. (1982) *Beginner's guide to the use of repertory grids in research,* Department of Sociology Occasional Paper No 1, Guildford: University of Surrey.

O'Connor, D. (1964) Locke, in O'Connor, D. (ed.) *A critical history of western philosophy* 204–219. MaMillan.

Oliver, A. (1986) Control of rapid prototyping in expert systems developments, in *Second International Expert Systems Conference* 247–252. Oxford: Learned Information.

Oliver, A. (1987a) How to make rapid prototyping effective when developing expert systems, in *Third International Expert Systems Conference* 45–48. Oxford: Learned Information.

Oliver, A. (1987b) Techniques for expert system testing and validation, in *Third International Expert Systems Conference*. 271–276. Oxford: Learned Information.

Quinlan, J. R. (1979) Discovering rules by induction from large collections of examples, in Michie, D. (ed.) *Expert systems in the electronic age*. 168–201. Edinburgh University Press.

Quinlan, J. R. (1986) Induction of decision trees. *Machine Learning, 1,* **1**, 81–106.

Oxman, R. & Gero, J. S. (1987) Using an expert system for design diagnosis and design synthesis, *Expert Systems* **4**(1), 4–15.

Partridge, D. (1986) *Artificial intelligence: applications to the future of software engineering*. Chichester: Ellis Horwood.

Payne, S. (1984) Task-action grammars, in Shackel, B. (ed.) *Interact '84 — First IFIP Conference on Human–Computer Interaction*. **1**, 139–144. Elsevier/North-Holland.

Payne, S. (1985) *Task action grammars: the mental representation of task languages in human–computer interaction*. Unpublished Ph.D. Dissertation, University of Sheffield, UK.

Payne, S. & Green, T. (1986) Task-action grammars: a model of the mental representation of task languages, *Human–Computer Interaction* **2**, 93–133.

Picht, H. & Draskau, J. (1985) *Terminology: an introduction*, No 2 in the Monograph Series of the Department of Linguistics and International Studies, University of Surrey, Guildford.

Polyanyi, M. (1966) *The tacit dimension*, New York: Doubleday.

Pope, M. L. & Keen, T. R. (1981) *Personal construct psychology and education*, London: Academic Press.

Popper, K. (1972) *Objective knowledge: an evolutionary approach*. Oxford University Press.

Pullum, G. (1987) Natural language interfaces and strategic computing, *AI & Society, 1,* 47–58.

Radley, A. R. (1973) Problems in the analysis and interpretation of repertory grids, in Bannister, D. (Chairman) (1973) *Repertory grid methods*, invited papers present at a workshop on Repertory Grids in November 1973 at Bedford College, London, British Psychological Society, Mathematical and Stastistical Psychology Section.

Rappaport, A. (1987) Cognitive primitives, in Boose, J. H. & Gaines, B. R. *Proceedings of Second AAAI sponsored Knowledge Acquisition for Knowledge Based Systems Workshop,* Banff, Canada, October.

Rasmussen, J. (1986) *Information processing and human–machine interaction: an approach to cognitive engineering*, Amsterdam: North-Holland.

Reason, P. (ed.) (1988) *Human inquiry in action*, Sage (in press).

Reason, P. & Rowan, J. (eds) (1981) *Human inquiry: a sourcebook of new paradigm research*, Chichester: Wiley.

Regoczei, S. & Plantinga, E. P. O. (1987) Creating the domain of discourse: ontology and inventory, *International Journ. of Man–Machine Studies* **27**, 235–250.

Reichgelt, H. & van Harmalen, F. (1986) Criteria for choosing representational languages and control regimes for expert systems, *The Knowledge Engineering Review* 2–17.

Reiss, G. (1986) Knowledge acquisition and the oleophilic advisor, in Robinson, G. & Cook, M. S. (eds) WESTEX-86, Proceedings of IEEE Western Conference on Knowledge-Based Engineering and Expert Systems.

Rosenman, M. A., Coyne, R. D. & Gero, J. S. (1987) Expert systems for design applications, in *Applications of KBS's: based on the proceedings of the second Australian conference*. Turing Institute in association with Addison-Wesley, 66–84.

Rumelhart, D. & McClelland, J. (1986) *Parallel distributed processing: explorations in the microstructure of cognition. Volume 1: Foundations*. MIT: Mass.

Rumelhart, D., Smolensky, P., McClelland, J. & Hinton, G. (1986) Schemata asnd sequential thought processes in PDP models, in *Parallel distributed processing: explorations in the microstructure of cognition. Volume 2: Psychological and biological models*, 7–57. Mass. MIT.

Schatz, U. H., Strahs, R. & Campbell, L. (1987) EXPERTAX: the issue of long-terrm maintenance, in *Third International Expert Systems Conference* 45–48. Oxford: Learned Information.

Schneider, W. & Shiffrin, R. (1977) Controlled and automatic human information processing: I. Detection, search and attention, *Psychological Review,* **84**, 1–66.

Schorr, H. (1987) IBM's artificial intelligence directions, Paper presentation at SHARE European Association Anniversary Meeting on 'Software Engineering'.

Schweickert, R., Burton, A. M., Taylor, N. K., Corlett, E. N., Shadbolt, N. R. & Hedgecock, A. P. (1987) Comparing knowledge elicitation techniques: a case study, *Artificial Intelligence Review* **1**, 245–253.

Schwartz, P. & Ogilvy, J. (1979) *The emergent paradigm: changing patterns of thought and belief*, Analytical Report 7, SRI International, Menlo Park, CA (quoted in Lincoln and Guba, *Naturalistic inquiry*).

SDL (1986) *CORE description*, Systems Designers Ltd.

Sell, P. (1985) *Expert Systems — A Practical Introduction*. Macmillan.

Shackel, B. (1986) Ergonomics in design and usability, in Harrison, M. and Monk, A. (eds) *People and computers: designing for usability* 44–64. Cambridge University Press.

Shannon, C. (1938) A symbolic analysis of relay and switching circuits, *Transactions of the American Institute of Electrical Engineers* **57**, 1–11.

Sharpe, W. (1985) Logic programming for the law, in Bramer, M. (ed.) *Research and Development in Expert Systems* 217–228, Cambridge University Press.

Sharratt, B. (1987) The incorporation of early interface evaluation into command language grammar, in Diaper, D. and Winder, R. (eds) *People and Computers III* 11–28. Cambridge University Press.

Shaw, M. L. G. (1980) *On becoming a personal scientist*, London: Academic Press.

Shaw, M. L. G. (1981) *Recent developments in personal construct technology*, London: Academic Press.

Shaw, M. L. G. & Gaines B. R. (1986) Interactive elicitation of knowledge from experts. *Future Computing Systems* **1**, 2, 151–190.

Shaw, M. L. G. & Gaines, B. R. (1987a) KITTEN: knowledge initiation and transfer tools for experts and novices, *International Journ. of Man–Machine Studies* **27**, 251–280.

Shaw, M. L. G. & Gaines, B. R. (1987b) An interactive knowledge-elicitation technique using personal construct psychology, in Kidd, A. L. (ed.) *Knowledge acquisition for expert systems: a practical handbook*, London: Plenum Press.

Shepard, R. (1981) Psychophysical complimentarity, in Kubovy, M. and Pomerantz, J. (eds) *Perceptual Organisation*. New Jersey: Lawrence Erlbaum.

Shepard, R. (1982) Perceptual and analogical bases of cognition, in Mehler, J., Walker, E. & Garrett, M. (eds) *Perspectives on mental representation: experimental and theoretical studies of cognitive processes and capacities*. New Jersey: Lawrence Erlbaum.

Shriffin, R., Dumais, S. & Schneider, W. (1981) Characteristics of automatism, in Long, J. and Baddeley, A. (eds) *Attention and performance IX*. New Jersey: Lawrence Erlbaum.

Shpilberg, D., Graham, L. & Schatz, H. (1986) Expertax: an expert system for corporate tax planning, in *Second International Expert Systems Conference*, 99–124. Oxford: Learned Information.

Shortliffe, E. H. & Buchanan, B. G. (1975) A model of inexact reasoning in medicine, *Mathematical Biosciences*, **23**, 351–379.

Slater, P. (1972) *Notes on INGRID 72*. Institute of Psychiatry: London.

Slater, P. E. (1987) *Building expert systems: cognitive emulation*, Chichester: Ellis Horwood.

Slater, P. E. (1987) Cognitive emulation in expert system design, *Knowledge Engineering Review* **2**, 27–42.

Small, D. & Weldon, L. (1983) An experimental study of natural and structured query languages, *Human Factors* **25**, 253–263.

Smith, S. & Mosier, J. (1984) The user interface to computer-based information systems: a survey of current software design practice, in Shackel, B. (ed.) *Interacte '84 — First IFIP Conference on Human–Computer Interaction*. 2, 35–39. Elsevier/North-Holland.

Spradley, J. P. (1979) *The ethnographic interview*, London: Holt, Rienhart & Winston.

Spradley, J. P. (1980) *Participant observation*, London: Holt, Rienhart & Winston.

Stacey, M. (1969) *Methods of social research*, Oxford: Pergamon Press.

Stewart, V. & Stewart, A. with Fonda, N. (1981) *Business applications of repertory grid*, London: McGraw-Hill.

Taylor, A. & Weaver, J. (1986) Knowledge elicitation: the problems of the Alvey DHSS large demonstrator policy application, Paper presented at the IEE Colloqium on Knowledge Elicitation, 25 March 1986, IEE Digest No.: 1986/42.

Tulving, E. (1974) Cue-dependent forgetting, *American Scientist* **62**, 74–82.

Totterdell, P. & Cooper, P. (1986) Design and evaluation of the AID adaptive front-end to Telecom Gold, in Harrison, M. and Monk, A. (eds) *People and Computers: Designing for Usability* 281–295. Cambridge University Press.

Trigano, P., Morizet-Mahoudeaux, P. & le Beux, P. (1986) DIAPHIL, a man–machine interface in natural language. Application to an expert system, in *Second International Expert Systems Conference* 391–398. Oxford: Learned Information.

van de Brug, A., Bachant, J. & McDermott, J. (1986) The taming of R1, *IEEE Expert*, Fall, 33–39.

Waldron, V. R. (1986) Interviewing for knowledge, *IEEE Transactions on Professional Communications*, **PC 29**, 2, 31–34.

Warnock, G. (1964) Kant, in O'Connor, D. (ed.) *A Critical History of Western Philosophy* 296–318. Macmillan.

Warren, N. (ed.) (1964) Theory and Methodology of George Kelly, the Report of a Symposium on Construct Theory held at Brunel College, London, Autumn 1964 (mimeo).

Wasson, P. & Shapiro, D. (1971) Natural and contrived experience in a reasoning problem, *Quarterly Journal of Experimental Psychology* **23**, 63–71.

Watling, J. (1964) Descartes, in O'Connor, D. (ed.) *A critical history of western philosophy* 170–186. Macmillan.

Webber, B. & Nilsson, N. (1981) Preface, in Webber, B. and Nilsson, N. (eds) *Readings in artificial intelligence* viii. California: Morgan Kaufmann.

Welbank, M. (1983) A review of knowledge acquisition techniques for expert systems, *British Telecommunications Research Laboratories Technical Report*, Martlesham Heath, Ipswich, England.

Welbank, M. (1987a) A survey of knowledge acquisition techniques, *SD Insight Report*, System Designers: Camberley UK.

Welbank, M. (1987b) Perspectives on knowledge acquisition, in Pavelin, C. J. and Wilson, M. D. (eds) Proceedings of the SERC Workshop on KNowledge Acquisition for Engineering Applications, *Rutherford Appleton Laboratory Report, RAL-87-055*, 14–20.

Welbank, M. (1987c) Knowledge acquisition: a survey and British telecom experience, in Addis, T., Boose, J. & Gaines, B. (eds) *Proceedings of the First European Workshop on Knowledge Acquisition for Knowledge-Based Systems*. Reading University: Reading, UK.

Welbank, M. (1987d) Knowledge acquisition update, *Insight Study No. 5*, Camberley: System Designers plc (restricted distribution).

Weilinga, B. J., Breuker, J. A. & van Someren, M. W. (1986) The KADS system: functional description, Deliverable T1.1, Esprit Project 1098, Department of Social Science Informatics, University of Amsterdam, Herengracht 196, 1016 BS Amsterdam, The Netherlands.

Wijesundera, D. A. & Harris, F. C. (1985) The integration of an expert system into the construction planning process, *Proc. of 2nd Int. Conf. on Civil and Structural Engineering Computing*, Vol. 2, pp. 399–405. (Describes CONPLANT).

Wilson, M. (1987) Task analysis of knowledge acquisition, in Pavelin, C. & Wilson, M. (eds) *Proceedings of a SERC Workshop on Knowledge Acquisition for Engineering Applications* 68–83. Rutherford Appleton Laboratory, RAL-87-055.

Wilson, M. D., Barnard, P. J. & MacLean, A. (1985) Analysing the learning of command sequences in a menu system, in Johnson, P. & Cook, S. (eds) *People and computers: designing the interface*, Cambridge University Press.

Wilson, M., Barnard, P. & MacLean, A. (1986) Task analysis in human computer interaction, *IBM Hursley Human Factors Report HF122*.

Wilson, M. D., Barnard, P. J., Green, T. R. G. & Maclean, A. (1988) Knowledge-based task analysis for human-computer systems, in van deer Veer, G. C., Green, T. R. G., Hoc, J.-M. & Murray, D. (eds) *Working with computers: theory versus outcome*. London: Academic Press.

Winograd, T. (1975) Frame representations and the declarative procedural controversy, in Bobrow, D. and Collins, A. (eds) *Representation and understanding: studies in cognitive science* 185–210. New York: Academic Press.

Winograd, T. (1983) *Language as a cognitive process*. London: Addison-Wesley.

Witkin, H. A. & Oltman, P. K. (1967) Cognitive style, *International Journal of Neurology* 6, 119–137.

Wright, G. & Ayton, P. (1987) Eliciting and modelling expert knowledge, *Decision Support Systems* 3, 13–26.

Wyatt, J. C. & Emerson, P. A. (1988) Paragmatic knowledge engineering: a new approach to difficult domains, in the conference proceedings of *Human and Organisational Issues of Expert Systems*, May 1988.

Young, R. & Gammack, J. (1987) Role of psychological techniques and intermediate representations in knowledge elicitation, in Addis, T., Boose, J. and Gaines, B. (eds) *Proceedings of the First European Workshop on Knowledge Acquisition for Knowledge Based Systems*.

Yourdon, E. (1979) *Structured walkthroughs*, Yourdon.

Yourdon, E. & Constantine, L. L. (1979) *Structured design: fundamentals of a discipline of computer program and systems design*, Prentice-Hall.

Zack, B. (1987) Selecting an application for knowledge-based system development, in *Third International Expert Systems Conference*, 257–270. Oxford: Learned Information.

Zelditch, M. (1962) Some methodological problems of field studies, in Brynner, J. & Stribley, K. M. (eds) (1979) *Social research: principles and procedures*, London: Longman in Association with the Open University.

Index